ONE WEEK LOAN

Representing the German nation

MANCHESTER
UNIVERSITY PRESS

Representing the German nation

History and identity in twentieth-century Germany

edited by
Mary Fulbrook and Martin Swales

Manchester University Press
Manchester and New York

distributed exclusively in the USA by St. Martin's Press

Published by Manchester University Press
Oxford Road, Manchester M13 9NR, UK
and Room 400, 175 Fifth Avenue, New York, NY 10010, USA
http://www.manchesteruniversitypress.co.uk

Distributed exclusively in the USA by
St. Martin's Press, Inc., 175 Fifth Avenue, New York,
NY 10010, USA

Distributed exclusively in Canada by
UBC Press, University of British Columbia, 2029 West Mall,
Vancouver, BC, Canada V6T 1Z2

British Library Cataloguing-in-Publication Data
A catalogue record for this book is available from the British Library

Library of Congress Cataloging-in-Publication Data applied for

ISBN 0 7190 5939 9 *hardback*

First published 2000

07 06 05 04 03 02 01 00   10 9 8 7 6 5 4 3 2 1

Typeset in Photina
by Northern Phototypesetting Co. Ltd, Bolton
Printed in Great Britain
by Bookcraft (Bath) Ltd, Midsomer Norton

Contents

1

Introduction: representation in literature and history

Mary Fulbrook and Martin Swales

How do we know about the past? How, if at all, can we gain a sense of 'real experience' of the past, as it was 'actually' experienced? How far do different forms of representation not only re-present – in the sense of making present once again – but also in effect construct, create, *new* conceptions of identity? And how do we – literary critics, historians, and scholars in related disciplines – reinterpret these texts and meanings? What criteria, if any, can we use to assess the authenticity of our own (re)interpretations of past interpretations and constructions?

Questions concerning the representation of 'reality' have for some time been central to debates in both literary criticism and historiography.[1] For those who accept the general message of postmodernism, the route to a past which has, by definition, gone forever is essentially shrouded in mystery. All we are left with is different readings, texts commenting upon texts.[2] But even for those who wish to adhere to some notion of 'telling the truth' about the past, serious problems are posed by the sheer variety of conflicting, often mutually incompatible paradigms for approaching that past.[3] The impact of postmodernism has sensitized even those who reject it (whether entirely, or in its more relativist implications) to the variety of ways in which cultural, political and historical representations serve not simply (or at all) to 'reconstruct' or 'reflect' the past, but also (or rather) to 'construct' or 'replace' it in a complex process of constructing contested identities in the present. Critical theory has, over the last two or three decades, thus confronted both history and literature with similar kinds of challenges to do with the 'texting' of the world of human interaction. It has sought to blur the distinction between the two disciplines by stressing, for example, the rhetoric of narrativity that informs both the work of history on the one hand and the work of novel fiction on the other. These controversial insights have led to a fundamental rethinking of different forms of human representation and construction of identity.

This is the general intellectual context to which this book is addressed. The contributors are all concerned, in different ways and with respect to different genres, with issues of representation, interpretation and identity. Modern Germany – with its dramatic political ruptures from late unification in 1871, through the short-lived and deeply riven Weimar democracy into the depths of the Nazi dictatorship, to the extraordinary experiment of two opposing German states, each with its own attempt to reappropriate and reinterpret a common past, up to the equally unparalleled experiment of reunification in 1990 – provides a superb case study, a historical tapestry of intertwining representations of contested identities, through which we can address such questions.

To take but the most central example: the Holocaust has often been treated as almost the limiting, defining case in controversies over representation and contemporary abuses of history. The 'appeal to Auschwitz' has been used as an emotive argument for the 'reality' of the past, a past which 'actually happened' and cannot be denied at the level of fact.[4] It has, too, been seen as a limiting case by those postmodernists who wish to argue, not that the 'real past' cannot be known as a set of factual or true individual statements, but rather that an (almost) infinite variety of 'emplotments' can be imaginatively imposed on a selection of those true statements.[5] Yet the variety of modes of reappropriation and representation of the Holocaust present serious challenges even for those who hold the traditional view that there was a real past, which has left real traces from which an attempt can be made at honest reconstruction.

We inevitably pay particular attention in this book to some of the ways in which this central event of the twentieth century left its ambiguous traces throughout the political and cultural lives of divided Germany. But there were, and are, always numerous strands to the often agonized debates over German identities, and we deal too with some of the key precursors to the Nazi abyss, as well as subsequent resonances and reverberations. Political, cultural and historical discourses have intermingled in a maelstrom of identity construction and reconstruction over the course of the turbulent twentieth century.

Through in-depth analysis of a select range of topics, we seek to bring together a variety of perspectives on theoretical debates in literature and history, and on the representation and construction of German identities in the twentieth century. Covering modes of representation ranging from newspapers, popular guidebooks, architecture, politicians' speeches and popular re-enactments, through the wilful and self-conscious fantasies and fictional worlds of novels, music, drama, film and fairy-tales, to the supposedly truthful representations of the past 'as it actually was' in the works of professional historians, the following chapters grapple with issues which have often been treated separately, or only brought together in the abstract discourse of theoretical debate. In spanning this range of topics, we seek to shed new light, too, on key moments and elements in the often agonized attempts to construct ever-renewed versions of German identity in the traumatized twentieth century.

First, however, a few words are in order on the issue of representation in literary and historical theory.

Representation in literary theory

The late 1960s saw waves of student unrest in Europe and America. That unrest made itself felt not only in the grand public spaces of the university campus and on the streets of the surrounding, often bemused social world but also in the seminar room. Those of us who were at the time professionally engaged in the teaching of literature will recall the intense climate of self-scrutiny that was prevalent. Questions as to the ethical value and the social relevance of literary study were omnipresent, constantly fuelled by a bad conscience about merely 'enjoying' literature. Theoretical discussion often supplanted any actual engagement with literary texts. Why, it was asked, were these texts prescribed on the reading list and not others? What constituted the canon of great literature? Why were 'high cultural' works exclusively represented, to the neglect of perhaps less complex texts that had enjoyed greater popularity, and by that token had had a demonstrably greater social impact? (At which point, interestingly, there was a curious intersection of fiercely high-minded, vigorously left-wing, anti-capitalist thinking with an acknowledgement of the market place as a site of genuine, rather than manipulated, social interaction.) The politicized generation of literary students of the late 1960s and early 1970s was, it has to be remembered, reacting against that particular trend in literary scholarship, often known as 'New Criticism', that came to the forefront in the aftermath of the Second World War. A weary, shattered world sought to pick up the pieces; and the study of literature was to help in this process by making available notions of heightened human cognition and of privileged linguistic utterance – and, by that token, of beauty and significance. Small wonder after the carnage of the war that literary value was sought not in a text's ability to express the complex tensions of socio-political interaction but rather in the comfort and uplift offered by the perfectly wrought artefact. By contrast, the students who took to the streets in 1968 had been born after the war. They had no need to offset the trauma of global political strife by the intense perfection of the great work of art. Rather, they sought to close the gap between 'literature' and 'life', between text and politics.

To historicize the radical demands of the student generation in the late 1960s is by no means to belittle its aspirations. Far from it. But equally it has to be said that there was at the time a rage for unmediated referentiality, for a prompt evaluation of literary texts according to accuracy of social portrayal and political acceptability. If the preceding tendency had justified the literary work because it ennobled and enriched the reader, because it gave access to a heightened sense of cognitive and moral complexity, the politicized tendency was sceptical of (aesthetic and other kinds of) privilege, and sought to justify the literary work by pragmatizing it. Such currents were to be detected in both Europe and North America. In West Germany there was a particular fervour to the debate, not least because much of the high aesthetic taste of the 1950s and early 1960s echoed the literary climate of the 1930s, when such aestheticism not only coexisted with, but, according to certain commentators, was partly responsible for Germany's slide into barbarism. The need felt, then, by German student radicals was not so much for a politicization of literary study; rather, literary study was seen as necessarily political (and nowhere more insidiously so than when the political agenda was left implicit, and therefore unexamined), and hence there was a burning desire to acknowledge the political force of the literary-critical enterprise – and to get the politics right.

All this meant, of course, that the ultimate justification for literary study was extra-literary. Perhaps in accordance with some such simple doctrine as that of the pendulum's swing, the political priorities of the late 1960s and early 1970s subsequently gave way to a re-literarization of literary study, to a re-textualization of the text. Yet the 'relevance' of literature espoused by the earlier generation would not go away; and hence the domains of society, politics and history now became in their turn heavily textualized. The truth of literature was, it was claimed, to be found in the notion that it admitted to, and held up for criticial interrogation, its textuality; and the more strenuously empirical disciplines had to be helped to realize that the source of their cognition was located in discourse analysis – and not in zealously accumulated and documented facts. Sceptical voices, by contrast, insisted that these new, headily textual doctrines derived their appeal from the fact that the promised political transformation of society did not come about in the late 1960s (Danny Le Rouge did not topple General de Gaulle). Hence it made sense to invoke the only transformation that was available (and available everywhere because totally harmless): the transformation of social reality into the stuff of literary discussion, into the focus of the literary seminar, into text. Other voices, conversely, highlighted the cognitive gain; they insisted that recent work in fields such as linguistics, sociology and anthropology helped the littérateurs to see that they no longer needed to apologize for the 'constructedness', the textuality, of their concerns – because their inquiry was deeply related to the workings of the social world 'out there'.

The particular battle for (as it were) the soul of literary criticism was, for obvious reasons, joined with especial fervour in respect of the referentiality of the literary text – and most urgently as far as notions of realism were at stake. The issues can be briefly summarized. The term 'realism' functions, as Stephan Kohl has shown, as both a perennial principle and as a period term.[6] As a perennial principle, it recurs constantly in aesthetic debate when there is a decisive shift in sensibility, when a particular age finds the inherited modes of literary representation stylized, artificial, 'untrue to life'. It is virtually impossible to find common ground in these various 'truths to life'; they are simply the neglected realm in the name of which any specific culture claims an extension of the traditional purview of art. In thematic terms, issues of social class, of religion or other beliefs, of violence, sexuality, work, race, colour can be involved; in stylistic terms matters to do with the acknowledgement of the vernacular, of prosiness, of inarticulacy, of freedom of form, of verse, of structure can constitute the great battle cry. All this is part of an unending dialectic by which aesthetic theory mediates between the twin imperatives of (to borrow Gombrich's terms) 'matching' and 'making', that is, copying the extra-literary world, and making an aesthetic artefact.[7]

There is, however, also the matter of realism as a period term that needs to be considered. This involves the emergence of a particular literary genre to prominence in the late eighteenth century: the novel. For many commentators, the novel, in its modern form, is the great expression of bourgeois culture; it arises with the mercantile ethos of early capitalism, and portrays an individualist world in which social mobility, the ups and downs of (economic and existential) risk-taking, form the staple diet of the narrative.[8] Above all else, the novel of bourgeois realism is secular, is unphilosophical and unselfconscious. It abundantly acknowledges the palpable world of social reality and of the battles of the individual human subject to stay afloat. Because of the triumphant worldliness of this form of narrative, it entails a textual performance that constantly seeks to conceal its own textuality, that seeks to present itself as disinterestedly transparent upon an extra-literary world of streets, houses, furniture, of institutions and socialized behaviour. This form of bourgeois novel realism may be a circumscribed period concept; but we should be under no illusions that that period is not still with us. Such novel fictions are alive and well, and are second nature to us – despite Roland Barthes's splendid demonstration that the 'effect of the real' is grounded in a particular form of rhetoric, one that acknowledges the sheer superabundance of materiality.[9] The novel that offers pages of description of London, Paris, New York is still very much dominant – in both highbrow and popular literature. Because of its seemingly unassailable strength as a convention that has forgotten that it is one, because of its endlessly advanced (and endlessly conceded) claim to express the way of the world in its sheer thereness, the realistic novel has been virulently criticized by theoreticians of a postmodern persuasion.

The attack on this form of literary realism has, broadly speaking, four strands.[10] First, it is false to assume that there is a literary text on the one hand, and an extra-literary thing called reality on the other, to which that text refers. What human beings know as reality around them is not simply unmediated facts and objects; it is, rather, a world rendered habitable (that is, intelligible) by an extensive economy of signs, symbols, conventions, rituals and assumptions. The literary text is, then, but one text in the corporate textuality of society. Secondly, literature is constituted by language; it cannot, therefore, produce a semblance of the world, but only a semblance of true discourse about the world. Thirdly, much theory of mimesis has, without realizing it, conflated two categories of representational truthfulness – *vraisemblance* (that is, what appears to be truthful, coherent and logical as an account of the world) and *bienséance* (that is, what is felt to be seemly or socially acceptable). Hence (so the argument runs) the work of traditional novel realism (the convincing story of the way we live now or lived then) does not in any thoroughgoing sense interrogate the world which it evokes. Rather, such a novel, in so far as it functions as the classic 'readable' text, confirms us, our ideology, our discourse, our assumptions of what is relevant or irrelevant, central or peripheral. In so doing, it underwrites tacit assumptions, making them seem ever more necessary, inalienably right – in a word, *natural*. Fourthly, the relative naivety of realism in cognitive terms, its readiness to take for granted the definition of self and world, is a particularly damaging property. Even its gestures of social criticism suggest only local dissent because the essential world-view is left intact. What looks like thoroughgoing criticism is mere tinkering which serves, in every line of the text, to confirm prevailing assumptions.

We have summarized the 'anti-realistic' implications of modern critical theory not in an effort to be modish but because it seems to us that behind all the unhelpful to-do about endless deferrals of meaning there are genuinely important insights to be gained. The insistence on the textuality of the text obliges us to take seriously the primary truth (so often overlooked in arguments to do with the materiality of literary realism) that literature, even realistic literature, is made not of objects (*res*) but of language. That is to say, where a work of narrative fiction describes an armchair in a character's room, it gives us, by definition, words, signifiers, and not the signified. The only way it could offer the latter is by enclosing an armchair with every copy of the text. The armchair is made of wood, horsehair, upholstery; whereas the text is made, irreducibly, of words. (One is reminded of René Magritte's splendidly accurate depiction of a pipe which bears the legend 'Ceci n'est pas une pipe' – 'this is not a pipe'.) But where a literary text invokes, as part of the story it has to tell, the assumptions, values, symbols and clichés that are in social circulation, there is an overlap of medium between the literary text and the socio-psychological processes it seeks to illuminate. The mentality that informs the characters' lives is couched in language – as is the worded text that re-creates it. The realistic novel is, then, particularly well placed to render not so much the material as the mental furniture of social living.[11]

What can we conclude from these considerations? In the foregoing discussion of the various possibilities of referential linkage between text and world, we have been seeking to spell out a set of hypotheses which accommodate both literary and historiographical concerns. We believe that literary critics and historians can best engage with the present theoretical climate not by retreating to fundamentalist positions but rather by seeking to capitalize on the interdisciplinarity made possible by the current state of theoretical debate about the humanities. The experiential world of any given age and culture is, of course, made of materialities, and leaves material traces; but it is also made of categories of significance (and they, too, can leave material traces). Perhaps one might put it as follows: in human affairs, matter comes to matter precisely when it is incorporated into a nexus of significance and interpretation, into categories of foreground and background, of centre and periphery. It is, then, not true to say that literature and historiography seek to mediate an unmediated world of raw experience (whatever that might be); rather, they mediate that which is already mediated. Moreover, in the wake of Foucaultian discourse analysis and New Historicism, it is surely acceptable to draw attention to the ways in which and the extent to which any age is weightily constituted by processes of (discursive) self-representation. In this context, issues of (national and other) identity are especially interesting. Even where the configurations of geography may be more clear-cut in the disposition of 'natural' frontiers than is the case with Germany, the concept of nationhood is one that is inseparable from language, reflectivity, discourse. And finally, it should be noted that in both novelistic and historical accounts of human experience, central events are made central by the input of a particular form of hermeneutic, by perceptions of causality, of momentousness, and so on. All of which is not to deny the force of contingency in human affairs; but it is to say that an account of those affairs that registered only random sequences would be unreadable – as both literature and history.

To argue in this way is not, of course, to conflate history and literature. A historical account is falsifiable in a way that a novel is not. Yet there are important overlaps. Jacques Derrida famously asserts in *De la Grammatologie* that 'il n'y a pas de hors-texte' (there is nothing outside the text).[12] Well, manifestly there is. But to say this should not prevent us from acknowledging how far textuality extends. Perhaps, finally, one can bring together two notions of veracity, one from a historian, one from a creative writer, that have an intriguing degree of common ground between them. We are thinking of Ranke's aspiration to get at the past 'wie es eigentlich gewesen (ist)' (how it actually was); and of Brecht's aphorism, 'Realismus ist nicht, wie die wirklichen Dinge sind; Realismus ist, wie die Dinge wirklich sind' (realism is not about the way real things are; realism is about the way things really are).[13] Common to both aperçus is the intensifiying force of the (as we might put it) ontological adverb – 'wirklich', 'eigentlich' – ('really' or 'actually'). The use of that adverb reminds us that the human quest to understand and articulate reality is not only a quest for facts; it is a quest for significances. What 'really' happened implies a category of signification and interpretation, and not simple, unmediated facticity. And that holds true for literary writers and for historians alike.

Representation in historical debates

Representation has long been a key and inescapable theme for literary critics. In the last quarter of the twentieth century – from the early 1970s onwards, perhaps – debates in literary theory increasingly affected the thinking of at least some members of the historical profession. What, then, is the state of play on the issue of representation among historians?

In one view, it is the task of the professional historian to re-present the past faithfully: to tell it 'as it actually was'. What has been called the historian's 'craft' entails, in this view, a degree of detective work in recovering the traces, which requires professional training in methods and skills; the reconstruction of what happened, what it was like, takes priority over any concern with the form of presentation of that past. Most practising historians in the Anglo-American world probably adhere – whatever their theoretical views – to some version of a model which says that it is their professional duty to re-present the past as faithfully as they can: to collate, with as much assiduity, skill and honesty as they have at their disposal, the traces of the past and to reconstruct from these traces (or 'sources') a picture which they then paint, as best they can, for an audience in the present. Although few would wish to adhere explicitly to a naive empiricist position, most historians in practice operate as though such a position (with appropriate qualifications and caveats) were viable. A significant proportion of practising historians feels quite happy to ignore 'theory' and simply get on with the nuts and bolts of the job of recovering the past and bringing it to the present.[14]

According to another, postmodernist view, history writing is in principle little different from the writing of literature. Narratives are not given in the surviving traces of the past, waiting to be dug up and mimetically reproduced by the historian; the imposition of a particular narrative which gives coherence and meaning to the bare bones of the past is more an art form, entailing the use of imagination, style and rhetoric.[15] The stories historians tell are constructed on the basis of a wilful selection of aspects of the past, leaving out much which could have been included, highlighting and downplaying, emphasizing and ignoring, almost at whim. Historians impose a shape, with a beginning, a middle, and a satisfying sense of closure in an artificially imposed end. 'Subjects' and 'plots' are created by the historians, not given in the record; even the very nature of the tale, whether comedy or tragedy, is an almost arbitrary choice. 'History itself', in the sense of the past which actually happened, did not actually happen in the way the historians tell the stories. And, on this basis, an almost infinite number of tales can in principle be told about the 'same' past. The apparent 'realism' of historical accounts – the sense that we are learning more about a real past, as it actually was – is more the outcome of literary artifice (the production of the 'truth effect') than genuinely mimetic representation.

Debates deriving explicitly from the postmodernist challenge have proliferated lately.[16] Attention is paid by some postmodernists not only to the ways in which historians shape their stories, but also to the character of the surviving traces which form the raw material of these stories. In the more extreme view, even these traces cannot provide unmediated access to a 'real' past.[17] Awareness of the underlying issues – the selection of elements from the past, the construction of conceptual frameworks through which to capture and represent them – is however far from new.[18] And these issues are important. At the heart of the debates – for all the changes in terminology and emergence of some new strands of argument – there is a key question: to what extent are historical accounts in some sense 'better', or at least more faithful, more accurate, representations of 'reality' (which can only be known through representations) than are, say, the creative (and more instantly gripping and easily accessible) works of novelists, dramatists, filmmakers?[19] If historians are no better at 'telling the truth' about the past than are creative writers or politicians (whose purposes are at least more transparent), on what basis can or could one even begin to assess the extent to which the latter provide faithful or distorted representations, since there would be no more reliable path back to the lost past against which to measure degrees of fidelity?

There is a second, closely related issue of – in many circumstances – comparable or even greater importance. Given that at least popular consumption of historical accounts is predicated on the willing suspension of disbelief (or the faith that what one is reading is true), what are the effects of different types of historical accounts for patterns of individual and collective identity? The role of value neutrality has been hotly contested over the last century: in changing strands, and veering from left to right and back again, the goal of 'objectivity' or value freedom has had its sustainers and detractors, its adherents and critics. Can history, conceived as 'telling the truth about the past as it actually was', aspire to a degree of political neutrality; or are all historical accounts inevitably, intrinsically, at least politically and morally coloured if not downright biased? Should one not only accept this to be the case, but also actually construct historical accounts with conscious, explicit political purposes?

These issues have been particularly contentious in Germany after the Holocaust. Representations of Germany's past have also been contributions to constructions of identity in Germany's present. And in divided Germany, with two opposing states glaring at each other across the Iron Curtain, history became an explicit political tool for the construction of new forms of historical consciousness and political culture – with each side claiming 'objectivity' and 'scientific truth' for its own interpretation.

Representation and identity in twentieth-century Germany

This book pursues some of these general theoretical issues through a range of specific examples and topics. We seek not to reach any collective agreement or present any collective view on these issues, which are too large and complex for any easy resolution in any one set of essays, but rather to illuminate the issues from a variety of angles and with respect to a variety of substantive media of representation.

We do however start from the common premise that all modes of representation – whether through literature in its narrative form, or through films, guidebooks, dramas, fairy-tales, political rituals and speeches, or the writings of professional historians – are essentially human creations which do not simply 'reflect' (in the sense of mimetic representation) some unproblematic, unmediated 'reality out there', like a passive mirror. Rather, they creatively interpret and refract (through particular conceptual prisms) complex worlds of significance and actively contribute to the construction of new forms of self-understanding in an always changing, ambiguous and positioned present. We take the peculiar (in many senses) case of modern Germany, where all forms of cultural representation have had particular resonance with political developments. Many of the chapters which follow deal, implicitly or explicitly, with that central event at the heart of twentieth-century German history: the roads into, and again out of, the abyss epitomized by Auschwitz. But they deal with this sometimes only tangentially, and with reference to omissions, silences, alternatives; they avoid on the whole the obvious neuralgic points which have been addressed in a very large literature more directly on Holocaust representation; and they deal too with other strands and developments in German cultural transformations in the twentieth century.

We begin very much on this point: the possibility of interpretations of German identity which are not simply premised on the knowledge of what came after. Using material ranging from the writings of academic philosophers and social theorists to the images of 'the Other' conveyed by popular cartoons in the press, Mark Hewitson analyses conceptions of national identity in Wilhelmine Germany. He pays particular attention to 'banal' nationalism, which is so often overlooked in the search for the roots of radical nationalism – or long-term malignancy – in German culture. Hewitson's careful analysis of representation in, as he puts it, its 'double sense of depiction and delegation' reveals how, for the majority of Germans before the First World War, the extension of mass media of communication such as newspapers, magazines and photography served in the main to strengthen a relatively securely held sense of German cultural identity over the long historical sweep. Greater knowledge and awareness of Germany's western neighbours and competitors – France, Britain, the USA – both underlined what were held to be uniquely German cultural characteristics (the contrast between *Kultur* and *Zivilisation*) and located Germany firmly within a (western) European heritage, in contrast to the Slavic peoples of Russia, or inferior 'primitive' peoples in colonial territories. But this form of 'banal' national identity shared implicitly by the vast majority of Wilhelmine Germans was not – in contrast to more extreme forms of nationalism emerging among a minority around the turn of the century – peculiarly racial, let alone racist, in tone. There was, in effect, increasing convergence between this banal nationalism and the more securely established conceptions of national identity in other European states with longer histories of unified political statehood.

Paradoxically, Hewitson argues, it was as a result of this increasing security of identity in Wilhelmine Germany that the effective taboo on discussions of constitutional issues began to be lifted in the decades preceding the First World War, when – in the other sense of representation – the growth of democratic political participation (at all levels, from discussion in the popular press, in leagues and grass-roots associations, to the demagogic activities of national parties) helped to raise explicit discussion of constitutional issues to new prominence. With a widening gap between banal conceptions and the more radical nationalism of extremists, the latter (who had particular influence on ruling elites and decision-makers) played a prominent role in the origins of the First World War – significantly, initially against Russia, perceived as more 'Other' than Germany's western European neighbours. Hewitson's very detailed reconstruction of this diversity of elements, and their patterns of combination under specific historical circumstances, shows just how labile and dependent on particular political conditions any construction of identity is.

Following the defeat of Germany in 1918, and the controversial attribution of primary war guilt in the widely detested Versailles Treaty, the new Weimar Republic had once again to embark on a process of identity construction. The Weimar Republic plays a pivotal role in twentieth-century conceptions of German identity: founded in the 'classical centre', home of Goethe and Schiller, associated with the first attempt at truly democratic forms of political representation and with new movements in cultural and social emancipation, despised and hated by the Nazis and rejected even by conservative nationalists politically as 'the system', socially and culturally as the depths of decadence, the Weimar Republic was returned to as a source of contested inspiration in the closing decades of the twentieth century.

To examine these broader issues, Deborah Smail and Corey Ross take a very specific and localized example. They consider what is almost a classic case of self-conscious identity construction and representation: images of Berlin, Germany's former and once again capital city of a united, democratic Germany, in the 1920s and the 1990s. Berlin – the divided city – has been almost paradigmatic of Germany's identity problems in the twentieth century. As Berlin continues to wrestle with its post-1989 identity, much of the reconstruction of the city has looked particularly to the Weimar period for inspiration and a sense of what is 'genuinely Berlin' – when, paradoxically, Berlin was busy reinventing itself from militaristic and monarchical capital of old Prussia (lost among the Brandenburg pine woods in the 'sandpit' of Europe) to a modern, world-class metropolitan centre on a glittering par with Paris, London or New York. (Not even the 'real' Berlin was without a significant element of invention.) Smail and Ross examine different representations of Weimar Berlin through the lenses not only of contemporary literary accounts – so widely used as models or mirrors of 'identity' – but also of guidebook literature, the claims of city planners and tourist offices, and commercial architecture. They argue that much of the myth of the 'Golden Twenties' can be traced back to the (remarkably mundane) efforts of city officials, planners and architects to present a cosmopolitan image of Berlin to the world; and that these glittering images were inevitably challenged, the cracks in their shallow glamour revealed, with the onset of economic depression – an argument which raises questions over the current and future status of the once again reinvented Berlin as symbol and centre of united Germany.

With the collapse of Weimar came, of course, the descent into the 'German catastrophe'. We are concerned here (as throughout the book) not with a detailed historical-political explanation of how this – or any other historical development – actually came about, but rather how it has been interpreted, represented, in the wider context of conceptions and constructions of German identity. Martin Swales takes the very telling example of one of Germany's greatest modern writers, who himself – almost against his will – came to reject his earlier stance of the 'un-political German'. Swales examines how it is that, in Thomas Mann's *Doktor Faustus*, the sombre and austere life of a great composer may be held to represent Germany's slide into barbarism in the late 1930s. He argues that the novel explores a particular, 'totalizing' cultural tendency which seeks to link the many strands of German spiritual life (inwardness, music, theology, Protestantism) and many of its key figures (Luther, Nietzsche) with the political catastrophe of Nazism. Swales contends that the novel submits this totalizing tendency to a historical critique. The Zeitblom figure – particularly in those moments when he reflects on the connections that sustain his account of the life of his friend (and fatherland) – alerts us to the fact that the grandiose symptomatology that connects everything with everything may be less a diagnosis of the catastrophe than its symptom and cause. In this sense, Mann's *Doktor Faustus* acts as its own critique, a critique of those processes of over-representation that played Germany so hideously false between 1933 and 1945.

In the second half of the twentieth century, the changed international context of Cold War and division dramatically altered the kaleidoscopic configuration of elements in constructions of German identity. Gone were the concerns of Germans in newly unified Imperial Germany to secure their place in a world of competing nation-states; gone were the cultural and commercial imperatives of Weimar modernism. In the two German states founded in the images of their occupying powers on the ruins of the Third Reich, attempts had to be made to 'overcome' the recent past and construct new – and yet mutually opposed – identities, differentially rooted in and yet rejecting different aspects of a common heritage. The Holocaust inevitably (and rightly) cast a long shadow over postwar constructions of identity – whether through obsessive examination and re-examination, in an endless and to some extent self-indulgent political culture of national shame in West Germany, or a spirit of officially proclaimed 'victory' and 'self-liberation' from the 'yoke of fascism' in the communist East Germany.[20] At the same time, this incessant concern with the recent past intersected with new issues and challenges to the construction of acceptable identities in a changing present. The chapters which follow all examine, through very detailed analysis of specific examples, aspects of this constantly recurring refrain in the later twentieth century.

Judith Beniston investigates two very different theatrical explorations of the Holocaust, Rolf Hochhuth's *Der Stellvertreter* and Peter Weiss's *Die Ermittlung*. She sees Hochhuth's drama as largely congruent with the viewpoints of West German historiography in the 1950s and 1960s. There is, for example, much mythologization of Nazism as the product of satanic forces (witness the demonic figure of the Doctor); in so far as possibilities of resistance are portrayed, they tend to be anchored in individuals rather than in broader social groupings or institutions. Some of those figures (one thinks, for example, of Gerstein) provide comfort in that they imply that, even in the midst of the terrible darkness, there is an alternative, uncontaminated Germany where Christian moral imperatives are still heeded. By contrast, Weiss's *Die Ermittlung*, for all that it is cast in the form of an oratorio, has no metaphysical or theological resonance; it is, rather, a secular drama that comprehends the Holocaust in rational, human terms – moreover in terms that marginalize the specifically Jewish suffering in favour of an interpretation in terms of broad classes and groups of victims. Thereby the play aligns itself, broadly speaking, with the German Democratic Republic (GDR) view of the Holocaust.

Mererid Puw Davies concentrates on two post-1945 texts, one a novel, the other a film, which interestingly make use of the genre of fairy-tales or folk-tales, which played such a central role in late eighteenth- and early nineteenth-century constructions of German identity as a *Kulturnation*. One particular, and particularly gruesome, *Märchen* reappears in a variety of later reworkings and reincarnations: that of Bluebeard. The central motifs here have to do with patriarchy, with gender and repression, and with violence. Puw Davies shows how this constellation lends itself to representations of and reflections on modern German identity – and particularly to questions concerning the spectre of the Holocaust as the return of the (psychically and historically) repressed realm. The use of *Märchen* material functions not as simple allegory; rather, in Puw Davies's reading, the friction between old and new modes of narrative, between the Grimm brothers and Auschwitz, sets up an interpretative field of force which liberates genuinely critical reflectivity.

Very different representations of the same tortured past can be found in the works of Bachmann and Duden. Adopting a Lacanian framework of interpretation, which she believes can provide important insights in this case, Stephanie Bird explores the problematic identification of women with victims of the Holocaust: in *Malina* and *Das Judasschaf* the female narrator defines her own sense of oppression within patriarchy in relation to the Nazi atrocities. However, far from privileging the narrator's perspective, the texts themselves question the role of victim identification as a strategy for the protagonists to ignore their own complicity in their oppression. Self-representation can be self-falsification. And this is a theme running through the chapters of literary analysis in this volume; Swales, Beniston, Bird and Puw Davies are all at pains to highlight the different ways in which literary texts can achieve important, cognitively valuable forms of critical self-consciousness.

Not all was negative exploration in postwar Germany. The GDR, in particular, sought (all too obviously) to establish and build up new constructions of identity in which Germans could take pride. And not all representation is of a 'purely' cultural form: arguably in most societies repeated rituals which are regularly and actively re-enacted are at least as important in securing unthinking, deeply held or 'everyday' understandings of identity as simply 'the way the world is'. Identities which need not be explicitly articulated, examined and re-examined, but are simply 'lived', may be more effective than those which are more like fragile plants which are repeatedly dug up to examine how well the roots are growing. But such re-enactments can be too obvious; and when they conflict with other elements of lived experience, they can even be counter-productive. Corey Ross turns to the construction of new forms of social identity through the politically willed 'staging' of the working class in the GDR. 'Representation' takes place not only through what is conventionally seen as 'culture' (novels, drama, film) but also through what Ross calls *Inszenierung*, an active 'staging' or acting out of new forms of social identity. For the ruling communist Socialist Unity Party (SED), the East German working class was to play a key role: it was the major actor in the historic mission of the SED to take Germany onto the higher plane of pure communism. But, as Ross shows, although the 'stage production' of the working class in the GDR did leave important traces in patterns of consciousness of social identity in East Germany, the effects were – to put it mildly – not always entirely those intended by the vanguard party of the working class. The official communist slogan, 'Everything for the good of the people' ('Alles zum Wohle des Volkes') was easily turned into the popular counter-slogan, with an implied 'but' at the start, 'we are the people' ('Wir sind das Volk'), when conditions were propitious in 1989.

Finally, Mary Fulbrook turns to the roles and writings of professional historians. The development of German historical writing after the Holocaust provides an interesting case study of the nature of history as a human enterprise – political, social and cultural, as well as more narrowly 'academic'. For one thing, any tale told about this particularly ghastly past was also, intrinsically and unavoidably, an indictment of certain villains in the continuing present. Degrees of complicity in the perpetration of mass murder might have very real consequences for legal proceedings, political involvement and material livelihood. There were vested interests on all sides in the kinds of tales that could or should be told about Germany's recent past. It was impossible for German 'contemporary history' (*Zeitgeschichte*) to be politically irrelevant. For another, historical consciousness was intimately bound up with the politics of divided Germany. Both East and West wished to represent themselves as having 'overcome' the Nazi era better than their Cold War opponent; and, within each Germany, history teaching was explicitly used as a tool for the transformation of political culture. Thus, the role of history in divided Germany after the Holocaust presents an almost extreme case study of the question of the extent and limits of history as an 'objective' enterprise committed to 'telling the truth about the past'. But it also, when set in a wider context, reveals the limits of the public impact of professional historical writing. There were all manner of dissonances, in both East and West Germany, between their (very different) public representations of a common past and the diversity of private memories or informal 'conversations' and re-presentations of the past.

Whither representation?

Taken together, the chapters in this book range over a number of constructions of identity in twentieth-century Germany. No attempt has been made to offer encyclopaedic coverage. Rather, we have allowed ourselves to take in-depth soundings, exploring the particular rhetorical strategies and media through which the various representations are attempted. And we have asked what these representations amount to. At every turn we have been mindful of the interplay between literary and cultural concerns on the one hand, and political and historical matters on the other. The issue of how a nation is represented – and hence constructed – is of surpassing importance, not least because 'representation' is a category both within art (aesthetic representation) and politics (representation of the people). In Hewitson's phrase, representation is a matter of both 'depiction' and 'delegation', a question which has centrally dogged German culture and politics from the

Kaiserreich, through the almost diametrically opposing conceptions of the *Volk* in Nazi Germany and the GDR, to the variety of democratic conceptions from Weimar to the present day. We have not sought to present an account of what, substantively, 'German identity in the twentieth century' is or has been held to consist in. Rather, we have focused on the range of forms of representation. We have presented select illustrations of the multiplicity of possible answers to the question of identity, seeking to illuminate the variety of means and media through which this question can be addressed, these answers constructed. We have sought to demonstrate just how contingent, ambiguous, and politically situated such representations are.

The wider theoretical questions raised at the start of this chapter clearly cannot be definitively answered purely by means of these case studies, and it would be absurd to suggest otherwise. But we would nevertheless claim more general significance for this collection of essays. For, in examining selected facets of representation and identity in twentieth-century Germany, two things above all become clear.

First, reflections on and of German identity are not merely representations, but at the same time also constructions, of differing and often conflicting versions of identity. Engagement with the past – in the sense not of a simple 'reality out there', but rather of a multitude of significances, symbolizations and attributions of meaning – is thus also, and always, participation in collective conversations about a complex present and a contested set of possible futures. And these conversations take place in real places, at real times; they interact, through different media, in plays for power and influence.

But secondly, and of undoubtedly equal importance: for all the intertextuality of these collective conversations, it has to be emphasized that we are not trapped in some endless vicious circle of essentially meaningless non-referentiality. Mutual understanding, empathy, translation across cultural and historical paradigms, can be both attempted and, to a significant degree, achieved; communication can lead to significant changes in perception, new insights and understandings. It may not, in principle, be possible to 'know the past as it really was', in all its lost entirety; but it is entirely possible to engage in genuinely meaningful, intersubjective communication about 'what is really significant about the past' in the present – and to do this without abandoning some notion of at least good faith or commitment to honesty, if not, perhaps, a more elusive, indefinable and absolute notion of historical truth.

The dialogue between historians and literary theorists can perhaps thus take us forward in our conceptions of representation and reality: in our understandings of the interconnections between the worlds of fantasy and exploration of human 'truths' through the play of the imagination, on the one hand, and – to return to Ranke and Brecht – what it was 'actually' like, how it was 'really' experienced, on the other. Perhaps we need, in the words of Shakespeare's Macbeth, to remind ourselves of the limiting case: "tis a tale told by an idiot, full of sound and fury, signifying nothing'. As postmodernists delight in telling us, there may be an arbitrary gap between 'signifier' and 'signified'; but this gap, however arbitrary, is not a void, for it is bridged – with that extraordinary human capacity for intersubjective communication and signification.

Notes

1 On literary theory, see for example Terry Eagleton, *Literary Theory: An Introduction*, 2nd edn (Oxford: Blackwell, 1996); for one recent response to the challenge of postmodernism to history, see Richard J. Evans, *In Defence of History* (London: Granta, 1997).

2 See for example Keith Jenkins, *Rethinking History* (London: Routledge, 1991) and *On 'What is History?'. From Carr and Elton to Rorty and White* (London: Routledge, 1995).

3 A problem which is not resolved by such essentially whiggish interpretations of the history of history as Joyce Appleby, Lynn Hunt and Margaret Jacobs, *Telling the Truth about History* (New York and London: W. W. Norton and Co., 1994).

4 Cf. for example Evans, *In Defence of History*, pp. 238–43.

5 Cf. Hayden White, 'Historical Emplotment and the Problem of Truth', in Saul Friedländer (ed.), *Probing the Limits of Representation* (Cambridge, Mass.: Harvard University Press, 1992), conceding that the Holocaust cannot sensibly be emplotted as comedy (notwithstanding the recent film *Life is Beautiful*).

6 Stephan Kohl, *Realismus: Theorie und Geschichte* (Munich: Fink, 1977).

7 E. H. Gombrich, *Art and Illusion: A Study in the Psychology of pictorial Representation* (Oxford: Phaidon, 1980), p. 24.

8 See Ian Watt, *The Rise of the Novel* (Harmondsworth: Penguin, 1963).

9 Roland Barthes, 'The Reality Effect', in Tzvetan Todorov (ed.), *French Literary Theory Today* (Cambridge: Cambridge University Press, 1982), pp. 11–17.

10 See Christopher Prendergast, *The Order of Mimesis* (Cambridge: Cambridge University Press, 1986).

11 See Lilian R. Furst, *'All is True': the Claims and Strategies of Realist Fiction* (Durham and London: Duke University Press, 1995); and Martin Swales, *Studies of German Prose in the Age of European Realism* (Lampeter: Mellen, 1995).

12 Jacques Derrida, *De la Grammatologie* (Paris: Seuil, 1967).

13 Bertolt Brecht, 'Katzgraben-Notate', in *Gesammelte Werke* (Werkausgabe Edition Suhrkamp) (Frankfurt am Main: Suhrkamp, 1967), vol. 16, p. 837.

14 Cf. for example the classic statement in Geoffrey Elton, *The Practice of History* (London: Fontana, 1969), who, for all his idiosyncrasies and prejudices (for example, against sociology), is not quite as naive about the ways in which historians' questions and narratives shape their material as some of his critics would have us believe; and, for a more recent how-to-do-history primer which is essentially premised on similar assumptions, John Tosh, *The Pursuit of History*, 2nd edn (London: Longman, 1991).

15 See particularly Hayden White, *The Content of the Form* (Baltimore and London: Johns Hopkins University Press, 1987).

16 See for example the debate with Patrick Joyce (and others) unleashed by Lawrence Stone, in *Past and Present*, no. 131 (May 1991), pp. 217–18; no. 133 (Nov. 1991), pp. 204–9; no. 135 (May 1992), pp. 189–94.

17 See particularly the debate between F. R. Ankersmit and Perez Zagorin on 'History and Postmodernism', where Ankersmit denies that the past has any role to play in adjudicating between competing accounts of the same question: articles in *History and Theory*, vol. 28, no. 2 (1989), pp. 137–53; vol. 29, no. 3 (1990), pp. 263–74 and 275–96.

18 See for example the lucid survey in Beverley Southgate, *History: What and Why? Ancient, Modern and Postmodern Perspectives* (London: Routledge, 1996). For a supreme example of a theorist grappling with many of the very same issues, but in a quite different historical context with different terms of debate, see the methodological essays of Max Weber.

19 Cf. particularly the essays by Swales, Beniston and Bird in this collection.

20 Cf. M. Fulbrook, *German National Identity after the Holocaust* (Cambridge: Polity Press, 1999).

Nation and *Nationalismus*: representation and national identity in Imperial Germany

Mark Hewitson

> In reality itself, things last for no time at all; through the restlessness, which they ... betray at all times, the form of each thing dissolves in the very moment of its coming into being; it lives, so to speak, only in the process of its own destruction. (Georg Simmel, *Philosophie des Geldes*, Leipzig, 1900)

To Georg Simmel, one of the three most important sociologists of the Wilhelmine era, modernity was characterized by flux and fragmentation. Representation and identity, which were central – although undefined – ideas in Simmel's work, could only be understood against the background of an all-embracing division of labour, the objectification of culture and the failure of individuals' subjective knowledge of the world to keep up with technology. The result of these processes, according to Simmel, was that contemporaries were faced with a 'bewildering multiplicity of styles'. A rift had opened up between 'objective' and 'subjective' culture: individuals were now surrounded by a confusing array of products and complex relationships, which they did not comprehend. This, in turn, reinforced a feeling of cultural relativism: 'The historicizing tendencies of our century, its incomparable ability to reproduce and give life to the most distant things – in a temporal as well as spatial sense – is merely the internal side of a general increase in adaptability and wide-ranging mobility.' Previously, individuals had defined themselves by their society's 'style' of life, as if, like their 'mother tongue', it were part of their own 'psychology'. By the turn of the century, they were confronted by 'a large number of styles', which effectively severed the connection between their mode of life and identity, just as, 'when we learn foreign languages', we experience the 'independent existence' of our own language. Objective styles of life and subjective experience were 'like two parties, between which exists a purely coincidental relationship of contacts, harmonies and disharmonies'. The principal question of the modern age, as far as Simmel was concerned, was whether individual psychology (or a subjective sense of identity) could be reconnected to the fleeting phenomena (or representations) of the external world.[1] Under such conditions, it appeared that representations of the nation would be too ephemeral, contradictory and autonomous to sustain a common national identity.

During the last twenty years or so, historians have come to accept many of the arguments about discontinuity – particularly between subjective individuals and their objective environment – which were articulated by Simmel and others more than a century ago. At best, a shared sense of attachment to a nation seems to be illusory, artificial and historically specific rather than natural and eternal, as had previously been assumed. 'Nations', which combine a cultural sense of belonging with a political will to achieve self-determination, are products of the eighteenth, nineteenth and twentieth centuries, and are already showing signs, according to scholars such as Eric Hobsbawm, of being eclipsed during the next century. 'National identity', from this perspective, is not analogous to individual identity, for it lacks a single will, a consistent personality and a coterminous physicality. Logically, it requires only a common – and possibly transient – sense of political and cultural affiliation: individuals are identical in feeling an attachment to the nation, even though the grounds for their attachment, as Celia Applegate has shown, are often divergent and dissonant. Historically, a sense of national identity has usually rested on a number of shared assumptions, beyond simple attachment: the majority of individuals within a nation, although not the same by any means with respect to their personalities, do hold *some* similar views, however temporary or unimportant. Thus, in Simmel's terms, subjective and objective culture are still connected to each other, albeit tenuously. These connections of identity are maintained by means of 'representation'. Individuals must be seen to be similar, and to act as a single group, rather than merely being similar. Representation is therefore necessary in its double sense of 'depiction', since the nation is – in Benedict Anderson's oft-repeated phrase – an imagined community, and in the sense of 'delegation', because certain individuals have to act on the nation's behalf, if it is to act at all. As Jürgen Habermas has demonstrated, these two meanings of the word are interrelated: the right to act on the nation's behalf rests, to a considerable extent, on a negotiated and often hegemonic consensus about how to imagine the nation. National identity results from 'a circulatory process that is generated through the legal institutionalization of citizens' communication'.[2]

Some Wilhelmine Germans were aware of this discursive basis of national identity. Certainly, that was what the historian Friedrich Meinecke, who was arguably the most sophisticated theorist of the nation in the prewar era, had in mind when he contrasted earlier nation-states, in which there was a clear distinction between rulers and the ruled, and more recent *Nationalstaaten*, in which almost all parties competed to gain recognition for their particular interpretation of national interest and identity. Meinecke also conceded that nations could be constructed by states (*Staatsnationen*) and that they had been transformed during and after the French Revolution into nation-states (*Nationalstaaten*). Nevertheless, both he and almost all of his contemporaries still saw nations as self-evident, primordial and natural entities, akin to living organisms: 'the nation ... cannot, of course, do without the totality, any more than the head can do without the body'. Despite making an analytical distinction between *Kulturnationen* and *Staatsnationen*, he assumed that virtually all nations had cultural elements which for centuries had remained 'vegetative'. Furthermore, they were communities of descent, deriving from tribal antecedents: 'a natural core based on blood relationship must be present in a nation', whereas a 'common place of residence', 'a common language', 'a common intellectual life, a common state or a federation of similar states' were not 'essential elements or characteristics of a nation'. Germany, Meinecke propounded, was an archetypal, natural *Kulturnation*, whose national consciousness extended back to the Middle Ages, even though the German nation-state only dated from 1871. Although there was still a 'duality' between the Prussian 'state-nation' (*Staatsnation*) and the German 'cultural nation' (*Kulturnation*), it was inevitable, Meinecke implied, that the Reich, which represented the culture of all Germans, would prevail.[3]

Modern-day historians, in attempting to explain the organicism of Wilhelmine conceptions of the nation, have tended to treat Germany as a special case, as a consequence of its late unification and rapid industrialization. There have been many variations on this theme since the 1960s, but most have concentrated on either culture or the state. To postwar American scholars like Hans Kohn, Fritz Stern and George Mosse, German national identity owed much more to culture, ethnicity or even race than its French or British counterparts, partly because of the absence of a German nation-state before 1871. Accordingly, *Deutschtum* could never be a question of voluntary attachment to a set of political ideals or institutions, as in the founding myth of the United States; rather, it was defined in terms of cultural or genetic attributes, frequently as an act of defence against alleged French or British predominance. During the post-unification era, such an exclusive definition of German identity could easily turn inwards, to root out 'aliens', or outwards, to subjugate 'inferior' neighbouring peoples. Recently, Harold James has extended the scope of these arguments by contending that the cultural 'building blocks of German national identity' were, in addition, contradictory and precarious, with the result, when they were combined with the 'incomplete' political institutions of the Reich, that 'Germany alone played great power politics with all the unfulfilled ambitions and romantic expectations of a movement for national awakening'. The First World War is then understood as 'a war to complete the incomplete nation'.[4]

James's thesis about the German state coincides, in large part, with that which is put forward by Fritz Fischer, Hans-Ulrich Wehler, Volker Berghahn and the Bielefeld school: the *Kaiserreich*, it is argued, was an incoherent, aristocratic and outdated system of government, increasingly out of kilter with the economic foundations and class composition of an industrializing society; the continuing power of this state, propped up by an expanding, independent and *Junker*-dominated army, had the double-edged effect of 'feudalizing' significant sections of the German middle classes and prompting Bernhard von Bülow and Theobald von Bethmann Hollweg to pursue a diversionary foreign policy of 'social imperialism'. Like James, most adherents of the Bielefeld school have depicted German nationalism as a means of escape – a *Flucht nach vorn* – from the conflicts and fragmentation of Wilhelmine society. They differ from James only in the degree of significance which they attach to the state. This is a line of thought that has since been taken further by John Breuilly, who effectively discounts many of the cultural underpinnings of the German national movement and idea. Instead, nationalism is described, though not exclusively, as a political reaction to the interventions and aspirations of the state: it was 'a consequence, not a cause of the new German nation-state'. Culture still has a role in sustaining national identity, particularly in Breuilly's more recent writings, but it is secondary to the German Empire, which itself stimulated and created a predominant conception of Germanness. The Reich, it is held, 'rather than being the product of one version of the national idea, was turning into its principal creator.'[5]

What unites most historians is their inclination to treat German nationalism as a pathology. Thus, Otto Dann, the author of the main German-language work on the subject, makes a distinction between 'patriotism', in which individual and group interests are subordinated to those of 'society as a whole', and 'nationalism', which results 'when the egalitarian basic consensus, on which a nation rests, is no longer respected'. To Dann and most other historians of Germany, the term 'nationalism' usually denotes radical, right-wing racism and chauvinism. In the wake of Anglo-American revisionism during the last two decades, some research has examined emancipatory nationalism, which had been intertwined with German liberalism for most of the nineteenth century, yet most of the literature on the *Kaiserreich* continues to focus on extra-parliamentary leagues, on the rightward shift of political parties and the creation of a national opposition, and on the popularity of anti-Semitism, militarism and imperialism. By contrast, this chapter looks at the everyday expressions of what has been termed 'banal nationalism'. It asks whether nationalism in the broad sense – the will amongst a group of people to form or maintain a nation-state – is indeed, as Ernest Gellner claims, a more or less general assumption in a society like Wilhelmine Germany, which stood on the brink of modernity.[6] In particular, it investigates the meaning of German identity in an age of transformation in the means of representation.

It is argued here that banal nationalism in Germany rested on surprisingly secure foundations, which prevented it from collapsing as the means of representation changed at the turn of the century. The chapter is divided into those sections which examine such changes in the means of communication and in the practices of political representation, and those which analyse the impact of such changes on German national identity. In particular, it is posited that the transformation of communication during the Wilhelmine era placed greater emphasis on German perceptions of the wider world, and that the alteration of political practices helped to turn national identity and national interest into objects of party debate. The next section shows how a strong sense of German identity was established during the course of the nineteenth and early twentieth centuries.

A German identity

'Nothing is more un-national than national isolation', declared Hans Delbrück, editor of the *Preußische Jahrbücher* and professor of history at Berlin University, during the centenary celebrations of the 'German wars of independence' in 1913. Like most other commentators, he based this judgement on a recognition of the open and receptive nature of German national identity. The nation's mission, it was argued, consisted in pooling and distilling the ideas of the world. As a consequence, Germany was believed to be both more philosophically and scientifically advanced, since it had synthesized and utilized the knowledge of other cultures, and more susceptible to collapse, as its own culture was transformed by the impact of foreign concepts and theories. 'Without overrating itself a people does not arrive at knowledge of itself at all', wrote Heinrich von Treitschke, Delbrück's colleague in Berlin and predecessor at the *Preußische Jahrbücher*: 'The Germans are always in danger of losing their nationality, because they have too little of this solid pride.'[7]

Recent historians of Germany have tended to sympathize with such anxiety. Because, until 1871, it lacked a political framework, which would have protected it against the incursions of Parisian *couture* and Westminster constitutionalism, German national identity, it has been claimed, became a confusing, composite construction of French, British, American, Swiss, Dutch, Italian and ancient Greek components. In the years before unification, writers and academics were able to dominate competing and contradictory discourses about the nation, fashioning 'Germany' to suit literary tastes and political predilections. From eighteenth-century patriotism and turn-of-the-century romanticism to democratic scepticism during the 1840s and realist admiration of the state in the 1850s, German conceptions of the nation oscillated unpredictably, it is held, because they depended on the social circumstances of poets and the vagaries of the book and newspaper trade. What was more, these conflicting versions of national identity continued to coexist with many other allegiances to kin, class, confession, profession, party, region and state. Until the late nineteenth century, loyalty to the nation allegedly remained secondary to a panoply of other affiliations. Even after 1871, such contradictions were not removed. Rather, they were compounded by the residue of an unresolved argument from the mid-nineteenth century about the geographical extent of Germany – an Austrian-dominated *Großdeutschland* or a Prussian-led *Kleindeutschland* – which had been translated by the 1890s, the argument runs, into pan-German yearnings for a 'Greater Reich' and into close ties between Austrian and German nationalism. Since the *Kaiserreich* had been established by Bismarck as a conservative, federal and monarchical compromise, designed to resist any shift towards a unitary nation-state, it could not be expected to invent a lustrous gallery of national symbols. Historians have not been surprised, then, to find that the German Empire never adopted a national anthem. This failure to create an artificial, political *Staatsnation*, it is asserted, led to the popularization of alternative, expansionist ethnic and racial definitions of a German *Volksnation*.[8]

Such interpretations of nineteenth- and early twentieth-century nationalism ignore a matrix of enduring images and ideas which constituted the core of German identity. Of the three possible bases of national particularity (cultural, genetic and political), culture, which was expressed in terms of a German 'character' and 'values', was the most significant. This did not mean, though, that loyalties to national political institutions were negligible. On the one hand, the Reich, because it was widely seen to have been economically successful, appeared to have fulfilled the fundamental voluntarist condition of a political nation, which was unusually prominent during an age of *Realpolitik*, by persuading citizens that it had acted in their best interests. The verdict of Paul Rohrbach, one of Wilhelmine Germany's most famous publicists, arguably echoed the view of the majority: 'Germany's rise has been favoured by the fact that the political and economic union of Germany coincided with the most wonderful technical progress that humanity had ever seen.' On the other hand, the political institutions of the Reich, although new, seemed to be the continuation of a long 'German' tradition. The notion of a strong, interventionist state, a system of codified, public law separate from politics, constitutional government, federalism and monarchy all went back, in the individual histories of Prussia, Bavaria, Saxony and the other states, to the start of the nineteenth century and beyond. Moreover, these traditions had been linked together between 1815 and 1867 within the practical structure of the German Confederation and within the persisting, ideological framework of the Holy Roman Empire: it was for this reason that no one thought to challenge the restoration of a German 'Reich' in 1871.[9]

Nonetheless, the absence of an overarching German state during the nineteenth century, which the existence of a confederation failed to counterbalance, prevented the emergence of seemingly self-evident connections between culture, territory and politics, which had characterized the formation of French and English nation-states. In the opinion of the economist

Adolph Wagner and of most other Wilhelmine commentators, the German 'territories' had been 'almost independent and half-sovereign' under the Holy Roman Empire and the Confederation, precluding the fulfilment of any of 'the nation's more general political and economic tasks'. Failed attempts 'to do without the great adhesive of the national community', as well as the desire 'to bind different nationalities in a common state', were proof that the nation-state (*Nationalstaat*) was 'the normal type', wrote Wagner's fellow-economist Gustav Cohn. Progress depended on the level of state organization. Since 'great nation-states' alone produced the highest forms of progress, Germany, which had for centuries lacked a territorial and political foundation, was reduced to 'laboriously catching up, when compared to the development of England or France, with what these had already achieved'. Under these circumstances, it had not been possible to derive a full sense of German identity from a set of political institutions. Germanness, in contrast to Englishness or Frenchness, had not, before 1871, been associated unthinkingly with a territorial nation-state. The main corollary of this fact, after unification, was the founding of German citizenship, when imperial legislation was eventually passed in 1913, on the principle of descent (*jus sanguinis*), not territory (*jus soli*). Thus, whereas French citizens included all those born on French soil and, by extension, in the theories of Ernest Renan and many of his compatriots, all those wishing to abide by France's constitution, citizens of the Reich were defined by their ancestors.[10]

This definition of citizenship, which was based on ethnicity or a myth of common ancestry, hinted at the uncertain boundary between the cultural and racial foundations of German identity. 'In its common "ethnic" sense', wrote the sociologist Max Weber, albeit in disagreement, '"nationality" [*Nationalität*] normally shares with "people" [*Volk*] at least the vague notion that a community of common descent must underpin it.' In an era before the threat of genocide was taken seriously, there were few obstacles to the use of racial stereotypes. A string of discoveries about evolution and genetic difference, which followed Darwin's publication of *On the Origin of Species* in 1859 and made biology the most modern of nineteenth-century sciences, encouraged German academics to speculate about the racial origins of cultural diversity and national identity. These speculations were fuelled by a long-standing historical interest in 'Germanic' tribes and by philological theories about an Indo-European family of languages, which appeared to distinguish central and western Europeans from the rest of humanity; they also incorporated pre-Darwinian typologies of racial form and beauty, and centuries-old certainty about the supposed superiority of whites over the so-called black and yellow races. The new discipline of anthropology, whose emergence in Germany during the 1860s was linked to the prospect of unification, came to accommodate all of these different strands. It enjoyed widespread academic interest and public support. As late as 1904, Weber, who was habitually cautious in his analysis of causes, still believed that 'the *anthropological* side of the problem' might explain the peculiarity of the western 'spirit', which had created capitalism: 'When we find again and again that, even in departments of life apparently mutually independent, certain types of rationalization have developed in the Occident, and only there, it would be natural to suspect that the most important reason lay in differences of heredity.' His admission that he was 'inclined to think the importance of biological heredity very great' betrayed the lasting popularity of racial social science during the Wilhelmine period.[11]

The advocates of race, however, failed to find specific, credible evidence for the genetic foundations of national identity or of broader cultural variations. This, according to his own testimony, was why Weber continued to look to the intellectual causes of western capitalism: 'in spite of the notable achievements of anthropological research, I see up to the present no way of exactly or even approximately measuring either the extent or, above all, the form of its influence on the development investigated here'. The main anthropological investigation of racial attributes was carried out in the 1870s and 1880s in the wake of the Franco-Prussian War, after Armand de Quatrefages, a well-known French anthropologist, had claimed that Prussians were Finnish in origin, and not Indo-European, as had been supposed. Through official letters to schoolteachers, Rudolf Virchow, the founder of German anthropology, supervised the examination of 15 million German, Austrian, Swiss and Belgian schoolchildren for traits such as blond hair and blue eyes. His findings refuted the assertions of Quatrefages, proving that both north Germans and Finns were on the whole blond, but it also revealed that south and west Germans were typically brown-eyed and dark-haired, which effectively disproved André Retzius's widely believed theory that superior long-heads had settled in Scandinavia, Germany, England and France, pushing indigenous broad-heads to European outposts such as Finland and Brittany. Other avenues of research such as craniometry, or the measuring of skulls, likewise found no convincing correlation between genes, language and nationality. Thus, amongst academics, the Aryan or Indo-European hypothesis, which posited that grammatical similarities between Sanskrit and the Romance and Germanic languages were best explained by the migration of so-called Aryans from India to Europe, was called into question. Although no such doubts were entertained by popular proselytizers of race like Houston Stewart Chamberlain, who continued to propound the racial superiority and exclusivity of the 'Germanic' peoples, they were usually reluctant to make clear distinctions between European nations. Chamberlain himself used the word 'Germane', which he traced back to Tacitus, to denote Celts, Teutons and Slavs. For most commentators, race was, at most, a semi-mythical backdrop to European ascendancy rather than a useful means to define German particularity. Even to a right-wing publicist like Delbrück, the idea that modern-day Germans were direct descendants of ancient *Germanen* was 'not correct'. 'Just like the Germans', he went on, 'all the other great cultural peoples – the English, French, Spanish, Italians – are also mixed races, fused together from the most heterogeneous of tribes through the stream of historical events.'[12]

Culture, given the distant and disparate nature of shared political events, constituted the core of German national identity. In its starkest form, it was expressed as the 'German character' or as a set of 'German values', which were renamed the 'ideas of 1914' during the First World War. Such character or values were, of course, an artificial construction, susceptible to change. 'National character is different in each epoch. The soul of the people (*Volksseele*) alters from day to day', wrote the playwright and journalist Max Nordau: 'If one wants examples: ... the German people of the preceding generation was effeminately sentimental, romantically enthusiastic; in short, emotional. In the present generation, it is hard and practical, coldly calculating, prone to act more than to speak, to calculate more than to daydream; in short, cogitative.' Nordau was aware – in a book entitled *Paradoxe* – that he was arguing against the grain. Most commentators assumed that there was a consistent code of German values which dated back to the Dark Ages and which had since been rooted in the increasingly rich and fertile soil of German culture. Every day, in newspapers and magazines, novels, poems and songs, cartoons and paintings, monuments and buildings, citizens of the Reich were exposed to different sides of a German character. Even academics appeared not to fear ridicule or criticism as, like Heinrich von Treitschke and Karl Lamprecht, they included references to national traits in their prestigious and widely read histories of Germany, or, like Hans Mayer and Alfred Kirchhoff, they contributed to works about *Das Deutsche Volkstum*, with chapters on 'German Landscapes and Tribes', 'German Morals and Customs', 'German Christianity', 'German Law', and 'German Education and Science'. According to such accounts, Germans were pious, introspective, deep, instinctive, privately maternal, outwardly masculine, loyal but credulous, passive but, when provoked, powerful: they were characterized, wrote Mayer, by 'a German depth in the life of feeling and thought, a loving devotion to the individual, an inclination for a cosy homeliness, a tendency towards the mystical, a high-aiming idealism, far-flung flights of fantasy, but also an overdeveloped individualism, a proclivity towards the fantastic and baroque, towards confused darkness and sentimentality'. Most of these and other values appear to have been collated during the Napoleonic wars as a deliberate counter-argument against France. This explains their coherence and longevity, since the neighbouring state, which remained the principal enemy of the German states throughout the nineteenth century, was depicted in much the same way during the entire period: as an atheist, over-rational and superficial society, rather than a community, and as a centralized and aggressive state.[13] In the course of the nineteenth and early twentieth centuries, Britain and, to a lesser extent, the United States could be fitted into the same scheme as a utilitarian addition to French rationalism. During the First World War, this set of binary oppositions was articulated as a struggle of German *Kultur* against French *Zivilisation*, and of German *Helden* against British *Händler*.

'German values' appeared to many observers by the end of the nineteenth century to be self-evident because they had been interwoven in a larger fabric of national symbols and legends. These, too, of course, had been invented or reinvented, usually in the period since 1815. Thus, the *Nibelungenlied* – a thirteenth-century poem which, in misinterpreted form, became the subject of Richard Wagner's *Ring* cycle – had been virtually ignored after its rediscovery in 1755 until it was taken up by Wagner and the playwright Friedrich Hebbel in the 1850s. Nevertheless, by the late nineteenth century, the symbolic firmament of German history appeared to be real, with each symbol constellated with a number of others. Two overlapping clusters of figures and legends were discernible. First, there were the heroes of the ancient 'Germanic' tribes and medieval kingdoms, including Arminius or 'Hermann', who had defeated the Romans at the battle of the Teutoburg forest in 9 AD, Siegfried, who was the tragic young protagonist of the *Nibelungenlied*, and Emperor Friedrich I or 'Barbarossa', who had allegedly waited since the twelfth century in the Thuringian Kyffhäuser mountain to come to the aid of the German nation. By the early nineteenth century, these myths of the *Germanen* and *Germanismus* already criss-crossed German culture, finding adherents as diverse as the philosopher Georg Wilhelm Friedrich Hegel, the historian Leopold von Ranke, and the poet Friedrich von Schlegel. In general, the myths reinforced each other and provided a context for more recent traditions: they referred to the woods, in which Hermann lived and died, to the mountains, where Barbarossa lay in wait, to the Rhine, into which Hagen threw the *Nibelungen* treasure, and to the rural, organic life of tribesmen, farmers and princes; they depicted struggles against infidels, with Barbarossa killed on his way back from a crusade, against the artifice and civilization of Rome, in the case of Hermann, and against outsiders; and they portrayed characters who were natural, chaste, warm, fertile and passive in the domestic circle of the family, free-spirited, autonomous, introspective and cooperative in the meetings and juries of the village or town, and loyal, protective, strong and violent in the battles of the tribes and Teutonic knights. Long-established symbols of Germany like 'deutscher Michel', which dated back to the early modern period, and 'Germania', which was invented in the late eighteenth century, were easily accommodated, with their respective references to rural simplicity and ancient fidelity, within a reinvented Germanic world. Similarly, modern representatives of the German tradition, such as Beethoven, Schiller, Goethe, Wagner and Nietzsche, were interpreted as independent-minded and deep-thinking successors of the *Germanen*. Although few Wilhelmine Germans would have disagreed with the assertions of right-wing cultural critics like Julius Langbehn, who claimed in his best-selling book *Rembrandt als Erzieher* that such representative figures were part of a broader Germanic culture including Rembrandt and Shakespeare, most assumed, like Langbehn himself, that Germany was the centre of this culture, just as Englishness was assumed to be the core of Britishness. As early as 1834, the popular *Brockhaus* encyclopaedia routinely equated 'germanisch' with 'deutsch'.[14]

Second, symbols and stories which had been associated with Prussia were attached to a wider German identity. On the one hand, many Prussian insignia, institutions and myths overlapped with – and had been derived from – those of the old Reich and the other German states. Thus, the one-headed eagle of the new Reich, which appeared on stamps and signs throughout Germany, not only resembled that of Prussia, but also that of the Holy Roman Empire, which was two-headed, of Alsace, Lübeck, Schwarzburg and Anhalt, and even of Austria-Hungary. Likewise, a Prussian monarch like Wilhelm I was quickly perceived, after 1871, to be both a typical representative of the German princes and to be the descendant, now holding court in Berlin not Vienna, of the old Holy Roman emperor. His historical role in Prussia – to defend the eastern marches of western Christianity against the Slavs – corresponded to that of his imperial Habsburg predecessors, who had defended the Holy Roman Empire against Russians and Turks. On the other hand, Prussia had been more closely associated than any other German state, in the opinion of a reading public, with the nineteenth-century national movement. Looking back, from the standpoint of the 1900s, the 'wars of independence', which culminated in a 'German' victory over Napoleonic forces – including those of Württemberg and Baden – at the battle of Leipzig in 1813, were often merged with the fate of Prussia, which had risen from the ashes after defeat at Jena in 1806. In 1913, during the centenary celebrations of the 'battle of the peoples' (*Völkerschlacht*), both supporters and critics regularly interchanged the words 'Prussia' and 'Germany', 'king' and 'kaiser'. In the same way, Prussia seemed to have led German resistance to France in 1840, so that songs like 'Die Wacht am Rhein' and 'Deutschland, Deutschland über alles', which the crisis produced, became, respectively, the favourite tune of Wilhelm I and the most-sung national hymn under Wilhelm II. Finally, in 1870, Prussia appeared to have coordinated a German war of defence against France and to have orchestrated the unification of the German nation, with the result that even the most critical and acerbic mouthpiece of the southern German states, the Munich satirical magazine *Simplicissimus*, found itself, thirty years later, helping to perpetuate the cult of the notoriously 'Prussian' Bismarck. This popular perception of Prussia as the creator and defender of the German nation, together with the legend of *Germanen* fending off the attacks of Romans and Slavs, served to transform the image of the Prussian officer and the idea of Prussian militarism into widely supported representations and conceptions of Germany as a whole. It also encouraged Wilhelmine Germans to portray Prussian characters like Wilhelm I, who as 'Barbablanca' was compared to Barbarossa, and Bismarck, who often appeared in the form and posture of Hermann, as heroes of the 'Germanic' Dark and Middle Ages. In short, despite critics' justified attempts to distinguish between them, the words 'preußisch', 'germanisch' and 'deutsch' had been woven together in a complex web of 'historical mythology'.[15]

German myths were disseminated on different levels. Historians and other academics presented an official, Prussian-led version of German history and identity, partly because they were conscious – as civil servants – of government control, especially after the imprisonment of the liberal historian Ludwig Quidde for *lèse-majesté* in 1896, and partly because they were ardent supporters of the Prussian state and German unification, perceiving themselves to be the heirs of mid-nineteenth-century, national-liberal historians such as Heinrich von Sybel and Johann Gustav Droysen. To the most famous historian of the imperial era, Heinrich von Treitschke, Prussia had taken Germany from the 'fairy-tale world of particularism' to the necessary harshness of a world of powerful nation-states. An almost irresistible Prussocentric movement towards the creation of a German Reich was seen to be the dominant, God-given idea behind German history, in accordance with the real-political, historicist, Protestant precepts of the historical discipline. Neo-Rankeans like Erich Marcks, Max Lehmann, Hermann Oncken, Erich Brandenburg and Max Lenz, whose calls for greater objectivity and detachment from politics had prevailed by the 1900s over the political activism of Treitschke and the Prussian school, continued to concentrate on the established pantheon of great Prussian leaders, producing biographies of Freiherr vom Stein, Field Marshal Hermann von Boyen, Bismarck and Wilhelm I, amongst others. Yet, throughout the historiography of the imperial period, Prussia remained subordinate to Germany. Consequently, despite hesitation, out-and-out supporters of the Prussian state like Ranke and left-liberal critics of Bismarck like the ancient historian Theodor Mommsen joined long-standing advocates of unification such as Treitschke, Sybel and Droysen in welcoming the inauguration of the *Kaiserreich* in 1871. Virtually all academics accepted what Treitschke, a student of the state and an opponent of cultural history, called 'a different picture and a different conception of the divinity' which marked out each national culture. This sense of German distinctiveness, which was frequently translated, even by outsiders in the historical profession like Karl Lamprecht, into a belief in German superiority, generally increased during the Wilhelmine era, as historians sought to link contemporary Germany, via Prussia, to a 'German' past of Teutonic knights, the Holy Roman Empire of the German Nation, Luther and the Reformation, and the 'wars of independence' between 1813 and 1815. By the early twentieth century, even a conservative historian and unflinching enthusiast of Prussia like Georg von Below took offence at being called 'just a Prussian' and retorted that he was German first, second and third. This harmony and hierarchy of loyalties was passed on to German citizens through the press, since historians like Hans Delbrück, Dietrich Schäfer and Theodor Schiemann were prolific journalists, and, more importantly, in history lessons in schools.[16]

Beyond such official views of German identity, there was an intricate web of images and ideas in paintings, cartoons, novels, poems, songs, operas, films, newspaper articles and photographs in magazines. In different ways, artists and writers mediated particular conceptions of Germanness, from mundane clichés, which were uttered in passing, to systematic or mystical reflections on the nature of the national 'soul' or 'spirit'. Few seem to have doubted the existence of a distinct German identity, although many refrained from speculating about it. Even Wilhelmine painters, many of whom rejected anti-French campaigns to preserve 'German' art in 1905 and 1911, disliked the notion of insularity, which one member of the Berlin Secession ridiculed as the artistic equivalent of 'healthy pork with sauerkraut' and 'Germanic unity gravy', rather than the idea of a separate German culture *per se*. 'Without doubt,' wrote the Secessionist Lovis Corinth, 'it is clear to every art connoisseur that there is a healthier striving and a more intense vitality in Germany today than in France, which was in the lead until now.' It was possible to gain a sense of German particularity, as Corinth obviously did, from the 'idealism' of 'Die Brücke', 'Der blaue Reiter' and other avant-garde movements, as well as from Anton von Werner's portraits of Bismarck and Arnold Böcklin's popular symbolic representations of Germanic mythology. In the same way, highbrow writers like Thomas Mann, who had already dreamed of writing a major work on *Kultur* and *Zivilisation* before 1914, and Stefan George, who distanced himself from foreign writers such as Zola, stood self-consciously within a German tradition. More important for the diffusion of a national mythology, however, was the propagation of typically German characters and legends in lower-brow literature. Best-selling novels such as Felix Dahn's *Ein Kampf um Rom* (1876), *Kleine Romane aus der Völkerwanderung* (1892–1901) and *Attila* (1895) recreated the helmets, spears, streaming banners and gigantic heroes of the Germanic era at the same time as the operas of Wagner became known to – if not seen by – a mass audience. Other popular works, such as those by Ludwig Ganghofer, Adolf Bartels and Franz Lienhard, depicted the warmth and wilderness of the German *Heimat* or, as in the westerns of Karl May, portrayed the well-meaning introspection and strength of German protagonists like Old Shatterhand. Together, these authors dominated the Wilhelmine book market, with some of their novels selling more than 500,000 copies.[17] They put forward, often in formulaic fashion, many of the accepted German values and traits of character which were repeated daily in the columns and cartoons of the press. It was these references, which rarely contradicted each other directly, that formed the mental landscape of turn-of-the-century Germans.

A specifically German landscape also seemed to be concrete, however, not just imagined. This effect was not merely an illusion created by the ideal-ization of an archetypal village, with high-roofed, timbered houses and a meandering river, such as had become commonplace on the postcards, enti-tled 'Grüße aus der Heimat', which had been brought onto the market in 1870. Rather, it was the consequence of deliberate attempts to build and enact a German identity. If 'styles' in Simmel's sense of fashion and mode of living were diverse, with commentators frequently deploring the lack of a German Paris, then public buildings and monuments were strikingly uni-form and national-minded, especially under the Empire, as the architects of town halls in Hamburg, Munich and countless other cities of the Reich refined the heavy, often bombastic, neo-gothic form which they believed, fol-lowing the early nineteenth-century architect Friedrich Schinkel, to be authentically German. In the course of the nineteenth century, monuments were erected to heroes of the distant past such as Luther and Hermann, whose statue in the Teutoburg forest was begun in 1819 and completed in 1875, and to cultural preceptors of the recent past like Herder, Schiller and Goethe: there were 800 of these in 1883, compared to 18 in 1800. After 1871, there was a rapid expansion of building work, as towns competed to put up statues to Bismarck and Wilhelm I, and as the great national mon-uments of the Niederwald (1877–83), Kyffhäuser mountain (1890–96), Porta Westfalica (1892), Deutsches Eck (1894–97), and the Nation-aldenkmal and Valhalla in Berlin (1890–97, 1896–1901) were constructed. Most of these monuments juxtaposed modern figures like Wilhelm I with his-torical and legendary characters such as Germania and Barbarossa. Many became the centrepiece of national rituals and ceremonies, as in 1913, when 43,000 runners took part in nine separate relays from the far corners of Ger-many, converging on the Völkerschlachtdenkmal near Leipzig in order to bring 'greetings from the people to the kaiser', as the press reports put it. Just prior to the inauguration of the monument, 275,000 gymnasts had taken part in the largest mass gathering in German history. Events such as these rested on a culture of public festivals and a network of associations, includ-ing gymnastic and choral societies, which had been established between 1815 and 1914. Almost all of them relied on private funding, granted a prominent place to 'the German people' and overlapped with numerous school ceremonies, which involved millions of children in addresses to the Hohenzollerns, the planting of national oak trees and the singing of 'Die Wacht am Rhein'.[18] By the 1900s, few young and middle-aged Germans had not, at one time or another, taken part in rituals to commemorate the nation.

Whether Germans welcomed such rituals was a separate question. Social-ists, in particular, it seemed to middle-class, nationalist newspapers like the *Hamburgischer Correspondent*, betrayed 'anxiety about love of the fatherland' (*Vaterlandsliebe*), refusing to participate in Sedan Day parades and other patriotic events. Yet much of the Social Democratic Party (SPD) and the majority of working-class Germans did accept significant parts of national mythology.[19] Throughout the Reich, by the early twentieth century, there were hardly any Germans, including socialists, who questioned the very existence of national identity: Germanness and the German fatherland were believed to be real, not figments of radical-nationalist imagination. At the same time, however, the *content* of national identity became a matter of dispute, as the old distinction between political and national affairs began to disintegrate, and as perceptions of Germany's position in the world were irreversibly transformed. The next section examines how changes in the means of representation obliged citizens of the Reich to reconsider what it was to be German.

Representation: photographs, newsreels and the mass press

Myths about Germany and a German identity had been constructed gradually during the course of the nineteenth century. Under the impact of political upheavals such as the restoration in 1815, revolution in 1848 and the wars of unification in the 1860s, symbols like the liberal black-red-gold flag had, by turns, been raised and lowered, just as festivals to the German nation had oscillated between support for and opposition to the political *status quo*. Notwithstanding shifts in the social composition and political disposition of nationalist movements and parties, however, there was a steady accumulation during the nineteenth century of national attributes and legends, which were acknowledged and repeated across the social and political spectrum. Such accumulation had been abetted by the spread of literacy, books and newspapers, which had made Bavarians, Saxons and Prussians aware of similarities between German states and had allowed national-minded poets, journalists and academics to present their case for German unification. By the 1900s, this relationship between the means of communication and national identity had altered. Now, as the sociologist Ferdinand Tönnies had recognized in 1887, much earlier than most of his compatriots, 'The press was not confined to national borders but was, in accordance with its proclivities and opportunities, thoroughly international.'[20] Perhaps for the first time, newspapers, magazines and, by 1910, films appeared to threaten the integrity of the nation.

The most serious menace seemed to be the exponential expansion of the press during the 1890s and 1900s, which resulted in part from technical advances in the cheap production of newsprint and in the printing process, and in part from increased demand. Newspaper circulation – and, in slightly lower proportion, the percentage of newspaper readers – increased dramatically. Between 1868 and 1900 the number of newspapers and magazines sent by post climbed from 150 million per annum to 1,200 million. It has been estimated that by 1912 five to six billion such publications were printed yearly, and that overall newspaper circulation alone amounted to 25.2 million, well in excess of the Reich's 15.2 million households. Academic commentators on the press, who began to organize themselves into a sub-discipline during the 1910s, recognized that these changes in circulation did not merely imply a greater number of readers, but a transformation of the press's role, as it became more pervasive and influential, effectively moving large parts of political discourse from face-to-face encounters in associations, parties and localities to the columns and cartoons of newspapers and magazines. The press, wrote one commentator, had become a 'great power', the 'strangest and strongest of the constitutive powers of our time'. Modern newspapers were 'omniscient and ubiquitous', hearing and seeing everything, even the 'secrets of the state and of family life', and rendering quarterly reports within the administration an 'anachronism', since reporters had already made the relevant facts known. Yet the growth of the press also meant that 'facts' were more often contested by journalists in other newspapers or in other sections of the same publication. Between 1900 and 1914, the number of journal titles doubled, from 3,300 to 6,500. This, in conjunction with increased overall circulation, meant that more Germans read more than one publication. During the 1910s, millions of readers also saw newsreels in the Reich's 2,500 cinemas. Confronted by so many interpretations of what Germany was, and what it was doing, citizens were likely to gain only a fleeting, relative sense of a common national identity.[21]

The way in which news was passed on to readers caused further confusion. By the 1900s, commentators had begun to discern a divergence between interpreted and uninterpreted, relevant and irrelevant information. The press, wrote one academic observer, had become preoccupied with 'appearances and, at best, momentary effects'. The existence of extensive news agencies like Wolffs Telegraphisches Büro and technologies such as the telephone, together with the necessity of filling ever-larger newspapers, had encouraged editors to relay a stream of unannotated facts to readers, so that 'even in the best cases, it is a question of an arbitrary picking out of single instances, whose true meaning is only recognisable in context'. The proclivity of the press was towards sensation and novelty, not towards 'true meaning'. At the same time, with the widespread introduction of photographs into mass-circulation weekly newspapers such as the *Berliner Illustrirte Zeitung* by 1900 and the advent of the newsreel in 1907, there had been a more general movement away from a culture of reading and storytelling to one of pictorial realism. Photographic images, although carefully selected and susceptible to distortion, purported to be real. They appeared, particularly before their instrumentalization during the First World War and the interwar period, to represent the objective but confusing disorder of the world, replacing the comfortable integrity of familiar myths with the abrupt and inexplicable disjunctions of reality. Even in caricature, which was based on a code of unexplained symbols, there had been a shift from literary references to nineteenth-century songs, operas, novels, poems and mythology in *Kladderadatsch* to the direct, grotesque, apocalyptic and film-like imagery of *Simplicissimus*. Modern city-dwellers, wrote the editor of the *Berliner Börsen-Courier* in 1914, had neither the time nor the inclination to treat newspapers as literature: they required hard facts in easily comprehended headlines and pictures. The 'modern newspaper is no longer read in the same way as its predecessors; no longer digested with a comfortable morning coffee or at the family table in the light of a paraffin lamp', he went on: 'Just think how many thousands if not millions of newspapers are now put hastily in a coat pocket and then, in the suburban train, electric tram, omnibus or underground, not studied anymore, but flicked through quickly for orientation.'[22] Under such conditions, as John Atkinson Hobson recognized in his study of British jingoism, national myths, far from being banished, found a ready and credulous audience. They had changed in nature, however, as far as a substantial number of readers were concerned: they were no longer transferred through the established conduits of a literary culture, but had to be recreated by means of headlines, photographs and film.

During the First World War, national myths were, in effect, recreated through a concerted use of the press and cinema, serving to consolidate a strong sense of national identity, which had been constructed during the course of the nineteenth century. Yet in the two decades before the First World War, in the absence of any large-scale orchestration of public opinion, many Wilhelmine Germans feared the disintegration of national identity, under the fragmentary impact of an expanding press. One of the principal causes of this disintegration, noted by Tönnies, was the fact that newspapers had outgrown national borders, despite being divided into sections on domestic and foreign affairs. Photographs and telegraphs enabled journalists to represent foreign nation-states, which were entirely mediated, in almost as immediate a way as they depicted Germany itself. Accordingly, news from abroad, which had dominated German political columns in the years before unification, when much of the reporting of German politics was censored, again became more prominent, after a lull during the 1870s and 1880s. Otto Groth, later author of a seminal work on the press in Germany, demonstrated in 1913, for example, that foreign coverage in the *Frankfurter Zeitung* for the preceding twenty-five years had, as a percentage, doubled.[23] As a result, German national identity depended, more than ever, on comparisons of the Reich with other nation-states and on perceptions of its position in the wider world.

German identity and the wider world

Because of the debate about Germany's responsibility for the outbreak of the First World War, there has been considerable discussion of the shortcomings of German national identity. During the last decade or so, a limited number of scholars have begun to question whether the leaders of the Reich and German public opinion acted in an aggressive manner at all. Most historians, however, rightly contend that the conduct of German foreign policy was offensive, not defensive, in the years before 1914. In general, they have argued either that aggressiveness resulted from uncertainty about Germany's stability at home and its position abroad, so that policy-makers came to favour an 'escape into war', or they have proposed that expansionism was an intrinsic part of a widespread ethnic and even racist sense of identity, which was predicated on the idea of German superiority, often in a Darwinian struggle for survival, but which in fact derived from the inadequacy of more benign cultural and political forms of identity.[24] In many instances, uncertainty about Germany's place in the world could, apparently, encourage expansionist racism, and vice versa. A shift towards world politics and changes in the means of communication, which presented other countries and continents in a much more immediate and vivid way, could be expected to have exacerbated such uncertainty and racism.

It is argued here that there was no straightforward relationship between an offensive, expansionist foreign policy, anxiety about the external predicament of the Reich, and cultural, ethnic and racial identity. The German government and army, it is true, acted offensively in 1914 and bore a greater responsibility for the outbreak and escalation of war than did the government of any other power. There was also widespread support for the idea of German expansion, either by acquiring colonies or defending economic markets. Yet such facts are not adequately explained by references to increasing anxiety about world politics or to the radical nature of German identity. Indeed, during the two decades before the First World War, it can be contended that most Germans' fears about the Reich's international position subsided and that their sense of identity came to include more pronounced attachments to political institutions, as in France, Britain and the United States. As has been seen, the majority of German citizens believed in the existence of a common national culture, in the natural competition of nation-states and in the superiority of white or European races. None of these sets of beliefs, however, distinguished Germany's populace from those of other countries. Thus, during the First World War, French and British writers, journalists and politicians were just as willing as their German counterparts to view the conflict as an ideological struggle between different systems of values.[25]

Like other Europeans, most Germans continued on the eve of the First World War to be convinced of the superiority of their own culture and race, despite changes in the means of communication and in the international predicament of the Reich. Although the balance of forces and alliances altered quickly, and although newspapers and magazines began to show foreign nation-states in a new light, many of the long-established international bulwarks of German identity remained in place. The commonplace assumption of racial and cultural superiority over the 'black' and 'yellow' races made imperialism seem natural, if sometimes expensive and impracticable. Left liberals and many socialists, although their parties were opposed to the acquisition of colonies on other grounds, upheld Germany's civilizing mission, complacently viewing the Reich as a less barbaric imperial power than France, Belgium and Britain. This point, which was made regularly in press reporting of the 'colonial atrocities' of neighbouring states, was demonstrated most graphically in the left-liberal, anti-imperial satirical magazine *Simplicissimus*, which repeatedly portrayed Africans and Chinese in stereotypical, barely human form, even though it also exposed the cruelty of colonial administrations. One cartoon, entitled 'Colonial Powers', compared regimes in four separate pictures: a Belgian administrator is shown roasting an African on a spit; French legionnaires play childish sexual games with heavy-limbed and apparently primitive African women; and a British soldier puts an African through a press in order to squeeze out money from his intestine. German officers, in contrast, are depicted with a line of giraffes, not Africans, which they are teaching to goose-step. *Simplicissimus* implied that imperialism was a European evil, worse in Belgian or British colonies than in their German equivalents. Nevertheless, the magazine's cartoonists continued to base their jokes on the assumption of European cultural and, in most cases, racial superiority. Even to the leader of the SPD, August Bebel, during the German colonial army's slaughtering of 70,000 Herero and Nama in southwest Africa between 1904 and 1907, it was evident that the massacred were 'a wild people, very low in culture', which he did not wish to support. In successive Reichstag debates, officials, conservatives, National Liberals and left liberals all denied that the Herero were a human 'people' at all. In a less explicit and absolute form, similar assumptions were made about the indigenous peoples of all continents except Europe. The test-case was the Far East, where Japan had already become a great power by the turn of the century: in general, the rise of the Japanese was incorporated, together with anxiety about Chinese demographic growth and emigration, within the broader racial and cultural notion of a 'yellow peril' (*die gelbe Gefahr*); in these terms, although they were still seen by the majority of Germans – including left-wing socialists like Franz Mehring – as a possible future menace, Japan and China were perceived by few commentators to constitute a direct threat to the security or economic fortunes of Europe. Even after Japan had defeated Russia in Manchuria in 1905, *Simplicissimus* continued to represent it as a small, ineffectual figure in the shape of a monkey or an insect.[26]

At times, Russians and other 'Slavs' were also depicted as racial inferiors. *Simplicissimus*, for example, showed them variously as primitive subhumans, lice and rats. On the whole, however, the Slavs provided a cultural rather than a racial foil for German identity, partly because they were sometimes included in the family of Aryan or Indo-European peoples. Russian culture, in particular, which had already been described as barbaric in the eighteenth century, came to represent 'Asia', menacing the borders of Germany and Europe. To the German left, such perceptions went back to the Karlsbad Decrees in 1819 and the revolutions of 1848 and 1849, when Russian armies had supported the reactionary policies of Austria-Hungary. By the mid-nineteenth century, it was common, as Friedrich Engels demonstrated, to slip from criticism of a despotic, centralized Russian state to denigration and subordination of entire Slavic cultures: 'Peoples, which have never had a history, which, from the very moment when they reached the first, rawest levels of civilization, fell under foreign domination or which were first forced up to the first stage of civilization, have no capacity for life, will never be able to attain any degree of independence.' Such hierarchies of culture persisted in socialist circles until the Russian Revolution in 1917. Thus, Bebel's declaration to the Reichstag in 1896 that 'the East' was character- ized by 'a lack of culture and a piece of barbarism', whereas 'true culture' found 'its home in central, southern and western Europe', was echoed in 1914 by an unofficial SPD press release justifying the party's decision to go to war:

> Defeat would be something unthinkable, something frightful. If war is the most horrible of all horrors, the frightfulness of this war will be intensified by the fact that it will not only be waged by civilized nations. We are sure that our comrades in uniform of all sorts and conditions will abstain from all unneces- sary cruelty, but we cannot have this trust in the motley hordes of the czar, and we will not have our women and children sacrificed to the bestiality of Cossacks.

On the German right, the picture was more complicated, with reactionaries like August von Haxthausen, who was one of the most well-known mid- nineteenth-century foreign observers of Russian culture, interpreting the peasant commune or 'mir' as a pre-revolutionary, pre-industrial barrier against European decadence. Most conservative commentators, however, saw Russia as a culture which had barely been touched by Greek thought, western Christianity, Roman law or the Enlightenment. By the 1900s, Rus- sia's defeat in the Crimean (1856) and Russo-Japanese wars (1905), spo- radic Russo-German hostility after St Petersburg had signed the Dual Alliance with France in 1894, and the collapse and partial restoration of tsarism in the bloody revolutions of 1905 and 1906 all allowed *émigré* Baltic Germans like Friedrich von Bernhardi and Theodor Schiemann, who domi- nated the academic study and newspaper reporting of Russian affairs, to dis- credit both state and society as the products of a foreign-dominated, backward and violent 'Unkultur'. This remained the dominant image of Rus- sia until the outbreak of the First World War, despite the efforts of the his- torian Otto Hoetzsch and a number of reform-minded conservatives to represent the Russian regime as an imitation of the German Empire in the

1910s. Most commentators, by contrasting themselves with their 'Asiatic' Russian or Slav neighbours, placed the Reich firmly in 'Europe'.[27]

Germany, according to most Wilhelmine onlookers, was part of a shared European culture which extended to British dominions and former colonies in North America and the Antipodes. This culture, which was characterized by Graeco-Roman philosophy, Christian morality, the science of the Enlightenment, industrial capitalism and imperialism, was divided into individual nation-states, competing for supremacy and survival. A failure to compete successfully, as Treitschke and others reminded their readers, would lead to eclipse, as in the case of Holland, or to annexation, as in Poland. By the early twentieth century, Germany was believed to be in competition with France, Britain and the United States for the intellectual and political leadership of the modern, 'European' world of *Kulturländer*. Although these rivals were treated as separate national entities, with their own geography and traditions, they were seen to share certain values, which were contrasted with German values: Germany, it was implied, offered the sole modern alternative system of thought and institutions to the dominant and overlapping systems of France, Britain and the United States. As has been seen, during the eighteenth and nineteenth centuries German culture had been defined primarily through a reaction against French administration, etiquette, learning and art, as these were manifested in the occupied territories of the Napoleonic wars, in the princely courts of the German states and in the monarchical, Bonapartist and republican regimes of the 'hereditary enemy' (*Erbfeind*) of the Confederation and the Reich. France, whose role as Germany's 'mentor and teacher' had – according to the liberal politician Friedrich Naumann in 1900 – only recently been challenged, appeared to have maintained a similar set of values throughout the preceding century. The French were, in the words of one widely read book, charming, polite, witty, flexible, boastful, superficial, tasteful, artificial, civilized, classical, sociable, conventional, individualist, egalitarian, centralized, nationalist and morally relativist. The neighbouring state's Roman heritage and its rejection of Protestantism were seen to have produced a rationalist culture which had fostered social conventionality, centralized administration and unhistorical political dogmatism: 'Rationalism', wrote the historian Karl Hillebrand, 'is the essential feature of the French mind [*Geist*].' From the mid-nineteenth century onwards, Britain, which had earlier been depicted as a 'Germanic' self-governing society, and the United States, which had been portrayed as a romantic, wild and free-spirited antithesis to Europe, were both gradually transformed, if German accounts were to be believed, into calculating, capitalist, industrial powers and oppressive, Puritan, empirical and materialist cultures, which more closely resembled the strict social form, rational science and commercialism of France. There were, of course, still thought to be marked differences between 'Romanism' and 'Germanism', and between the 'Old' and 'New World', as Karl Lamprecht spelled out in his popular diary of

Americana in 1906: 'If the present American civilization disappeared: what would remain for posterity? Practically nothing ... It has to be expressed in no uncertain terms: vis-à-vis the old culture of the European population, both the Germanic and the Romanic, the Americans are still behind.' Yet, with the democratization of British politics, the growth of French financial capitalism and the emergence of French, British and American positivism, few Germans questioned the political and cultural propinquity of France, the United Kingdom and the United States, for it seemed that the populations of all three countries were preoccupied with external form, observation, numbers, utility and, increasingly, equality. The majority of Wilhelmine commentators assumed that Germany was different.[28]

A sense of national particularity, which had in some respects been reinforced by a series of international comparisons, was not, as some historians claim, an explosive and unpredictable by-product of Germans' anxieties about the Reich's position in the world. As could be expected in an age of *Weltpolitik* and of photographs in newspapers, magazines and encyclopaedias which presented New York skyscrapers and Japanese warships to an unaccustomed public, there was considerable discussion and uncertainty about Germany's transformation into a 'world empire' or 'world state'. The popular prediction that the future belonged to vast trading areas and blocs of territory such as Greater Britain, Russia and the United States compounded existing convictions about a national struggle for survival and prompted liberals like Max Weber to view German unification as 'a youthful prank', which would have been better left undone 'if it was meant to be the end and not the starting point of a German policy of world power'. The idea that the Reich had to expand or decline was widely believed. It was not seen by most Germans, however, as a sufficient reason for war, nor was it perceived to be a constant or overriding aim of Germany's foreign policy. The fact that neither the United States, which had not come into conflict with the Reich until the late 1880s over Samoa, nor Russia, which had been weakened by defeat in the Russo-Japanese War and revolution in 1905, constituted direct threats to German national security over the short term, meant that attention remained fixed on Europe. During the 1900s and 1910s, as in the nineteenth century, France remained the principal military threat to the Reich, and Britain the main economic threat. Accordingly, Wilhelmine newspapers and magazines, although devoting more attention to extra-European powers than in previous decades, continued to concentrate on the Reich's western neighbours: in a comparative survey of the four major party publications, 35.5 per cent of articles for the years 1900, 1906 and 1912 were on France, 30.4 per cent on Britain, 23.85 per cent on Russia and 10.35 per cent on the United States; in the leading political journals, 30.65 per cent of articles for the years between 1898 and 1914 were on Britain, 29.15 per cent on France, 27.25 per cent on Russia and 12.95 per cent on the United States. Since much of this reporting went into considerable detail and included uninterpreted information from news agencies, it is not surprising that changes in the European balance of power in favour of Germany rapidly, if still distortedly, found their way into print.[29]

When Wilhelmine observers measured the progress of the Reich against a French yardstick, they had every reason to feel confident. German depictions of France's decadence can be traced back to criticisms during the revolutionary and Napoleonic wars of the atheism and artificiality of French society. They became more common during the second half of the nineteenth century, as national-minded German historians and journalists revealed the 'frivolity' and 'hollowness' of the Second Empire, the 'hypocrisy' of France's claim to represent 'civilization' in 1870, and the 'instability' and 'corruption' of the Third Republic. Yet such representations were juxtaposed with the historical accounts of the early nineteenth century by authors like Karl von Rotteck and Karl Theodor Welcker, which were overwhelmingly laudatory, and with justifiedly positive appraisals of French power even after 1870, which rested on increasingly voluminous and precise reports in German newspapers. According to such reportage, Germany had only surpassed France militarily during the late 1890s when 'republicanization' – which became a cross-party label during the Dreyfus affair for unwarranted political interference – was widely believed to have destroyed military discipline, strategy and armament. By the 1900s, most correspondents shared Bülow's belief that the French army had been undermined, despite the government's efforts to maintain forces (with about five million conscripts and reserves in 1914) as large as those of Germany: 'one must ask oneself if an army which contains so many contradictory elements and such a spirit of revolt will be united enough to succeed against an external enemy'. With a demographic deficit of 23 million by 1910, compared to 5 million in 1880, France simply could not keep up with Germany. This was the meaning of the *Simplicissimus* cartoon '30-Year Military Service: A Picture of the Future', which appeared in 1913 at the time of the French law increasing the length of conscription from two to three years: it envisaged a couple of tired, quinquagenarian French soldiers telling each other they should not complain, for 'Who knows how long the next generation will have to serve!' When such prophecies were combined with the realization, around 1900, that Germany's economy had outgrown that of France, making the Reich the largest and most powerful economic bloc on the European mainland, many Wilhelmine Germans began to feel, like the economist Adolph Wagner, that 'The German is again emerging as the major people'.[30]

Such judgements were based on comparisons with Britain as well as France, as Wagner's addendum made clear: 'If anyone is to be first among equals, then it will be he [the German] and not the Frenchman or the Briton.' This perceived reversal of British and German fortunes was just as important as the Reich's alleged ascendancy *vis-à-vis* France, for the British Empire not only constituted Germany's principal economic rival, but was also a 'world state' and the main obstacle to German maritime and colonial ambitions. For much of the nineteenth century, Britain had been admired by liberals for its balanced, constitutional system of government, its robust parliamentary style of politics, its defence of basic freedoms of association, assembly and expression, and its pursuit of free trade and unencumbered industrial growth. It had also been praised by many conservatives – and a significant number of liberals – for its aristocratic parties, its incremental, historical approach to policy-making, its tradition of common law, its deferential, Protestant and patriotic society, and its 'Germanic' and dynastic ties to the states of the Confederation. These images of Britain altered decisively between 1871 and 1914, as German academics and journalists began to emphasize the self-interest of British foreign policy, the geo-political implications of British imperialism and the wider ramifications of Britain's relative economic decline. Conservatives, Catholics and National Liberals, who were already suspicious of what Ludwig von Gerlach termed the 'advancing democracy' of 'old England' after the 1867 Reform Bill, led the way in revising German attitudes. Treitschke, a National Liberal deputy who came to vote with the Free Conservatives, marked the transition. In the 1850s and early 1860s, he had been convinced that 'Admiration is the first feeling which the study of English history calls forth in everyone'. During the early 1870s, he had gradually given up the idea of transferring British political institutions to Germany, since the monarchical and state traditions of the *Kaiserreich* were better suited to German conditions. Finally, from the mid-1870s onwards, he came to contrast the two countries, making a distinction between 'Anglo-Saxon' and 'Teutonic' cultures, and concentrated on unmasking the arrogance, inhumanity, hypocrisy and selfish materialism of British foreign policy: 'In the halls of parliament', he declared, 'one heard only shameless British commercial morality, which, with the Bible in the right hand and the opium pipe in the left, spreads the benefits of civilization around the world.' In the 1900s, a long line of liberal and conservative successors to Treitschke, including historians and economists like Dietrich Schäfer, Hermann Oncken, Friedrich Meinecke and Gerhard von Schulze-Gävernitz, went on to show how the expansion of the British Empire had been the fortuitous consequence of Britain's advantageous trading position as an island and of its duplicitous policy of divide and rule on the European mainland, which allowed it to acquire colonies in the eighteenth and nineteenth centuries with little opposition from other powers. Thus, historians often overlooked the industrial and administrative causes of British imperialism. Many concurred with Otto Hintze that Britain had, by the early twentieth century, become a cautious, uncompetitive 'pensioners' state' (*Rentnerstaat*), attaining 'a satisfied, stationary condition' which was 'not favourable to the needs of a national and political extension of power, to the striving for Anglo-Saxon domination of the world'. Revisionist social imperialists in the SPD and left-liberal imperialists around Friedrich Naumann expressed similar points of view.[31] Compared to Britain and France, Germany seemed to have grown stronger since unification in 1871.

In the historiographical debate about international politics and national identity, most historians have argued either that Wilhelmine Germans defined themselves increasingly in terms of ethnicity and race, which allowed the subjugation of neighbouring peoples, or that they became more and more anxious about the domestic stability and international predicament of the Reich, which pushed them to plan or risk war as a means of escape or diversion. Some historians have combined the two sets of arguments, pointing to the absence of a coherent and credible cultural and political identity as an explanation of Germans' 'flight' (*Flucht*) towards conflict *and* race. However, from the evidence examined here, the premises of such arguments appear flawed: the majority of Germans appear to have had a strong sense of cultural – rather than purely racial – identity, defining themselves primarily with reference to France and Britain, and they seem to have been confident about the Reich's position in Europe and, consequently, in the world. How can this sense of confidence and 'European' identity be reconciled with German responsibility for the outbreak, in 1914, of a European war which was supported by most sections of Wilhelmine society? The most convincing answer points to the exceptional circumstances of July 1914, when Russia, which was depicted by Germans in a different way from 'European' states like France and Britain, had become the principal enemy of the Reich.

In general, in the decades before the First World War, Germans had had to moderate some of the more extreme characterizations of both Germany itself and Germany's old enemies and rivals, as a stream of information from telegraphic agencies, countless series of photographs and detailed reports from correspondents in mass-circulation newspapers had helped to level some of the distinctions that had previously been drawn between 'home' and 'abroad', making foreign nation-states seem at once more mundane and less powerful. Although images of these nation-states still passed through the filter of established identities, leading to significant divergences between the far left and radical right, a more or less commonplace, stable and realistic view of France and Britain was discernible in the prewar era. Neither country, it was widely agreed, had either the means or the will to launch an offensive against the Reich. During the Moroccan crises in 1905 and 1911, when Berlin came into conflict with London and Paris, this assessment of Germany's position in Europe prompted socialists, left liberals and left-wing Catholics, representing the majority of the German electorate, to oppose war and encouraged right-wing Catholics, National Liberals and conservatives to support it. In 1914, this division of the political nation, which rested on competing representations of Germany's national interest, was concealed by the government's successful policy of putting Russia, in the words of the Head of the Naval Cabinet, 'in the wrong'.[32] Unlike France and Britain, Russia served to unite most of the German nation behind a plausible 'war of defence', not only because the tsarist state was the long-standing bugbear of the German left, but because Russia seemed alien: like Japan and other extra-European regions and states, Russia was depicted less consistently and realistically in the German press than were 'European' states. By casting Russia as the aggressor, the Reich government was able to risk war and retain the support of the German left. Yet any belligerent, anti-Russian coalition was likely to be temporary and conditional, as Bethmann was aware, given the willingness of the German left – and parts of the right – to question the aims and purposes of the Reich's foreign policy and war effort. In this sense, the unity of the *Burgfrieden* and the 'August days' was deceptive: it obscured a fundamental debate about the nature of Germany's national interest and about which parties had the right to represent it.

Political representation and national affairs

In Germany, the question of political representation was usually subordinated to that of the state. In most German political thought, which had been heavily influenced by Idealism and Cameralism, the 'state' was believed to have preceded 'politics' and the 'nation' by centuries. To the conservative historian Treitschke, the *Staat* had 'existed as long as history' and was 'as essential to humanity as language'. In his lectures on *Politik*, posthumously published as a book, he divided the subject into five parts, all of which centred on the state. Most Wilhelmine academics agreed with Treitschke that social organization had been achieved by means of power, rather than by mutual agreement or cultural affinity: 'the state ... does not ask on principle about beliefs, it demands obedience.... Empires have survived for centuries as powerful, highly developed states without this inner consent from their subjects.' Thus, Gustav Cohn, a liberal economist, wrote in similar vein 'that the advancing culture of peoples had been preoccupied initially, and for many centuries, with the securing of *domination* and *order*'. The state had imposed internal order on populations and protected them against external enemies. Over time, it had come to exercise power with a degree of consent, which it eventually formalized as laws. It was at this point that the legal and historical disciplines, which – in the absence of a separate faculty – effectively combined to teach politics, began to diverge: to historians, including many historical economists, law was underpinned by a long-established tradition of coercion, which had become consensual, whilst to legal positivists, who had dominated their field since the mid-nineteenth century, law rested on a consensus of reason. The corollary for politics, however, was the same: a duality emerged between, on the one hand, a supposedly neutral state, army and law, which represented the interests of the whole, and, on the other, the allegedly partisan activity of politics, which allowed the representation and negotiation of sectional interests in society. Even the progressive Heidelberg professor Georg Jellinek, who had upset legal positivists by suggesting that the state could be examined politically, nonetheless maintained a distinction between *Staatsrecht* and *Politik* in his work, which was divided into a 'social theory of the state' and a 'constitutional and legal theory': 'Scientifically, there are two main ways to regard the state ... One is the legal, the other the political way of understanding the human collectivity.' The persistence of this duality between state and politics necessarily affected the conceptualization of 'political representation', creating an opposition between officials in government, who acted on behalf of a whole society, and party politicians, who spoke for a part of the electorate or for a particular interest-group. To the liberal historian Friedrich Meinecke, only the state had the capacity to recognize and the right to portray and realize – to 'represent' in its double sense – the interests of the whole. It was widely assumed that politicians would not be able to detach themselves from their own class, regional and confessional backgrounds or from the demands of their political constituencies. As a result, old liberals like the economist Wilhelm Roscher and younger liberals like Max Weber tended to emphasize the shortcomings and contradictions of democratic representation, respectively warning of the tyranny of the majority and the dangers of bureaucratization. These reservations were shared, in one form or another, by all German parties except the SPD.[33]

During the imperial era, a number of pronounced changes in political practice appeared to compound the problem of political representation, complicating the dichotomy between the state and politics. First, the division of responsibilities between the different levels of government and representation – local, state and Reich – was ambiguous, partly because the constitution of 1871 had envisaged a loose federation of powerful states with only a small, overarching authority at the level of the Reich. The *de facto* transfer of functions and public attention to a central 'government' of Reich ministers and to the Reichstag lacked an adequate constitutional or theoretical foundation. Second, the growth and bureaucratization of parties during the 1890s and 1900s, which the sociologist Robert Michels termed 'the oligarchical tendencies of organization', strengthened party structures, but also distanced party leaders from their voters, turning them, according to their critics, into the functionaries of self-serving political 'machines'. By 1914, the SPD, which was the largest party in Europe and an organizational model for other German parties, had forty-three regional organizations, seventy-four newspapers and an annual budget of 1.1 million Reichsmarks. Third, political parties, spurred on by extra-parliamentary associations like the Navy League, strove to escape their traditional social and regional *milieux* and appeal to a mass electorate. In this respect, the efforts of the Social Democrats, with their one million members and 4.2 million voters, were matched by those of the Centre party, which counted on the support of the 850,000-member Volksverein für das katholische Deutschland, and the Con-

servative party, which had founded the 330,000-member Bund der Land-
wirte in 1893 specifically to recruit the smaller peasantry of central and
western Germany to its cause. Although this type of mass membership
seemed to make parties into genuinely representative organizations, representation in such circumstances, in the opinion of Georg Simmel and other
commentators, became a mere fetish for numbers, rather than reflecting the
interests and relationships of society as a whole.[34] Fourth, parties seemed to
have given up broad, inclusive political programmes, transforming themselves into narrow economic interest-groups. Thus, despite the emergence of
mass-membership organizations, Germany's political spectrum appeared to
have become more and more fragmented. By the 1900s, it could be argued
that the only party attaching much importance to 'ideology' was the SPD,
which claimed to represent a coherent and universal system of ideas, it was
said, merely to disguise the sectional interests of the working classes. Finally,
the centre of gravity of German politics had moved to the left, particularly
from the turn of the century onwards. In 1912, the previously ostracized
Social Democratic party had become, with 110 seats, the single largest
group in the Reichstag, creating the possibility of liberal-socialist majorities
in the chamber and behind-the-scenes deals with the Reich government. At
the same time, a conservative 'national opposition' was formed, which
began to criticize ministers, for the first time in a concerted way, from the
right. By the 1910s, at the latest, it was difficult for contemporaries to avoid
the question of political representation: who, asked newspapers and politicians, had the right to represent what?

The question coincided with a separate debate about national interest and
the right to represent the nation-state. This debate had begun, virtually
unnoticed, in the 1890s, but only came to the attention of the German public from the mid-1900s onwards. Previously, it had been widely assumed
that 'national affairs' were sacrosanct, beyond the scope of party politics. In
1902, Alfred Kirchhoff, one of the main academic authorities on the nation-
state, still balked at the fact that 'each party in our political life lays a claim
to the predicate "national"'. The practice, he implied, was both novel and
unjustifiable: 'Yet all these national organizations in reality follow factional
policies in the first instance.... If political particularism is, happily, in the
process of dying out, parliamentary narrow-mindedness has nevertheless
often produced results which bring Austrian conditions to mind and which
must surely be painful for those truly national-minded Germans who are not
blinded by the interests of faction.' After unification in 1871, the idea of the
nation, which had functioned until that date as an illicit means of political
criticism, was fused with that of the state. The National Association was dis-
banded and many of its members, who had previously been critics of the
princely states, became ardent defenders of the German Empire. Despite Bismarck's inclination to ignore the national idea altogether, denouncing it as
a 'swindle' and refusing to adopt a national flag, the *Kaiserreich* was quickly

accepted as a nation-state by most of the German public, as Meinecke correctly observed. Consequently, concepts of the nation, which had always been presented as objective descriptions rather than ideological prescriptions, were also included, along with the new polity, within the tradition of state neutrality. Moreover, common fears during the Bismarckian era about the fragility of the political and national settlements of 1871 served to increase the sacrosanctity of each in a self-perpetuating process of mutual reinforcement. Any denigration of the rickety structure of the German Empire was perceived to be an attack on the German nation, and vice versa. The persistence of the myth that particularism constituted a real danger to the Reich was one indication of this process. As was demonstrated during the *Kulturkampf* in the 1870s and during the proscription of the SPD in the 1880s, political labels like 'Reichsfeind' were used interchangeably with national ones such as 'vaterlandslos'. Catholics and socialists were branded 'anti-national' in order to pre-empt discussion and criticism of the polity and the nation: national identity and the political regime were felt to be the untouchable foundations of politics. By the late 1900s, such connections between the state, national identity and the polity had been unravelled. 'In older nation-states', wrote Meinecke, 'there was, as a rule, no doubt about who was the head and who constituted the limbs which responded to it. Yet, in younger nation-states, where the most diverse individualities and social groups seize the idea of the nation and project themselves onto it, there is no end to the doubt and struggle over the issue.' Now, for the first time since the 1860s, 'politics' became, amongst other things, a controversial but open debate about representing the nation. The next section shows how this debate helped to give an exaggerated impression of the significance of radical German nationalism in the prewar period.[35]

Nationalism and the politics of identity

The years between 1890 and 1914 have usually been portrayed by historians as an era of nationalism, different in kind from the rest of the nineteenth century. This was the period, it is argued, when an emancipatory national movement of the left, which had dictated concepts of the nation in the mid-nineteenth century, was eclipsed by the xenophobic, integral nationalism of the right. The first anti-Semitic organization was founded in 1879, the Society for Germandom Abroad in 1881, the German Language Association in 1886, the Colonial Society in 1887, the Pan-German League in 1891, the German Society for the Eastern Marches in 1894, the Navy League in 1898, the Kyffhäuser Association in 1899, the Imperial League to Combat Social Democracy in 1904, the Patriotic Book League in 1908 and the Army League in 1912. Many of these mass-membership organizations were based on the notion of political, linguistic or racial defence and expansion. Partly as a response to their success, it is contended, many of the German parties moved to the right, calling into question the existing borders of the *Kaiser-reich*, traditional levels of military expenditure and conscription, and the government's naval, colonial and foreign policies. The resonance of such ideas was allegedly so great that significant sections of the left-liberal parties and the SPD repudiated their anti-imperial past and began to call for the expansion of the Reich. This new, cross-party emphasis on foreign policy was motivated to a considerable degree, the argument runs, by a national-minded or politically self-interested desire to deflect attention from the domestic failings of the German Empire, with its contradictory institutions, stalemated parties and class conflict. The Reich government, buffeted from all sides, gradually gave way to the demands of the radical right and adopted an aggressive policy of prestige and brinkmanship abroad. Such social imperialism, which had been used with increasing regularity since the Bismarckian era, had proved popular in almost all sections of German society, it is held. Notwithstanding anxiety about the Reich's international position and the inadequacy of national identity, German nationalism and the 'escape into war' in 1914, most historians still agree with Fritz Fischer, is to be understood primarily as the consequence of tensions and conflicts at home.[36]

Anglo-American revisionism during the last two decades, despite altering common perceptions of many aspects of German history, has had less impact on analyses of German nationalism. Although research has been redirected away from the state and the instrumentalization of national sentiment towards the realignments of the German right and the democratization of politics, historians rarely distinguish banal from radical nationalism and, as a result, they still assume that extreme nationalism was widespread or even preponderant between 1890 and 1914.[37] Such assumptions mean that they have attempted to trace the infusion of anti-Semitic, racist, xenophobic and integral nationalist ideas into different sections of Wilhelmine society, including working-class milieux, rather than starting with an investigation of everyday concepts of the nation and asking at what point banal nationalism, which was characteristic of almost all European countries, became radical or dangerous. From this latter perspective, it appears that the majority of Wilhelmine Germans were more, not less, wary and sceptical of strong expressions of national belonging and national interest than in previous decades. Thus, whilst it is true that national identity in Germany had been defined, to a greater extent than in Britain or France, in terms of culture and ethnicity, not political affiliation or history, and that national affairs, which comprised matters of state, military security and foreign policy, had enjoyed an unusual degree of exemption from political scrutiny and debate, it was movement *away* from these definitions of identity and this type of exemption which created the false impression that mainstream German nationalism had become more extreme. In fact, what had changed was the extent to which Wilhelmine parties, press and public were prepared openly to discuss questions of national identity and national interest. Such discussion, though it alienated and radicalized part of the German right and unsettled much of the centre, helped to demonstrate the particularity of Germany's system of government, making the political components of German identity more salient, just as it helped to clarify what was central to German culture and what was peculiar about the Reich's international position. That the discussion occurred at all was an indication of increased confidence – on the part of the government and majority public opinion – about the stability and solidity of the German nation-state.

By the turn of the twentieth century, most German commentators treated the Reich as a normal nation-state, comparable to Britain, the Netherlands, Denmark, Sweden, Switzerland or France. Even critics of the structure of the German Empire like Friedrich Meinecke, who drew attention to the continuing duality or 'schizophrenia' between 'old Prussia' and the 'new Reich', remained certain that 'the goal to which everything is directed is an all-inclusive community of the German nation-state, a community so strong that it is able to tolerate, utilize and overcome all the separate nationalities of its individual members'. In spite of the popularity of the *großdeutsch* idea in 1848, the divisiveness of a German 'civil war' in 1866, the existence of German-speaking populations outside the borders of the Reich and Polish-, French- and Danish-speaking nationalities within them, as well as the persistence or exacerbation of regional, confessional and class divisions, the Reich had quickly been accepted as a *Nationalstaat*, in contrast to other recently unified nation-states such as Italy. Advocates of a parliamentary regime like the left liberal Friedrich Naumann admitted that the German polity had stood the test of time, becoming 'a solid political body'. 'The danger that we shall again sink back into a confusion of small states [*Kleinstaaterei*] can be regarded as having been removed', he went on: 'The fear that this constitution would only be an interlude has not been borne out by events.' Supposed supporters of *Großdeutschland* in the Centre party, anxious to overcome their reputation during the *Kulturkampf* as enemies of the Reich, generally refrained from calling for a revision of the borders of 1871. Indeed, the assertion of the influential Catholic publicist Carl Bachem that the founder of the *kleindeutsch* Empire, Bismarck, was the 'greatest German statesman of the modern age' was closer to the party line in the Wilhelmine period, as German Catholics severed their links with their Polish counterparts in eastern Prussia, than were demands for a redrawing of the Reich's borders. Social Democrats were less charitable to Bismarck, but they, too, habitually acknowledged the validity of the nation-state and its borders, even if SPD politicians took care, in the words of the Bavarian reformist Georg von Vollmar, 'not to mistake the fatherland for its present rulers'. In this respect, the view of the revisionist Eduard Bernstein that 'great differences exist in different lands' probably reflected majority opinion in the party: 'Peculiarities of geographical situation, rooted customs of national life, inherited institutions, and traditions of all kinds create a difference of mind which only slowly submits to the influence of [industrial] development.' Even though German workers did not yet have the full rights and entitlements of citizenship, Bernstein continued, it could not be 'a matter of indifference to German Social Democracy whether the German nation, which has indeed carried out, and is carrying out, its honourable share in the civilizing work of the world, should be repressed in the council of the nations'. During the main debate about the nation in the SPD, at the time of the Stuttgart conference of the Second International in 1907, the party's leader August Bebel, along with most other Social Democratic deputies, applauded Gustav Noske's call in the Reichstag for the defence of an independent German nation. Despite their support for a revolutionary general strike at the outbreak of any war, the left wing of the SPD, likewise, claimed that 'their nationality was worthy and their fatherland dear'.[38]

As the German nation-state began to seem self-evident and secure from both internal and external enemies, it gradually became an object of political discussion. By the 1900s, as Meinecke noted, virtually all social and political groups claimed the right to reinterpret the nation and to debate national affairs. Because of the novelty of this type of debate, many Wilhelmine onlookers expressed concern about the instability and insufficiency of German patriotism, and about the possible disintegration of the German nation-state. 'In Germany, even the love of country has not found a valid form of expression', wrote Walther Rathenau, a left-liberal publicist and chairman of the electricity company AEG: 'Servile devotion and the noisy patriotism of business societies are not balanced by a secure national consciousness.' Previously, national sentiment had constituted an unspoken assumption of German politics, not a topic for party disputation: the label 'vaterlandslos' was used to exclude groupings like the Centre party and the SPD from the political nation. Now, public controversy about national affairs helped to produce a multitude of different readings of national interest and identity, and to consolidate and radicalize a minority movement of right-wing nationalists, which found a focus in the extra-parliamentary leagues and parts of the National Liberal and conservative parties. To August Keim, later leader of the Army League, this 'fragmentation' showed the necessity of 'a crusade of national education' so that the 'development of our inner unity and thereby the completion of the work of our national unification', which was derived from 'the blood-brotherhood of the German tribes', could at last occur; to his colleague and leader of the Pan-German League, Heinrich Claß, it evinced that German politics had been subverted by Jews, who had exploited popular disaffection over the diplomatic failures of the Reich government and created an alliance amongst socialist, liberal, Catholic, Polish, Danish, Alsatian and Hanoverian enemies of the state. Keim, Claß and other radical nationalists claimed to exercise a monopoly over the expression and meaning of German patriotism, extending the tradition of the 'national' or 'state-supporting' parties of the 1870s and 1880s, which had successfully ostracized Catholics and socialists by pointing to their supposed lack of patriotic feeling. Such a strategy failed during the 1900s and 1910s because Catholics and socialists resisted attempts to build a national consensus against them, putting forward their own patriotic credentials and their own vision of the nation, and because the state-supporting parties themselves were prepared to discuss national affairs, revealing in the process an unsuspected diversity of opinions.[39]

Strident and unprecedented disputes about the identity, interest and policy of the German nation, together with the repeated assertions of league members that they alone were truly national, convinced observers like Rathenau that a 'secure national consciousness' did not exist. In other words, such manifestations failed to persuade him that the 'noisy patriotism of business societies' was to be equated with the views of the majority. Many Germans agreed with the conservative Hans Delbrück 'that the Pan-Germans were a small, almost comical sect with no significance' in the 1890s and 1900s, even if the *Alldeutscher Verband* appeared to have become more influential in the 1910s. Most Germans, including a significant number on the right, did not hold radical nationalist ideas. Excluding affiliates, only the Navy League amongst the so-called 'national associations' (*nationale Verbände*) had a membership of more than 100,000, and even its highest figure of 330,000 was less than a third of the SPD's prewar total. Allowing for overlapping membership between leagues, it has been estimated that the 'German-national' public numbered several hundred thousands from an electorate of 14.5 million in 1912. Of the 12.2 million who voted in the same year, 8.25 million supported the Social Democratic, Centre, left-liberal and minority-nationality parties, which had few, if any, connections with national associations. In addition, many Conservative and National Liberal party voters had little sympathy for radical nationalism. Instead, a significant number of Germans preferred what Meinecke called an 'active, free idea of the nation'. It was for this reason that members of leagues were frequently ridiculed in the press as 'Teutschen' and 'Teutsch-Nationale', depicted as top-hatted, over-weight, bearded and credulous old men indulging in frivolous 'Deutschtümelei'. Even the language of radical nationalism was challenged and mocked. One cartoon in *Simplicissimus* translated distorted 'patriotic' words into pictures: the 'people' (*das Volk*) was represented as a motley, pompous procession of decorated, black-suited septuagenarians. The caricaturist assumed, without further commentary, that his readers would understand the emancipatory, inclusive, heroic connotations of the term *Volk*.[40] By the 1900s, it was evident that national feeling, which had been seen during the 1880s as a uniform qualification for full political participation, had taken a variety of forms, all of which were open to party discussion and political satire. The novelty of this debate about the German nation in itself caused considerable anxiety and precipitated the radicalization of the far right, which, in turn, created the illusion that the Wilhelmine period was an age of extreme nationalism. Yet the fact that the debate took place was a sign that the old division in Germany between politics and the nation had begun to disappear.

Political discussion of national affairs was most visible in the areas of foreign policy and constitutional reform. In both cases, contemporaries' fears of national disintegration and modern historians' condemnations of radical and popular nationalism prove, on closer inspection, to be exaggerated. Party scrutiny and criticism of foreign policy became obvious during the first Moroccan crisis in 1905–6, as the German government was forced to cede to France, which was backed by most of the international community, at the conference of Algeciras. To the left, Bülow and Wilhelm II had acted too aggressively, failing to cajole the Quai d'Orsay into making concessions over the 'Tunisification' of Morocco; to the right, the Chancellor and the Kaiser had lost their nerve, missing the opportunity of inflicting a humiliating defeat on the 'hereditary enemy' and of destroying the Entente Cordiale. 'Now we will take the liberty of criticising ... and it will be well in the future if the people of Germany will show more interest in foreign affairs', wrote the moderate leader of the National Liberals, Ernst Bassermann, in 1906: 'The times are past when we remained silent before such a state of things.' Outside observers like the British ambassador in Berlin, Sir Frank Lascelles, concurred that 'the change' which had 'come over public opinion' during the 1890s and 1900s, becoming 'apparent' only in the course of the Moroccan crisis, was 'remarkable'. 'This, and similar questions,' he went on, 'were symptomatic of a general feeling that the foreign affairs of Germany were not skilfully dealt with.' Britain's envoy in Munich made similar observations a year later: 'A generation ago, the German public took but little interest in general foreign affairs ... Things have changed since then.' During the second Moroccan crisis in 1911–12, as the government again stopped short of conflict with few tangible gains, criticism of official policy-making increased. It continued unabated until the outbreak of the First World War, obscuring substantial points of agreement between parties and encouraging an overestimation of the importance of radical nationalists. Although hysterical censure of the government and eye-catching predictions of national collapse came from German-national circles, the majority of Wilhelmine Germans, as has been seen, shared a less threatening set of images of the Reich's western European rivals than had their predecessors. Unlike extreme nationalists, most were opposed to the notion of an offensive or preventive war. Discussion of national affairs had itself created, to a large degree, a misleading impression of nationalist agitation.[41]

The clamour of the far right was heightened by the controversy about constitutional reform, which reached its peak between 1908 and 1914. It was caused by the same set of circumstances – namely, changes in the nature of political representation and the breaking of the taboo surrounding national affairs – that had produced disputes about foreign policy. Furthermore, the immediate causes of the two controversies also overlapped, so that many reformers were concerned, above all, to find constitutional solutions to diplomatic mistakes. Thus, it was no coincidence that the *Daily Telegraph* affair, which was provoked by Wilhelm II's tactless revelations about German hatred of Britain, started the crisis in 1908 by pushing some political parties to countenance the complete replacement of Germany's system of government. This sense of constitutional crisis was maintained by a series of events, which lasted until the outbreak of war and included the formation of the 'grand bloc' in Baden in 1909, reform of the Reich's finances and Prussian franchise agitation in 1910, discussion of an Alsatian constitution and Germany's failure during the second Moroccan crisis in 1911, the emergence of the SPD as the largest single Reichstag party, the imposition of a Centre-party government on the king of Bavaria and the introduction of *de facto* votes of censure during Reichstag interpellations in 1912, and the Zabern incident in 1913, during which a Prussian lieutenant was allowed to imprison Alsatian municipal officials with impunity. Looking back, it was the novelty of the discussion itself which struck contemporaries. 'In the last twenty years, one could regularly hear and read that the time of theoretical constitutional questions was over, for the constitution, as it was fashioned by Bismarck's hand, was to be accepted as the fixed property of the German people', admitted Naumann, a proponent of reform, in 1908: 'Almost every one of us who entered politics in the 1880s and 1890s has lived through a period in which he was rather indifferent to genuine constitutional questions.' Once again, sections of the German right reacted hysterically, moved to panic more by the very existence of a debate about the reform of the national polity than by the content of that debate. The warning of one journalist of 'attempts to institute pure parliamentarism by means of incisive force' was typical of radical, right-wing responses to what was perceived to be an impending catastrophe. In the event, most Germans accepted the Reich's system of government and virtually none, as Naumann conceded, were willing to die in order to replace it with a parliamentary regime. Certainly, disagreements emerged as politicians and journalists began to scrutinize the merits and faults of different types of political regime, but these disagreements did not portend the collapse of the German nation-state, contrary to the expectations of the far right.[42]

Political discussion of national affairs helped to relativize most Germans' perceptions of the nation-state, at the same time as it fundamentalized the attitudes of a minority of radical nationalists. Thus, even in the sphere of foreign policy, where prejudice, distortion and dispute were particularly pronounced, a large number of Germans had gained a clearer and more realistic picture of France, Britain, the United States and other *Kulturländer*. Consequently, the majority of the German electorate, as has been seen, had misgivings about entering into a war against such states. Partly because of debates about foreign policy in the press and in the parties, many Wilhelmine Germans were now prepared to assess national interest for themselves, rather than blindly acceding to *raison d'état*. In the area of constitutional reform, there was less apriorism and more substantial agreement. After reading long and detailed reports on the strengths and weaknesses of the *Kaiserreich* in the press, where the Empire was compared to the allegedly ailing parliamentary regimes of western European states, most Germans came to support, with varying degrees of enthusiasm, what Otto Hintze called the 'unique Prussian-German system' of constitutional government.[43] Whereas parliamentary polities were characterized by dominant lower chambers or political parties, since governments were appointed and dismissed by parliament, Germany's constitutional regime appeared to protect the neutrality or at least the independence of the executive, with the Kaiser retaining the power of ministerial appointment and dismissal. A considerable number of left liberals and virtually all socialists rejected this type of government. Many, however, had come during the course of constitutional debate to acknowledge that Germany stood in a different political tradition, which had been shaped by constitutional monarchy (*konstitutionelle Monarchie*) and the law-governed state (*Rechtsstaat*), from that of its western neighbours. In this limited sense, a political component had been added to German national identity, even amidst widespread questioning of citizens' loyalties to the political institutions of the German Empire. Arguably, during the first twenty-five years of the *Kaiserreich*, citizens were meant to be loyal to the state, the army and the nation, whether at home or abroad, without engaging in discussion or attaching conditions. Over the next twenty years, this fiction had slowly been abandoned and national affairs had been subjected to public interrogation. The overall result, notwithstanding a countervailing proclivity towards extreme nationalism, was a moderation and relativization – but not destruction – of Germans' attachment to the nation-state and to the idea of a German identity.

Despite the unprecedented acrimony of public criticism, the German Empire was not on the brink of collapse from the turn of the century onwards. Nor was it seriously threatened by a right-wing *coup d'état* or a left-wing revolution. During the late 1900s and early 1910s, most parties had agreed with Hintze that Germany's system of government did 'not appear, precisely when compared to England, to be an incomplete stage of development on the way to parliamentarism, but rather a separate constitutional form, ... which has an historical and political background quite different to that of the parliamentary system'. During both the *Daily Telegraph* affair and the Zabern incident, the majority of Reichstag deputies, by maintaining that votes of no-confidence were designed to censure but not dismiss governments, had refused to introduce a parliamentary regime. Even after the SPD had become the largest political grouping in the lower chamber in 1912, parties had managed to cooperate with the government, one year later, to pass the first direct property tax and the largest military increases in the

Reich's history, 'bringing about', in the words of one of Bethmann's collaborators, 'the greatest financial reform and increase in military preparedness [since 1870], despite such bitterly opposed parties'. Learning from the mistakes of Bülow, the new Chancellor had retained the support of Wilhelm II and had weathered political storms from the right, over finance reforms in 1909 and 1913, and from the left, over the failure to alter the Prussian franchise in 1910 and over the Zabern incident three years later. To an unanticipated degree, his policy of 'diagonals', gaining support from different parties from one issue to another, had met with success. For the first time, socialists had voted for government bills, such as those introducing a democratic constitution in Alsace in 1911 and a direct property tax in 1913. Even to conservative outside observers like the Austrian ambassador, writing in June 1914, such cooperation had served to bolster the administration's position: 'In matters of domestic politics, Bethmann's authority has never been questioned.' Consequently, contrary to the claims of modern historians, neither the Reich government nor the German public were pushed primarily by political tensions and party stalemate at home towards a diversionary policy of adventure and war abroad. Although many league members and some conservatives sought refuge from the transformation of domestic politics and the open discussion of national affairs in radical nationalism and an aggressive foreign policy, most Wilhelmine Germans looked on internal political developments with greater equanimity. For them, national identity and national interest were still related, above all, to a moderate and increasingly relative sense of a common German culture and to a more realistic assessment of Germany's changing position in the world.[44]

Conclusion

During the prewar period, banal nationalism in Germany came to resemble more closely that of other western European countries. Most Germans' sense of national identity was more similar to that of their French and British counterparts in 1914 than it had been in 1871. However, although German nationalism as a whole had moved closer to the various nationalisms of states like Britain, Denmark, France and the Netherlands, it still diverged from them in more significant ways than they differed from each other. First, the cultural component of German identity was more pronounced, and the political component less evident, than in countries with longer histories of a shared state and common political institutions. The argument presented in this chapter concerns only the *consistency* of cultural identity, which was as dense and credible as that of Germany's neighbours, and the *tendency* of perceptions of national particularity, which included an increasing number of political elements, towards moderation and relativity, as in other European states. As a direct result of such a tendency and such consistency, the majority of Wilhelmine Germans do not seem to have found the idea of race more

attractive or compelling, particularly as a means of distinguishing themselves from other Europeans, than their French or British equivalents. Secondly, radical nationalism in Germany was different in *content* and in *scope*
from that which emerged in neighbouring countries. Thus, a minority of
extreme German nationalists were deeply affected by a unique conjunction
of events and processes – most notably, the tardiness of unification, a long-
standing distinction between politics and the state, the rapidity of industrialization, the deepening of class conflict and the scientization of race – which
distinguished late nineteenth- and early twentieth-century Germany from
other states. Partly as a consequence, radical nationalists in the Reich were
more numerous and overlapped to a greater extent with German ruling
elites than in the Third Republic or in the parliamentary monarchy of the
United Kingdom. Yet, according to the thesis put forward here, this radicalization of a minority of Wilhelmine nationalists produced a counter-reaction
amongst the majority and widened the gap between banal and extreme
nationalism. Finally, nationalism in general – both banal and radical – had
a greater *impact* on German policy-making than it did in the rest of western
Europe or in the United States. This impact was not merely the upshot of
radical-nationalist influence: many moderate nationalists, too, were conscious of Germany's anomalous position as a late arrival in an already established system of European states and as a country at the outer edge of
'Europe', and they were prepared, accordingly, to countenance a more offensive policy towards Russia and a more disdainful attitude to the continental
balance of power, which was often treated as a British instrument against
the Reich. Such differences of outlook, though, did not mean that most Germans were more willing than Britons, in all instances, to go to war. Certainly, as has been seen, they demonstrated a greater willingness to enter
into a war with Russia. Nevertheless, overall, increased confidence about the
Reich's position in Europe and more accurate, less threatening images of
Britain and France helped to ensure that the majority of Wilhelmine Germans were more likely to oppose and question the necessity of war during
the 1900s and 1910s than had been their grandparents in 1870.

This chapter has shown how changes in representation – in the double
sense of depiction and delegation – transformed conceptions of German identity, so that everyday expressions of German nationalism became more similar to those of other western European nationalisms. Historians have tended
to ignore such convergence. On the one hand, they have treated nationalism as a pathology and have refused to make a distinction between banal
and radical forms of national identity. The absence of this distinction has led
them to neglect both the density and complexity, and the moderation and
relativization of commonplace definitions of Germanness during the Wilhelmine era. On the other hand, historians have been deceived by the contradictory impact of modern representation on national identity. With the
growth of the press, the development of political organizations, the democ-

ratization of politics and the breaking of the taboo concerning the discussion of national affairs, competition on the part of newspapers, parties, leagues and officials for the right to represent the German nation gave the impression that nationalism had become more significant and more extreme. One obvious explanation for the rise of nationalism appeared to be linked, in Simmel's terms, to the flux and fragmentation of representation, which had undermined a sense of identity and had reinforced a feeling of *anomie*. More and more desperate and radical reinventions of a common national identity, it is held, were attempts to compensate a widely felt loss of meaning. In fact, however, German identity was much more intricate and durable than some contemporaries and many later historians believed. As a result, the diversity of representations of the nation during the 1890s, 1900s and 1910s served mainly to moderate and relativize most Germans' sense of national identity, not to destroy it. This was the paradox of nationalism in Germany, where a virtual interdiction had been placed on the discussion of national affairs after the 1870s: the gradual lifting of that interdiction, which allowed a fragmentary debate about the nation to take place, derived *inter alia* from a new-found confidence in the strength, popularity and longevity of the German nation.

Notes

1 G. Simmel, 'Die Arbeitsteilung als Ursache für das Auseinandertreten der subjektiven und der objektiven Kultur' (1900), in H.-J. Dahme and O. Rammstedt (eds), *Georg Simmel: Schriften zur Soziologie* (Frankfurt: Suhrkamp, 1983), pp. 116–18.

2 E.J. Hobsbawm, *Nations and Nationalism since 1780* (Cambridge: Cambridge University Press, 1990), pp. 163–83; C. Applegate, *A Nation of Provincials: The German Idea of Heimat* (Berkeley: University of California Press, 1990); B. Anderson, *Imagined Communities*, rev. edn (London: Verso, 1991); J. Habermas, 'Reply to Grimm', in P. Gowan and P. Anderson (eds), *The Question of Europe* (London: Verso, 1997), p. 264. Also J. Habermas, *Staatsbürgerschaft und nationale Identität* (St Gallen: Erher, 1992).

3 F. Meinecke, *Cosmopolitanism and the National State* (Princeton: Princeton University Press, 1970), pp. 1, 14, 16.

4 H. Kohn, *The Mind of Germany* (London: Macmillan, 1961); F. Stern, *The Politics of Cultural Despair* (Berkeley: University of California Press, 1961); G. L. Mosse, *The Crisis of German Ideology* (New York: Weidenfeld & Nicolson, 1964); H. James, *A German Identity, 1770–1990* (London: Weidenfeld & Nicolson, 1989), pp. 33, 110.

5 F. Fischer, *War of Illusions* (London: Chatto & Windus, 1975); H.-U. Wehler, *The German Empire, 1871–1918* (Oxford: Berg, 1985); V. Berghahn, *Imperial Germany, 1871–1914* (Oxford: Berghahn, 1994); J. Breuilly, *The Formation of the First German Nation-State, 1800–1871* (London: Macmillan, 1996), p. 113; J. Breuilly, 'The National Idea in Modern German History', in M. Fulbrook (ed.), *German History since 1800* (London: Arnold, 1997), p. 570.

6 O. Dann, *Nation und Nationalismus in Deutschland, 1770–1990*, 3rd rev. edn (Munich: C. H. Beck, 1996), pp. 16, 20. G. Eley, *From Unification to Nazism* (London: Allen & Unwin, 1986), pp. 60–109, has reconsidered the everyday bases of German nationalism, but his main work remains *Reshaping the German Right* (New Haven: Yale University Press, 1980), which concentrates on the Navy League. M. Billig, *Banal Nationalism* (London: Sage, 1995). E. Gellner, *Nations and Nationalism* (Oxford: Blackwell, 1983).

7 H. Delbrück, 'Was ist national?' (1913), in *Vor und nach dem Weltkrieg: politische und historische Aufsätze, 1902–1925* (Berlin: Strollberg, 1926), p. 380; H. von Treitschke, *Selections from Treitschke's Lectures on Politics* (London: Gowans & Gray, 1914), p. 10.

8 H. James, *A German Identity*, pp. 8–33; B. Giesen, *Die Intellektuellen und die Nation* (Frankfurt am Main: Suhrkamp, 1993), pp. 102–235; M. Hughes, *Nationalism and Society: Germany, 1800–1945* (London: Arnold, 1988), p. 15; I. Geiss, *The Question of German Unification, 1806–1996* (London: Routledge, 1997), pp. 51–65; Dann, *Nation und Nationalismus*, pp. 185, 200–4; E. Hobsbawm, 'Mass-Producing Traditions, 1870–1914', in E. Hobsbawm and T. Ranger (eds), *The Invention of Tradition* (Cambridge: Cambridge University Press, 1983), pp. 273–9.

9 P. Rohrbach in *Jugend*, 1912, cited in James, *A German Identity*, p. 83. L. Dumont, *German Ideology: From France to Germany and Back* (Chicago: University of Chicago Press, 1994), p. 22, on the Reich.

10 A. Wagner, *Vom Territorialstaat zur Weltmacht* (Berlin: n.p., 1900), pp. 6, 8; G. Cohn, *System der Nationalökonomie*, vol. 1 (Stuttgart: n.p., 1885), pp. 448–9, 445. R. Brubaker, *Citizenship and Nationhood in France and Germany* (Cambridge, Mass: Harvard University Press, 1992), pp. 85–137.

11 M. Weber, *Wirtschaft und Gesellschaft* (Tübingen: Mohr, 1976), p. 242; and *The Protestant Ethic and the Spirit of Capitalism* (London: Unwin, 1987), p. 30. G. L. Mosse, *Towards the Final Solution* (London: Dent, 1978). On anthropology, P. Weindling, *Health, Race and German Politics between National Unification and Nazism, 1870–1945* (Cambridge: Cambridge University Press, 1989), pp. 48–59.

12 H. Delbrück, *Regierung und Volkswille* (Berlin: Stilte, 1914), pp. 3–4.

13 M. Nordau, cited in U. Gerhard and J. Link, 'Zum Anteil der Kollektivsymbolik an den Nationalstereotypen', in J. Link and W. Wülfing (eds), *Nationale Mythen und Symbole in der zweiten Hälfte des 19. Jahrhunderts* (Stuttgart: Klett-Cotta, 1991), p. 17. H. Mayer (ed.), *Das Deutsche Volkstum*, 2nd rev. edn (Leipzig: n.p., 1903), p. 34. M. Jeismann, *Das Vaterland der Feinde* (Stuttgart: Klett-Cotta, 1992) and Dumont, *German Ideology*, on the definition of a German identity *vis-à-vis* France.

14 Kohn, *The Mind of Germany*, pp. 189–207; K. von See, 'Das Nibelungenlied – ein Nationalepos?', in *Barbar, Germane, Arier* (Heidelberg: Winter, 1994), pp. 83–134; H. Gollwitzer, 'Zum politischen Germanismus des 19. Jahrhunderts', in *Festschrift für Hermann Heimpel*, vol. 1 (Göttingen: Vandenhoeck & Ruprecht, 1971), pp. 282–356; L. Gall, *Germania: Eine deutsche Marianne?* (Bonn: Bouvier, 1993). J. Langbehn, *Rembrandt als Erzieher* (Leipzig: n.p., 1890); E. Keller, *Nationalismus und Literatur* (Bern: Francke, 1970), pp. 17–21; Stern, *The Politics of Cultural Despair*, pp. 97–180. M. Titzmann, 'Die Konzeption der "Germanen" in der deutschen Literatur des 19. Jahrhunderts', in Link and Wülfing (eds), *Nationale Mythen und Symbole*, p. 127.

15 W. Siemann, 'Krieg und Frieden in historischen Gedenkfeiern des Jahres 1913',

in D. Düding *et al.* (eds), *Öffentliche Festkultur* (Reinbek: Rowohlt, 1988), pp. 302–14. D. B. Dennis, *Beethoven in German Politics* (New Haven: Yale University Press, 1996), p. 49, and H. Hattenhauer, *Deutsche Nationalsymbole* (Munich: Olzog, 1984), p. 56, on 1840; A. T. Allen, *Satire and Society in Wilhelmine Germany* (Kentucky: University Press of Kentucky, 1984), pp. 95–102, on 1870–71. W. Wülfing, K. Bruns and R. Parr, *Historische Mythologie der Deutschen, 1798–1918* (Munich, 1991).

16 S. Berger, *The Search for Normality* (Oxford: Berghahn, 1997), pp. 1–35; S. Berger *et al.* (eds), *Writing National Histories* (London: Routledge, 1999), pp. 15–21, 97–110; G. G. Iggers, *The German Conception of History*, rev. edn (New Hampshire: Wesleyan University Press, 1983), pp. 3–228. Treitschke, *Selections from Treitschke's Lectures on Politics*, p. 10. On schools, J. H. Schoeps, 'Die Deutschen und ihre Identität: Zwischen Kyffhäusermythos und Verfassungspatriotismus', in P. Krüger (ed.), *Deutschland, deutscher Staat, deutsche Nation* (Marburg: Hitzeroth, 1993), pp. 92–5; A. Kelly, 'The Franco-German War and Unification in German History Schoolbooks', in W. Pape (ed.), *1870/71–1989/90: German Unifications and the Change of Literary Discourse* (Berlin: de Gruyter, 1993), pp. 37–60.

17 Walter Bondy, cited in P. Paret, *The Berlin Secession* (Cambridge, Mass: Belknap, 1980), p. 191; L. Corinth, cited in R. Manheim, 'Kunst und Nation im spätwilhelminischen Deutschland', in O. Dann (ed.), *Die deutsche Nation* (Vierow: SH-Verlag, 1994), p. 78. On S. George and T. Mann, W. Lepenies, *Between Literature and Science: The Rise of Sociology* (Cambridge: Cambridge University Press, 1988), pp. 203–312. On F. Dahn, K. von See, *Die Ideen von 1789 und die Ideen von 1914* (Frankfurt am Main: Athenaion, 1974), pp. 91–5. G. Mosse, 'Was die Deutschen wirklich lasen', in R. Grimm and J. Hermand (eds), *Popularität und Trivialität* (Frankfurt am Main: n.p., 1974), pp. 101–20; U.-K. Ketelsen, *Völkisch-nationale und nationalsozialistische Literatur in Deutschland, 1890–1945* (Stuttgart: Metzler, 1976), pp. 33–52; Titzmann, 'Die Konzeption der "Germanen", pp. 120–45.

18 A. Confino, *The Nation as a Local Metaphor* (Chapel Hill: University of North Carolina Press, 1997), pp. 158–89. T. Nipperdey, 'Nationalidee und Nationaldenkmal in Deutschland im 19. Jahrhundert', in *Gesellschaft, Kultur, Theorie* (Göttingen: Vandenhoeck & Ruprecht, 1976), p. 153. F. Schmoll, *Verewigte Nation* (Tübingen: Silverberg, 1995). Düding *et al.* (eds), *Öffentliche Festkultur*, pp. 67–88, 166–90, 278–320; Hobsbawm, 'Mass-Producing Traditions', p. 277; T. von Elsner, *Kaisertage: Die Hamburger und das Wilhelminische Deutschland im Spiegel öffentlicher Festkultur* (Frankfurt am Main: Peter Lang, 1991).

19 *Hamburgische Correspondent*, 1912, cited in Elsner, *Kaisertage*, p. 370. R. J. Evans, *Proletarians and Politics* (London: Harvester Wheatsheaf, 1990), pp. 124–91.

20 F. Tönnies, *Gemeinschaft und Gesellschaft*, 8th edn (Leipzig: Buske, 1935), p. 237.

21 H. Diez, *Das Zeitungswesen* (Leipzig: Teubner, 1910), pp. 1–2. Statistics, respectively, from T. Nipperdey, *Deutsche Geschichte*, 3rd rev. edn, vol. 1 (Munich: Beck, 1993), p. 809; Berghahn, *Imperial Germany*, p. 16; K. Koszyk, *Deutsche Presse im 19. Jahrhundert* (Berlin: Colloquium Verlag, 1966), pp. 304–8.

22 Diez, *Das Zeitungswesen*, pp. 141–3. Allen, *Satire and Society in Wilhelmine Germany*, p. 225. A. Haas, *Das moderne Zeitungswesen in Deutschland* (Berlin: n.p., 1914), p. 10.

23 O. Groth, 'Der Stoff der Zeitungen', in W. Schulz (ed.), *Der Inhalt der Zeitungen* (Düsseldorf: RBDuVG, 1970), pp. 115–17.

24 The latter argument about racism has been made most forcefully by Mosse, *The Crisis of German Ideology*, and the former about a *Flucht nach vorn*, by Fischer, *War of Illusions*. More details of this historiographical debate are given in M. Hewitson, 'Germany and France before the First World War: A Reassessment of Wilhelmine Foreign Policy', *English Historical Review* (forthcoming 2000).

25 R. N. Stromberg, *Redemption by War* (Kansas: Regents Press, 1982), pp. 137–50.

26 Allen, *Satire and Society in Wilhelmine Germany*, pp. 124–5. H. W. Smith, 'The Talk of Genocide, the Rhetoric of Miscegenation: Notes on Debates in the German Reichstag Concerning Southwest Africa, 1904–1914', in S. Friedrichsmeyer *et al.* (eds), *The Imperialist Imagination* (Ann Arbor: University of Michigan Press, 1998), pp. 107–23. H. Gollwitzer, *Die gelbe Gefahr* (Göttingen: Vandenhoeck & Ruprecht, 1962), pp. 163–218; J. Kreiner (ed.), *Deutschland-Japan: Historische Kontakte* (Bonn: Bouvier, 1984), pp. 115–32. *Simplicissimus*, 23 May 1905, no. 8, vol. 10.

27 F.Engels, cited in L. Kopolew, 'Zunächst war Waffenbrüderschaft', in M. Keller (ed.), *Russen und Rußland aus deutscher Sicht*, vol. 3 (Munich: Fink, 1992), p. 51. A. Bebel, cited in N. Stargardt, *The German Idea of Militarism* (Cambridge: Cambridge University Press, 1994), p. 59; F. Stampfer, cited in P. Scheidemann, *Memoirs of a Social Democrat*, vol. 1 (London: Hodder & Stoughton, 1929), p. 189. C. Schmidt, 'Ein deutscher Slawophile? August von Haxthausen und die Wiederentdeckung der russischen Bauerngemeinde 1843/44', in Keller (ed.), *Russen und Rußland*, vol. 3, pp. 196–216; G. Voigt, *Rußland in der deutschen Geschichtsschreibung, 1843–1945* (Berlin: Akademie Verlag, 1994), pp. 66–114; D. Groh, *Rußland im Blick Europas*, 2nd edn (Frankfurt am Main: Suhrkamp, 1988), pp. 97–412; T. R. E. Paddock, 'Still Stuck at Sevastopol: The Depiction of Russia during the Russo-Japanese War and the Beginning of the First World War in the German Press', *German History*, vol. 16 (1998), pp. 358–76.

28 Treitschke, *Selections from Treitschke's Lectures on Politics*, p. 20. F. Naumann, in *Hilfe*, 1900, no.28; O. A. H. Schmitz, *Das Land der Wirklichkeit*, 5th edn (Munich: n.p., 1914), pp. 22–3, 38, 56–7, 61, 67–8, 73, 111, 114–15, 142, 146; K. Hillebrand, *Frankreich und die Franzosen*, 4th edn (Strasbourg: n.p., 1898), p. 9. K. Lamprecht, cited in F. Trommler, 'Inventing the Enemy: German–American Cultural Relations, 1900–1917', in H.-J. Schröder (ed.), *Confrontation and Cooperation: Germany and the United States in the Era of World War I* (Oxford: Berg, 1993), p. 113; D. E. Barclay and E. Glaser-Schmidt (eds), *Transatlantic Images and Perceptions: Germany and America since 1776* (Cambridge: Cambridge University Press, 1997), pp. 65–86, 109–30; D. Diner, *America in the Eyes of the Germans* (Princeton: Markus Wiener, 1996), pp. 3–51; C. E. McClelland, *The German Historians and England* (Cambridge: Cambridge University Press, 1971); P. M. Kennedy, *The Rise of the Anglo-German Antagonism, 1860–1914* (London: Allen & Unwin, 1980), pp. 59–145, 306–437.

29 M. Weber, *Gesammelte Politische Schriften* (Tübingen: n.p., 1958), p. 23; W. J. Mommsen, *Max Weber and German Politics, 1890–1920* (Chicago: University of Chicago Press, 1984), pp. 68–90. Reportage is examined more fully in M. Hewitson, *National Identity and Political Thought in Germany: Wilhelmine Depictions of the French Third Republic, 1898–1914* (Oxford, forthcoming); Hewitson, 'Germany and France before the First World War', on the question of enmity and threats to national security.

30 H.-O. Sieburg, *Deutschland und Frankreich in der Geschichtsschreibung des neunzehnten Jahrhunderts*, 2 vols (Wiesbaden: n.p., 1954–58); Jeismann, *Das Vaterland der Feinde*, pp. 27–102, 241–95. B. von Bülow memorandum, 15 May 1909, *Auswärtiges Amt Bonn*, R6605, A8510; *Simplicissimus*, 17 March 1913, no. 51; A. Wagner, cited in Kennedy, *The Rise of the Anglo-German Antagonism*, p. 310. Also, G. Krumeich, 'La puissance militaire française vue de l'Allemagne autour de 1900', in P. Milza and R. Poidevin (eds), *La Puissance française à la belle époque* (Brussels: Editions complexe, 1992), pp. 199–210; H. Kaelble, 'Wahrnehmung der Industrialisierung: Die französische Gesellschaft im Bild der Deutschen zwischen 1891 und 1914', in W. Süß (ed.), *Übergänge: Zeitgeschichte zwischen Utopie und Machbarkeit* (Berlin: Dunker & Humblot, 1989), pp. 123–38. The arguments here are made in more detail in M. Hewitson, 'German Public Opinion and the Question of Industrial Modernity: Wilhelmine Depictions of the French Economy', *European Review of History*, vol. 7 (2000), pp. 45–61.
31 L. von Gerlach, cited in Kennedy, *The Rise of the Anglo-German Antagonism*, p. 73; Treitschke, cited in McClelland, *The German Historians and England*, pp. 168, 184; O. Hintze, cited in W. Schenk, *Die deutsch-englische Rivalität vor dem Ersten Weltkrieg in der Sicht deutscher Historiker* (Aarau: Keller, 1967), p. 77.
32 G.A.v.Müller, cited in N. Ferguson, 'Public Finance and National Security', *Past and Present*, vol. 142 (1994), p. 18.
33 H. von Treitschke, *Politik*, 2nd rev. edn, vol. 1 (Leipzig: n.p., 1899), pp. 1, 32; G. Cohn, *System der Nationalökonomie*, vol. 2 (Stuttgart: n.p., 1885–98), p. 50; G. Jellinek, 'Eine Naturlehre des Staates', in *Ausgewählte Schriften und Reden*, vol. 2 (Berlin: n.p., 1911), p. 320; Iggers, *The German Conception of History*, p. 202, on Meinecke; D. Beetham, *Max Weber and the Theory of Modern Politics*, 2nd edn (Cambridge: Polity, 1985), pp. 63–94; W. Roscher, *Politik* (Stuttgart: n.p., 1892), pp. 308–472.
34 A. Mitzman, *Sociology and Estrangement*, revised edn (New Brunswick: Transaction Books, 1987), pp. 267–338, on Michels; G. Simmel, 'Die quantitative Bestimmtheit der Gruppe' (1908), in *Schriften zur Soziologie*, pp. 243–63.
35 A. Kirchhoff, *Was ist national?* (Halle: Gebauer-Schwetschke, 1902), p. 41; F. Meinecke, *Weltbürgertum und Nationalstaat*, 7th edn (Berlin: n.p., 1927), p. 18.
36 See above. Also, W. J. Mommsen, *Imperial Germany, 1867–1918* (London: Arnold, 1995), pp. 75–100, 163–204.
37 D. Blackbourn, *Germany, 1780–1918* (London: Fontana, 1997), pp. 424–40; Eley, *Reshaping the German Right*; G. Eley, 'State Formation, Nationalism and Political Culture', in *From Unification to Nazism*, pp. 61–84.
38 Meinecke, *Cosmopolitanism and the National State*, pp. 368, 374; F. Naumann, 'Die Umwandlung der deutschen Reichsverfassung', *Patria*, 1908, p. 95; C. Bachem, cited in H. W. Smith, *German Nationalism and Religious Conflict* (Princeton: Princeton University Press, 1995), pp. 61–78, 138–40, 185–205; G. Vollmar and other references to the SPD, in D. Groh and P. Brandt, *'Vaterlandslose Gesellen': Sozialdemokratie und Nation, 1860–1990* (Munich: C. H. Beck, 1992), pp. 112–57; E. Bernstein, *Evolutionary Socialism* (New York: Schocken, 1952), pp. 165–6, 170.
39 W. Rathenau, cited in Allen, *Satire and Society in Wilhelmine Germany*, p. 76; A. Keim, cited in Eley, *Reshaping the German Right*, pp. 265–6.
40 H. Delbrück and F. Meinecke, cited in R. Chickering, *We Men Who Feel Most Ger-*

man (London: Allen & Unwin, 1984), pp. 283, 285, 296; *Simplicissimus*, 1897, shown in Stargardt, *The German Idea of Militarism*, p. 37.

41 E. Bassermann, F. Lascelles and F. Cartwright, cited in P. G. Lauren, *Diplomats and Bureaucrats* (Stanford: Hoover Institution Press, 1976), pp. 55, 57, 59.

42 Naumann, 'Die Umwandlung der deutschen Verfassung', pp. 84, 97; *Deutsche Tageszeitung*, 13 December 1913.

43 O. Hintze, 'Das monarchische Prinzip und die konstitutionelle Verfassung' (1911), in G. Oestreich (ed.), *Staat und Verfassung*, 2nd rev. edn (Göttingen: Vandenhoeck & Ruprecht, 1962), p. 359.

44 Hintze, 'Das monarchische Prinzip und die konstitutionelle Verfassung', pp. 364–5; A. Wahnschaffe and L. von Szögény-Marich, cited in K. Jarausch, *The Enigmatic Chancellor: Bethmann Hollweg and the Hubris of Imperial Germany* (New Haven: Yale University Press, 1973), p. 105.

3

New Berlins and new Germanies: history, myth and the German capital in the 1920s and 1990s

Deborah Smail and Corey Ross

Berlin is currently the largest construction site in Europe. With the fall of the Wall, the city's politicians and planners have been faced with the enormous task of not only reconnecting East–West transportation lines, rebuilding the 'no man's land' in the historic heart of the city, repairing the structural damage of decades of neglect under the GDR and preparing for the arrival of the German government, but also throughout the process finding suitable forms that express the city's new role in reunified Germany and the world at large. The practical and symbolic aspects of this reconstruction task are inextricably linked with each other, and are of central importance in the symbolism of the new Germany. Berlin has in many respects served as a metaphor of divided Germany since the end of the Second World War, the land between the two great political systems, a kind of microcosm of Germany – or even Europe – as a whole. Yet the collapse of the GDR and reunification has by no means ended this symbolic role of Berlin. Rather, it has served to reinforce it as the two sides of the city, like the two sides of country as a whole, slowly grow together, the new construction projects covering over the evidence of the Cold War and Allied occupation so recently dominant in the city's physical and political topography. Indeed, the fact that reunified Germany has been popularly dubbed the '*Berliner Republik*' and that the '*neue Mitte*' around Potsdamer Platz has been paralleled with the new centre in German politics after the 1998 elections has to do with more than the mere choice of capital city or tawdry political wordplay. They both reflect the sense that the city's recent past of division and future as a reunited city strikingly symbolize the past, present and future of Germany at large.[1]

As the reconstruction of Berlin continues, certain areas of the city are becoming associated not only with the future of the city, or even the future of Germany, but also the future of Europe. These sites include the Potsdamer Platz, where some of Europe's biggest businesses are setting up headquarters among new cinemas, casinos, residential apartments, a shopping mall and the new museums of the nearby Kulturforum; the Reichstag with its new glass cupola; Lehrter Bahnhof, which previously bordered on no man's land but which now will be a central station where northbound and southbound trains will cross with eastbound and westbound trains; and the area in and around the Friedrichstrasse, the site of numerous new large-scale office buildings (based mainly on speculation) and a series of new shops ranging from normal high street chains to *haute couture* boutiques. Indeed, if a recent article in the *Guardian* is any indication, it would appear that the image of Berlin that is now emerging is precisely the one that many city planners wished for. With the title 'All Roads Lead to Berlin', the article describes Berlin as a 'phoenix', a 'new international megalopolis' and a 'monster rising from the Prussian sands'.[2]

Such language vividly brings to mind scenes from Fritz Lang's *Metropolis* – a film that has always been associated with 1920s Berlin. Indeed, the *Guardian* rather explicitly makes this connection in its choice of illustrations: a photo of cranes and scaffolding around the Reichstag next to a still from Lang's cinema vision of Berlin as the city of the future. This is no coincidence. In fact, much of the current reconstruction effort in the city has looked to the Weimar period – the only other time the city was unified under a democratic government – for inspiration and for a sense of what is genuinely 'Berlin'. This period is broadly considered the city's heyday, a time of intense cultural and intellectual ferment, a kind of blossoming of unfettered creativity following the constraints of rigid Wilhelmine morality and eventually succumbing to the brutally proscriptive suppression of National Socialism. The name of the new 'Marlene Dietrich Platz' in what used to be no man's land is perhaps the most obvious (though by no means only) example of the attempts to invoke this 'Golden Twenties' past in the hope that Berlin will once again recover a degree of its vitality and glory after the decades of political repression and Cold War division. When looking for traditions to celebrate, for past reflections of what Berlin 'ought to be', for positive symbols of a new civic identity, the 'Golden Twenties' beckon as a time of progress, openness and promise.

But the 1920s was also a period of a very self-conscious, not to mention self-interested, questioning of what Berlin represented, how it embodied the broader spirit of the age, what made it unique and how it should be presented to the world. In both its physicality and image, 'Berlin' was as much in a process of reinvention then as it is now. In a sense, the city planners, politicians, journalists and writers concerned with the new Berlin of the 1990s are in some ways re-inventing an old invention, reappropriating and popularizing some of the long-lived myths of 1920s Berlin as a means of connecting with some of the brighter periods of the city's past – an important connection for shaping the imagination and conception of Berlin as the capital of a progressive, democratic and united Germany after 1990. Yet image-making for the city was also precisely what their 1920s counterparts were doing.

In this chapter we will be looking at some of the ways in which images of 1920s Berlin have parallelled, inspired and influenced the physical and metaphoric recasting of Berlin since 1990. The city was then, as it is now, the subject of much deliberate, stage-managed hype as the 'place to be' and the 'up-and-coming' capital of Europe. New building projects, although on a smaller scale than the current Potsdamer Platz developments, aimed to create a model consumer paradise and busy commercial centres. Progress in transportation links, like the current work at Lehrter Bahnhof and around the city's airports, aimed at placing Berlin at the centre of European business and trade, and cultural life, both elite and popular, was seen to be blossoming.

Although the years between First World War and Nazi takeover of power are generally referred to as the 'Weimar' period, it was Berlin, not the pleasant provincial town in Thuringia, that came to symbolize the social, political and cultural developments of the time. Previously the capital of Prussian monarchical pomp and militaristic display, Berlin was recast during the 1920s into a dynamic and cosmopolitan capital of a progressive German state. This new Berlin was born largely on the pages of feuilleton, in the skilful self-marketing of artists and the silver screen of popular film – cultural personalities and artefacts which have survived in popular memory and drawn immense scholarly interest, ranging from the films of Fritz Lang to the paintings and personae of the likes of Otto Dix and Georg Grosz to the writings of Kurt Tucholsky, Egon Erwin Kisch and Siegfried Kracauer to Alfred Döblin's famous novel *Berlin Alexanderplatz*. The enduring myth of Berlin has made it the centre of artistic and architectural modernism; of 'rationalization' and commerce; of entertainment, mass culture, and sexual liberation. Common to most of this imagery are the quintessentially 'modern' themes of speed, commotion and traffic, masses of people moving to and fro, lights and nightlife, a new sexual permissiveness and shifting gender roles, the illuminated throngs visiting the film cinemas, and of course the American-style musical shows and 'girls' that simultaneously combined elements of militaristic display, factory precision and the idea of the independent, no-nonsense, sexually liberated 'flapper'.

These well-known and well-studied cultural elites were not the only generators and propagators of a 'new', modern, cosmopolitan and 'happening' Berlin during the latter half of the 1920s. Then, as now, city officials were intimately involved in conjuring up this image, above all the Berlin Tourist Office. The reason for this was essentially pragmatic, and indeed was much the same as today: to attract tourists and business to the city.[3] In 1927 the Tourist Office launched a broad campaign called 'Jeder Einmal in Berlin', whose goal was to promote Berlin as a business and tourist attraction.[4] It published an official guidebook to the city, *Jeder Einmal in Berlin. Offizieller Führer für Berlin und Umgebung*, which amounted to an attempt on the part of city officials to present a coherent image of Berlin as an up-and-coming world-city of international stature, a metropolis of modernity and a centre of culture that everyone should visit. In its opening pages, the director of the Tourist Office, Adolf Schick, presented the city as:

The Weltstadt *of order and beauty,*
the *city of work,*
the *most active* Weltstadt *of the continent,*
the *European centre of economics and transport,*
the *city of music and theatre*
the *great city of sport,*
the *metropolis with the most beautiful surroundings!*[5]

Naturally, an important part of constructing this image was to present Berlin on a par with other unquestioned world-cities such as London, Paris and New York. The various sections of the guide try to impress the reader with the size, economic importance and diversity of the city, and to convince him/her that in all areas of life, Berlin was, at best, on a par with New York, Paris and London and, at worst, not so far behind that it need be ashamed. The colonies of foreigners living in Berlin at the time were cited as a sign of Berlin's cosmopolitanism and international stature. Around 130,000 Russians, Czechs, Hungarians, Dutch, Austrians and others 'have chosen Berlin as their permanent place of residence and give its streets, its restaurants and places of entertainment the international character of New York, London or Paris'.[6] They also brought with them a sense of the exotic, which any self-respecting world-city needed to have. 'Oh, how international, indeed, how exotic this city is for those who know it. We have Chinese restaurants, Japanese venues, Dutch cocoa-lounges ..., we have a Persian school in the Bismarckstrasse, a Muslim colony on Hohenzollerndamm with a proper mosque, a Buddhist cloister in Frohnau and a rich exotic-corner at the film-extras market in the old amusement park.'

It was understandably in the realm of cultural life – both elite and popular – that city officials made their most unqualified claims for Berlin's *Weltstadt* status. Alongside the more standard information on museums, theatres and concert halls in the guide, the city is fêted simultaneously as a centre of artistic creativity as well as a capital of pleasure and amusement (*Vergnügen*), all the while retaining a sense of speed and 'tempo': 'Two o'clock in the morning. We're very hot and thankful for the wind that fans a bit of coolness along the Kurfürstendamm ... But one cannot yet be tired at two a.m. in Berlin. Closing time only comes at three. Shall we continue?'[7]

But setting Berlin on a par with other world-cities could only go so far towards propagating it as a true *Weltstadt*. In presenting itself in so many ways as equal to New York, Paris and London, the city also needed to be distinguished from them. London had Westminster and its palaces, Paris its boulevards and Eiffel Tower and New York its skyscrapers to set them apart from one another and to provide each with its own symbols and national associations. Berlin could, according to the guide, offer almost anything these other cities could. But what attractive features could it offer that the others did not have? What unique and distinctive features did it possess that made it special – indeed, that made it 'German'?

The Brandenburg Gate was the most distinguished architectural symbol of the city and indeed was used as the basis for the official 'Jeder Einmal in Berlin' symbol. Yet it does not feature all that prominently in the marketing of the city, presumably because it actually presented little to look at and was patently underwhelming in comparison with the Eiffel Tower or Manhattan's skyscrapers. The answer was found in what were seen as the traditionally 'German' virtues of order, discipline and cleanliness, older Wilhelmine values which could complement Berlin's supposed 'tempo' and vitality in such a way as to avoid some of the less attractive aspects of other world-cities. To offer an illustration, in a 1929 urban planning journal on *The New Berlin*, city councillor Walter Behrendt argued that 'a new, immensely strong vitality has seized the city, perceptible to everyone who lives in it or enters it from outside, tangible above all in the flying tempo that prevails here and that carries along everyone who stands under its influence. Foreigners coming from Paris or London affirm that Berlin is currently the liveliest city in Europe.' Whereas Paris was deemed a mere showpiece (albeit an elegant one), the '*Weltstadt* of yesterday', and New York a young and lively yet 'rampant, wildly sprouting growth, undisciplined [*zuchtlos*] and without form', Berlin had the ability to be the best of all worlds: elegant, young and orderly, a truly twentieth-century city unlike Paris, but without the social and architectural chaos of the great American metropolis.[8] Moreover, this notion of 'disciplined' growth, of the potential of rational urban planning, was seen not only as more socially enlightened than New York's slums, it was also quintessentially 'modern'. The new social housing developments on the outskirts of town, especially those around Britz, were celebrated for leaving the old centre behind: 'In this periphery of Berlin one hears – not so noisily as in the centre, but perhaps even more strongly – the heartbeat of the present. Here the ideas of modern city-planning speak most loudly.'[9]

Of course the desire of many Berliners to compete with other cities was not limited to the Weimar years. It has a long history, and heavily influenced city-planning well before the First World War.[10] Much of this competitiveness prior to the 1920s tended to be backward-looking and imitative; city planners often tried to create an air of historical importance simply unattainable in comparison with London or Paris. In his collection of feuilletons on *fin-de-siècle* Berlin, Arthur Eloesser criticized these 'speedy culture-makers who within a few years want to achieve a target for which other European capitals needed centuries' and the 'undignified imitation and rash desire to do things better'.[11] The decade of stagnation from the outbreak of war in 1914 to the end of inflation precluded many such construction projects in any event. By then it was clear that Berlin could not compete with these other European capitals in terms of its past, and perhaps not quite even in terms of its present. But it could be presented as a world-city of the future, and indeed this was what the official advertising for the city emphasized – not at all unlike current images of Berlin as the great construction site of the 1990s, the 'heartland, the engine-room of a united Europe in the 21st century'.[12] As an American correspondent for the *Chicago Tribune* summed it up in the official guidebook: 'Berlin, the youngest of Europe's cosmopolitan capitals, spurred onward by the ambition to be the town where there "is always something doing" is throbbing with a new rhythm of life all her own. ... Noted for her sternness in the past, Berlin now is going about the business of enjoying the gay sides of life with the same thoroughness that marked her growth into Europe's most modern, most healthful city.'[13] Besides comparing favourably to other *Weltstädte*, Berlin during the latter half of the 1920s was also claimed to compare favourably to its own 'stern' past, its prewar image of Prussian militarism and monarchy while at the same time retaining a salutary degree of Wilhelmine orderliness that putatively set it apart from other world-cities.

Probably the most spectacular attempt to market this image of Berlin to the world was the 'Berlin in Lights' (*Berlin im Licht*) festival of October 1928, which literally spotlighted what city officials, businessmen and many cultural commentators thought Berlin stood for. Sponsored by the Tourist Office, the Verein Berliner Kaufleute und Industrieller[14] and almost 150 other business associations, 'Berlin in Lights' was a four-day spectacle of illumination designed to demonstrate the city's brilliance. It included a festival of light at Tempelhof airport, an official 'Light Ball', a parade of automobile lights and a procession of illuminated advertisements – all central symbols of 1920s modernity.[15] In the official opening of the festival, Berlin was claimed to be the 'new European city of light'. Gustav Böß, the city's mayor, claimed that 'Berlin is becoming a city of light, it is already well on the way. ... I know: Paris, London and New York are still ahead of us. But soon we will have caught up with them!'[16]

It was no coincidence that the organizers of 'Berlin in Lights' concentrated events particularly in the West End of the city around the Kurfürstendamm, Tauentzienstrasse (or 'Street of All Nations', as it was called during the spectacle) and Kaiser-Wilhelm-Memorial Church. In terms of symbolism, this area was widely regarded as the most 'modern' and 'democratic' side of Berlin. Perhaps more importantly, it was also a growing centre of commerce and 'mass' consumption – that is, retail shopping and nightlife – as the financial support and sponsorship from the Verein Berliner Kaufleute und Industrieller testifies. Initially developed as a predominantly residential area around the turn of the century, by the 1920s the West End had become a fashionable wealthy suburb for the liberal and often Anglophile elites in the professions, finance, commerce and culture, a relatively large proportion of whom were Jewish. It also quickly became a kind of counter-city-centre to the historic palace area and commercial centre around the Friedrichstrasse, which had been the liveliest area of the city before the war. As one contemporary remarked, if the Friedrichstrasse were not home to the largest train station in Berlin, it would surely have died out, not least because of its proximity to the old monarchical buildings, for the 'democratic West', the area of the city's 'new rulers', was 'drawing away its life-blood'.[17]

For many, the West End was indeed the very embodiment of the 'new Berlin' and its spirit: Americanized, intensely commercial, dynamic and modern, international. It was a centre of nightlife, of cafés, bars and the new 'mass' restaurants, the most famous among them the Hotel Kempinski. It was also the centre of modern visual imagery: not just the new and immensely popular film cinemas, but also of neon lights, show windows and modern advertisement generally, which made increasing use of the erotic over the course of the 1920s, reflecting changing gender roles and notions of sexuality. It was even the home of that most 'modern' object of all, the automobile. By the end of the 1920s, the Auguste-Viktoria Platz actually overtook Potsdamer Platz as the busiest traffic intersection in Europe, with some 3,250 vehicles per hour.[18] As Christian Bouchholtz had already enthusiastically put it in 1921: 'The spirit of the Ku'damm, – the first time one has a taste of it one feels changed by it and cannot do without it. For it is young, ambitious and free!'[19]

Indeed, the West End's very physicality was deemed more 'progressive' than that of the historic city centre. Much of its new commercial architecture had adopted the relatively simple forms of the international style, often referred to as *Neue Sachlichkeit*. The ornate façades of Wilhelmine buildings were stripped of their stone ornamentation and replaced with plain supports upon which neon advertisements could be mounted. The size of shop windows was also increased and greater emphasis placed on product displays and their effective illumination. The significance of this new commercial architecture was hotly discussed in many newspapers and journals, with opinions ranging from emphatic approval to wary scepticism – echoing the architectural debates surrounding Potsdamer Platz and the new Spreebogen government quarter in the 1990s. For Walter Behrendt, the lights and new shop façades, along with the increase in traffic, were *the* signs that Berlin was 'the liveliest city of Europe'.[20] For the architects, the illuminated architecture signified the dawning of a new architectural spirit, one which celebrated the new republican era by rejecting the monarchical *Prunk* of the Wilhelmine past and adopting, instead, a modern international language which stressed functionality and simplicity of form in the service of business and the consumer. In short, the West End was more or less universally seen as symbolizing much of the spirit of the new progressive age.

This was, of course, precisely why right-wing circles deplored and attacked it so bitterly. Whereas the West End's supporters saw in it the shimmering promise of the future, others saw in it all that was wrong with Germany at the time. By the 1920s there was already a well-established tradition of anti-metropolitan and anti-cosmopolitan polemics dating from around the turn of the century, which saw the modern metropolis of speed, mass consumption and 'Americanization' as anything but a model for the future. Widely viewed as a centre of wealth, commerce, and liberal cosmopolitanism, the West End was simultaneously the object of social envy, nationalistic hatred and conservative chauvinism among right-wing propagandists. In the right-wing press the West End in general, and the Kurfürstendamm in particular, became a cliché for the 'nouveau riche', the 'war profiteers' and 'parasites', the 'November criminals', and so forth, usually with strong anti-Semitic undertones. Moreover, the area's nightlife, mass cultural venues and advertising were attacked as immoral and degenerate. Particular targets of scorn were the subversive tones of American jazz, the dance culture that accompanied it, the suggestive use of women's bodies in advertisement and the independent, sexually liberated attitude of the modern flapper. Precisely those qualities that were celebrated in the Republican press as the embodying the 'spirit of the age' – modern, liberal and internationalist – were lambasted in the right-wing press as atavistic, immoral and unnatural, indeed as quintessentially 'undeutsch'. In other words, what some considered the liveliest and up-and-coming area of the German capital city was for others the very opposite of what it meant to be 'German'.[21]

With the onset of economic depression in 1929, this anti-cosmopolitan, anti-metropolitan sentiment became more mainstream. Broadly speaking, the more Berlin's crisis became apparent, the more the entire idea of Berlin as the up-and-coming *Weltstadt* conjured up in feuilleton, film and official festivals began to disintegrate. Suddenly the evaluations changed: all the images of modernity, progress and cosmopolitanism that had previously been celebrated were now interpreted more negatively.

This was clearly the case in literary journalism. As the economic and political crisis worsened, the international heterogeneity in Berlin that had previously been celebrated in liberal feuilleton during the years of relative prosperity was now seen as a threat. To Heinrich Hauser, an emphatic protagonist of *Neue Sachlichkeit*, the city's Chinese and Jews were no longer an exotic asset, but were 'eerie, because they can change as quickly as actors' faces ... The earth itself rejects them, the instinct of healthy nations withstands them.'[22] Likewise, the cosmopolitan Berlin, the swarming centre of commerce and industry, was increasingly seen as a 'nomadic camp'; it was a 'city of nomads' and of 'enormous, rootless streams of people'.[23] Even the 'modern' and 'progressive' commercial district in the West End rapidly lost its gloss. To Siegfried Kracauer, the Kurfürstendamm became the 'Street Without Memory', an 'incorporation of emptily flowing time in which nothing can last' and in which the constant change and fluidity wrought by raw commercial forces 'wipes out memories'.[24] What is more, the previous fascination with lights and night life was now seen as a fraud, the glamour and glitter of the nightclubs a deceptive yet threadbare veil over the misery of their patrons: 'The brighter the lights, the gloomier the crowd'.[25]

The ambiguities and deceptiveness of the 'Golden Twenties' myth also became a topos in the creative literature of the early 1930s. Street scenes around the Kurfürstendamm and Potsdamer Platz, while still retaining a certain magic of festive illumination, now have more ominous elements with poverty and prostitution becoming increasingly visible. In the opening pages of Erich Kästner's best-selling 1931 novel *Fabian*, the area is described as a 'fairground' (*Rummelplatz*) in which tacky advertisements for unneeded products and questionable locales rain down over the pedestrians.[26] In Gabriele Tergit's 1931 novel *Käsebier erobert den Kurfürstendamm*, the area is described as a 'dead city in which cholera had lived. Or was it like in the gold-digging cities of America when the gold had run out? To let, to let, to let, house by house. The shops closed. House by house.'[27] In Irmgard Keun's 1932 novel *Das kunstseidene Mädchen*, scenes of economic plight and prostitution regularly disrupt the attempts of the protagonist, the eighteen-year-old unemployed typist Doris, to experience Berlin as the cosmopolitan and magical city which she assumes and wants it to be:

> In the *Haus Vaterland* there are wonderful, elegant staircases like in a palace with duchesses strutting about – and landscapes and turkish and wine ... The people are all in such a hurry – sometimes they are all pale in the light, then the girls' dresses don't look paid for and the men actually cannot afford the wine – but is no one happy? Now everything is getting dark – where is my bright [*helles*] Berlin?[28]

In 1931, the writer Curt Moreck published a self-consciously unofficial guidebook to Berlin as counterpart to the official *Jeder einmal in Berlin* guide: the *Führer durch das 'lasterhafte' Berlin*. Though in tone, style and content the book still wants in many ways to propagate and believe the idea of the up-and-coming *Weltstadt*, the young metropolis where 'something is always doing', it is no longer quite convinced of the myth itself. It is thus self-contradictory, ambiguous, and rather sarcastic in its portrayal of Berlin, and reveals instead a less glamorous side of many of the themes in the official guide. Although at first described as lively and entertaining, Berlin's cabaret is nonetheless deemed a 'weak' and 'pale copy' of cabaret in Paris.[29] Even in celebrating 'Berlin's internationalism', it comments that the city's nightlife in general 'would like to be international, but at its core it does not manage to transcend the specifically Berlinesque'.[30] While the Kurfürstendamm is still celebrated as 'Berlin's display window, ... Berlin's youngest street, the fresh artery of the new West', and the public in it as 'the youthful figures' who have 'toned their muscles on the sports' fields and in the waters of the Havel lakes',[31] some of the bars in the street are described as phony attempts at cosmopolitanism in which the men 'want to be taken for gentlemen' and the women 'colour their hair blond and style it like Greta Garbo because up to now no other prototype of sex appeal has been discovered and one cannot imitate Marlene Dietrich's long legs'.[32] The myths and images of the up-and-coming capital of the 'Golden Twenties' are still alive, but they cannot help revealing that they are, in the end, only images.

Clearly, the economic crisis radically changed how Berlin was represented and portrayed in broader public discourse during the Weimar years – not least because so much of the 'Golden Twenties' *Weltstadt* image was based on a new economic optimism during the years of so-called 'relative stability' between the hyperinflation of 1923 and depression of 1929. Even so, these myths have proved remarkably long-lived and still to this day – even more than before the fall of the Wall in 1989 – inform understandings of the city. In the media, the image of Berlin as the centre of the 'Golden Twenties' and metropolis of modernism has been conjured up with renewed vigour since 1989. In a cover story shortly after the fall of the Wall, *Time International* rather romantically recalled the 1920s as a time when 'Berlin swirled to the dusky voice of Marlene Dietrich, the topless dancing of Josephine Baker, the bittersweet syncopation of Kurt Weill. The city became avant-garde in everything (including hedonism): the glass skyscrapers of Mies van der Rohe, the atonal music of Arnold Schoenberg, the plays of Bertolt Brecht, the films of Fritz Lang, the cosmic explorations of Albert Einstein.'[33]

As in the 1920s, there have of course been dissenting voices that object to the Berlin myth. One example is Michael Bienert's book on *The Imaginary Metropolis*, which studies the efforts of cultural elites and city officials to cultivate precisely this image of Berlin in the 1920s and gives the overall impression of a city desperately trying, but inevitably failing, to live up to that unattainable image. Another example is Detlef Briesen's agenda-driven book *Berlin: Overrated Metropolis*, released in 1992 shortly after the decision to move the capital there from Bonn. Representing a kind of apex of the anti-metropolitan (or at least anti-Berlin) and decidedly *West* German polemics against the decision to move, this book argues, far less subtly than Bienert's, that the Berlin of the past was not all it was touted to be, and that the Berlin of the future will be just as bad – by and large replacing the positive connotations with the myth of unfriendly, 'ugly' or 'Prussian' Berlin.

But generally speaking, this connection with the past has been taken up with relish in the 'new Berlin' of the 1990s. The architecture of the Friedrichstrasse development is a clear invocation of 1920s styles, in particular the rounded cupola of the 'Galeries Lafayette', imitating the 1920s restructuring of the Mosse publishing house at a nearby site, and the eclectic cubist/*Neue Sachlichkeit* architecture of the new 'Friedrichstadt Passagen' building. There are also numerous references to the 1920s at Potsdamer Platz, from the traffic signal tower (to remind people that this was once the busiest square in Europe) to the aforementioned Marlene Dietrich Platz. It is here in former no man's land, the single largest construction site in Europe stretching from Potsdamer Platz in the south to the Lehrter Bahnhof in the north, that most political and media attention has been focused. The city built a special 'Infobox' specifically for the purpose of viewing the construction site and for informing tourists out about what stood there before the bombings as well as what will occupy this most symbolic space in the centre of the new German capital. And it is here that some of the greatest controversy has taken place over the new construction efforts and what they symbolize for the twenty-first century and the new millenium.

In a curious parallel to the conflicting views on Weimar Berlin, both the critics and proponents of the *'neue Mitte'* around Potsdamer Platz by and large agree on what it represents: an important connection between East and West Berlin (pragmatically, in terms of transport connections, but also as a physical embodiment of the unification process); a new economic vitality at the heart of the city after the years of forced division that quite literally kept this heart from beating; a new centre of government for Germany; and more generally speaking, a powerful symbol that Berlin is once again on its way to becoming a major world metropolis – 'Berlin: metropolis of tomorrow' as the cover of *Der Spiegel* optimistically proclaimed as early as Christmas 1989. Nine years later, the October 1998 cover of the magazine *Deutschland* uses the rather typical images of construction to convey this sense of unified Berlin as an up-and-coming city symbolic of the enhanced status of unified Germany as a whole in the world: against a backdrop of a forest of cranes working on the Reichstag are the words 'Journey through Germany in the microcosm of the metropoli'.[34]

Again, the disagreement lies in how one interprets these developments and how far they can be seen to live up to the inflated rhetoric and expectations surrounding them. For proponents, the *'neue Mitte'*, with its huge, ultra-modern corporate, government, office and cultural complexes, symbolizes the fruits of German unification, the success of Germany's market economy, and more broadly, given its location in the former no man's land, a sense that Berlin, and with it Germany as a whole, has simultaneously 'moved on' from the postwar period of division into a new historical epoch and at the same time returned to a state of relative 'normality' – i.e. the modern normality of the nation-state. This general sense of a new age and a bright new future is what Gerhard Schröder and the SPD pundits are trying to get across by drawing an explicit connection – hardly a mere play on words – between the *'neue Mitte'* of Berlin and the *'neue Mitte'* of German politics: the newly-elected centrist SPD that will govern Germany into the next millenium.

For critics, the reconstruction effort around former no man's land symbolizes rather the inordinate power of West German business interests, the imposing nature of the unification process and the stifling of plurality under the weight of bureaucratic planning. The swift eviction of the nomadic caravaners who had given the grim Potsdamer Platz colour for a number of years was heavily criticized in some left-wing quarters, and the decision to outlaw the popular Turkish pastime of weekend picnicking on certain meadows of the *Tiergarten* near the new government complex has been exceedingly unpopular. Moreover, as regards the plans for a national Holocaust Memorial in the area between Potsdamer Platz and the Brandenburg Gate, many Germans – as well as many Jewish parties in Germany and elsewhere – are rather disconcerted by the feeling that it could represent a desire to 'move on' from this aspect of Germany's history as well, a kind of symbolic 'bottom line' drawn under this greatest burden of German national memory.

The past is always difficult to harness effectively, especially for a city with a past as difficult as that of Berlin. It is precisely the oppressive weight of the memory of National Socialism and the brutal division of the Cold War that makes the connections with the democratic and supposedly 'modern' and 'progressive' Berlin of the 1920s so important as a foundation of positive civic tradition. In the turbulent history of the city, the 'new Berlins' of the 1920s and 1990s share a number of important characteristics that link them together in the popular imagination. Both have been centres of revolution that fundamentally changed the political order of Germany; both are unified under a democratic government; both are the capital city of a rapidly changing Germany; both are widely viewed as a microcosm of the country as a whole; both have been touted as the new, up-and-coming 'place to be'; and both serve, each in their own time, as a symbolic bone of contention about which direction Germany is taking.

Yet there is one more parallel that should briefly be drawn before concluding. In view of the current economic difficulties in Germany, it is hard to avoid the question of whether the end of the post-unification boom in Berlin might eventually lead to a similar transformation of the city's image as occurred in the years after 1929. Already some of the gloss has worn off the initial post-*Wende* optimism about the new German capital. Whatever the hype about the new Lehrter Bahnhof, the fact is that direct services from Berlin to Vienna and Prague have recently been cancelled. And however much talk there has been of Berlin as Europe's gateway to the emerging markets of the former Soviet bloc, these markets still by and large remain to materialize. If the high unemployment figures are not brought under control and the questionable office speculation in anticipation of the government's move from Bonn proves to be a financial quagmire, will Berlin's image change from that of the dynamic construction site of a modern, glittering new centre of politics, commerce and culture to a symbol of the mismanagement of unification and a new economic pessimism? Today as in the 1920s, it seems that representations of a 'new Berlin' as the symbol of a changing Germany are inextricably tied to the vagaries of its economy.

Notes

1 There has been a remarkable wave of popular and scholarly interest in Berlin and its history since the fall of the Wall, and not just in Germany. For recent works in English, see Alexandra Richie, *Faust's Metropolis: A History of Berlin* (London: Harper Collins, 1998); Ronald Taylor, *Berlin and its Culture: A Historical Portrait* (New Haven: Yale University Press, 1997).

2 Neal Ascherson, 'All Roads Lead to Berlin', *Guardian G2*, 16 November 1998, pp. 2–3.

3 The Ausstellungs-, Messe- und Fremdenverkehrs- Amt der Stadt Berlin, created in 1927 by combining the city's Tourist Office with the Department for Trade Fairs and Exhibitions.

4 For a description of these activities, see ibid. A logo was designed with the motto 'Jeder Einmal in Berlin' written across the columns of the Brandenburg Gate. Businesses used the logo on their letter heads, the post office franked mail with it, posters were made and sent out to tourist offices in Germany and abroad, a song based on the slogan was produced and sung in a touring revue, even a recording was made and sent out to radio stations.

5 Adolf Schick, 'Warum "Jeder Einmal in Berlin"?', in *Jeder Einmal in Berlin. Offizieller Führer für Berlin und Umgebung* (Berlin: Rothophot, 1928), p. 15.

6 Erich Busch, in ibid., p. 32.

7 Peter Sachse, 'Wege des Vergnügungsreisenden', in ibid., p. 124; Eugenio Xammar, in 'Ausländer in Berlin über Berlin', in ibid., p. 24.

8 Walter Behrendt, 'Berlin wird Hauptstadt – Metropole im Herzen Europas', *Das Neue Berlin*, vol. 1 (1929), pp. 98, 100.

9 *Jeder Einmal in Berlin. Offizieller Führer*, p. 53.

10 M. Bienert, *Die eingebildete Metropole: Berlin im Feuilleton der Weimarer Republik* (Stuttgart: Metzler, 1992), p. 99.

11 Arthur Eloesser, *Die Straße meiner Jugend* (Berlin: Fleischel, 1919), pp. 8f.

12 Ascherson, 'All Roads Lead to Berlin'.

13 *Jeder Einmal in Berlin. Offizieller Führer*, pp. 22–3.

14 The Verein Berliner Kaufleute und Industrieller produced their own contribution to the notion of a cosmopolitan Berlin with their book, *Berlins Aufstieg zur Weltstadt: Ein Gedenkbuch* (Berlin: Hobbing, 1929).

15 *Berliner Tageblatt*, 13 October 1928.

16 Gustav Böß in *Berliner Tageblatt*, 14 October 1928.

17 Curt Moreck, *Führer durch das 'lasterhafte' Berlin*, (Berlin 1931), pp.12–20.

18 Karl-Heinz Metzger and Ulrich Dunker, *Der Kurfürstendamm. Leben und Mythos des Boulevards in 100 Jahren deutscher Geschichte* (Berlin: Konopka, 1986), p. 108.

19 Christian Bouchholtz, '*Kurfürstendamm*', (Berlin: Axel Juncker Verlag, 1921), p. 9.

20 Behrendt, 'Berlin wird Haupstadt', p. 98.

21 For an overview in English, see Derek Glass (ed.), *Berlin: Literary Images of a City* (Berlin: Schmidt Verlag, 1989).

22 Heinrich Hauser, 'Berlin ist Deutschland', in *Die Tat*, vol. 24 (1932/33), p. 568, cited in E. Schütz, 'Beyond Glittering Reflections of Asphalt', in T. Kniesche and S. Brockmaun (eds), *Dancing on a Volcano: Essays on the Culture of the Weimar Republic* (Columbia, S.C.: Camden House, 1994), pp. 119–26.

23 E. Michel, 'Der abwesende Berliner', *Berliner Tageblatt*, 7 July 1932; R. Korherr, 'Berlin', *Süddeutsche Monatshefte*, vol. 27 (1930), pp. 389, 393, cited in Schütz, 'Beyond Glittering Reflections'.
24 S. Kracauer, 'Strasse ohne Erinnerung', *Frankfurter Allgemeine Zeitung*, 16 December 1932.
25 Ibid.
26 Erich Kästner, *Fabian*, (Munich: dtv, 1989), p. 12.
27 Gabriele Tergit, *Käsebier erobert den Kurfürstendamm* (Berlin: Arani, 1988), p. 201.
28 Irmgard Keun, *Das kunstseidene Mädchen* (Munich: dtv, 1989), pp. 73–4.
29 Moreck, *Führer*, pp. 107–8.
30 Ibid., p. 114.
31 Ibid., pp. 38–40.
32 Ibid., p. 114.
33 Otto Friedrich, 'The Capital Once Again', *Time International*, 19 March 1990, p. 11.
34 'Deutschlandreise im Mikrokosmus der Metropolen', *Deutschland: Zeitschrift für Politik, Kultur, Wirtschaft und Wissenschaft*, October 1998.

4

The over-representations of history? Reflections on Thomas Mann's *Doktor Faustus*

Martin Swales

The title and subtitle of Thomas Mann's sombre novel of 1947, which offers an anguished reckoning with the history and culture of Germany, read *Doktor Faustus: Das Leben des deutschen Tonsetzers Adrian Leverkühn erzählt von einem Freunde* (The Life of the German Composer Adrian Leverkühn told by a friend). The priorities are interesting; the immediate psychological and realistic foreground of the text – the life of the composer Adrian Leverkühn as told by his friend Serenus Zeitblom – is relegated to the subtitle. The main title names an emblematic figure from German cultural history – Faust. Moreover, the subtitle has more than its fair share of cultural intimation: the composer is not referred to as a 'Komponist', but by the archaic and etymologically Germanic noun 'Tonsetzer'. And, in case we missed the point, the adjective 'deutsch' is added by way of qualifier to the noun. In other words, the emblematics of Germany are very much to the fore on the title page; much representativeness is in evidence. And, as we shall see, issues of how Germany has been – and is – represented both by and to herself and by and to others are central to the novel's purpose. It is interesting to consider whether the adjective 'deutsch' in the subtitle is, as it were, exclusive or inclusive. Does it bespeak an attempt to assert the splendid isolation of Germanness? Or does it reach beyond itself, seeking to explain Germanness to the world outside and beyond Germany? This is one of the major themes of the novel: how does Germanness break through to the world outside? One form of breakthrough – to European modernism – is at the heart of the novel's cultural-historical argument. And, in a very different sense, the events that form the insistent backdrop to Zeitblom's narrative act – the destruction of Germany in the years between 1943 and 1945 – are the nemesis that follows the catastrophic intervention of Germany into the world order that was the obsessive expansionism of the Third Reich. The novel ends on a note of lament, lament for both the 'friend' and the 'fatherland'. The question that confronts us is: how does the one come to represent the other?

A great deal of work has been done on this issue.[1] And I wish to offer a brief overview and summary of what the critical discussion thus far has already achieved. My concern in this chapter is less to work through those arguments again than to ask *how* the various complex acts of representation are achieved. What, in other words, is the rhetoric of representation in Thomas Mann's text?

Clearly, the most powerful intimations of representativeness are those which invoke Leverkühn's life and selfhood as reincarnation of energies within the German cultural tradition. One formative presence (and the one invoked in the novel's title) is that of the *Faust* legend – particularly the 1587 *Volksbuch*. Here we are concerned with a potent narrative which essentially derives from (but is by no means confined to) the German tradition, and which expresses the liberation and destructiveness brought about by the individualist, secular, scientific energies of modernity. The governing intertext is not Goethe's magnificently conciliatory version of the legend but that older narrative which ends with Faust's damnation. In a sense, Goethe's *Faust* is conspicuous by its absence. Just as Leverkühn's last great work, the *Doktor Fausti Weheklag*, seeks to 'take back' the humane vision of Beethoven's Choral Symphony, so too does Thomas Mann's *Doktor Faustus* 'take back' the Goethean affirmation. There are, it is worth noting, a number of parallels between the protagonist of the *Volksbuch* and Leverkühn. Both are born in Thuringia; both devote themselves initially to theology; both delight in exploring the universe, in 'speculating the elements' and accept the Devil's help in their quest for greater knowledge and experience. Both bewail their fate at the end of their lives, making confession to their friends. Their life story is recorded by their surviving assistants, Wagner and Zeitblom. Adrian is, of course, acutely aware that he has a literary-cultural ancestor. He enjoys employing a pastiche sixteenth-century German; he often stylizes himself with reference to the 1587 *Volksbuch*. His final work is, beyond all parody and knowingness, the acknowledgement of the existential truth inherent in the old legend of damnation.

In this sense Leverkühn can be seen to embody the dark, spiritually stressful strand in German culture. To the *Faust* narrative is added the presence of Luther. The *Volksbuch* itself is, of course, a work deeply embedded in the spirit of Protestantism. Adrian's theology professor, Kumpf, with his fierce belief that religious faith dialectically generates the forces of demonology and his bombarding of the Devil with a bread roll from his table, manifestly recalls Luther. Luther (like Faust and Leverkühn) comes from Thuringia. Leverkühn's birthplace Kaisersaschern is a town that is clearly imbued with the spiritual ethos of Protestantism, one that conjoins the modern energies of scepticism with an atavistic sense of self-disparagement and sinfulness. Those who hail from Kaisersaschern, it seems, suffer from a mismatch between inwardness and outwardness. In these senses, then, Leverkühn's destiny is deeply and intensely Germanic.

This latter-day Faust is a musician. And here again a potent strand of the German cultural tradition comes into play. Leverkühn's destruction by syphilitically induced madness produces echoes of Beethoven, Schubert, Schumann, Wolf. More importantly, music is central to the whole discursive argument of Thomas Mann's novel. Its implications extend beyond the artistic sphere and generate conceptual patterns that embrace philosophy and politics. Music, we learn, expresses relationships between (harmonic, melodic) individuality and (polyphonic, cultic) objectivity. It enshrines notions of hierarchy, of dominance and subservience, of leaders and led, of order and freedom. Moreover, just as music works with an interplay of vertical statements (chords, harmonic textures) and linear, horizontal articulation (melody, sonata and other forms), so too it has both an ahistorical (vertical) ontology and an abundant (horizontal) historicity. That is to say: in ontological terms, music is, as Leverkühn puts it, ambiguity raised to the status of a system; it is, at one level, pure disembodied form, a source of insubstantial delight like pure mathematics; and, at another level, it is sheer eruptive energy, unadorned pulse, visceral emotion. In historical terms, music provides a formal correlative for notions of order and progression, of departure and homecoming; moreover, at certain stressful points in its history (and Leverkühn's creative career is coterminous with one such) it seeks, as it were, to deny its own historicity and to assert its groundedness in primal materiality, in the physics of certain frequencies that validate the octave, the fifth, and the third at an experiential level situated quite beyond contingent historical-cum-cultural conditioning. But such moments of longing for the ontological are themselves historically bounded. In these ontological and historical senses, then, the phenomenon of music provides a complex contextuality of signification for Adrian's career, one that converts the particularity of his creative endeavour into a powerful symptomatology of the German soul and of its history in the first half of the twentieth century.

Moreover, there are further strands to that symptomatology. Leverkühn may be a composer; but the inscape of his creativity makes him a philosophical spirit, one whose most obvious antecedent is Nietzsche. The parallels work both at the level of biographical event and at the level of mentality. In terms of their biography, both (yet again!) come from Thuringia; both attend the University of Leipzig; both are tormented throughout their creative lives by violent migraine headaches, conceivably deriving from a syphilitic infection contracted in a visit to a brothel; both send a friend as mediator to propose to a young woman on their behalf, and are rebuffed. And finally, both consume themselves in the strenuousness of their creative tasks, collapsing into insanity for the last decade of their lives, before dying on the same day (25 August). The parallels are not only outward, but also inward. Both conjoin a high degree of irony and self-awareness with a desperate quest for authenticity beyond knowingness and parody. Both are aware of the spiritual barrenness of the modern age, of the scandalous void left by the demise of religious faith; both are part complicit in, part fiercely critical of, the manoeuvres by which modern culture will seek to recapture forfeited certainties. Psychologically and philosophically, Nietzsche and Leverkühn are by turns utterly cerebral and tormentedly passionate to the point of self-immolation. Leverkühn's surname, with its intimations of 'living dangerously', clearly aligns him with the Nietzschean ethos of strenuousness.

Hitherto, for obvious reasons, I have concentrated particularly on Leverkühn. But his biographer Serenus Zeitblom also partakes of representativeness by virtue of a powerful cultural legacy. He is a humanist, and the lineage of his mindset goes back to the early sixteenth century, to that humanist critique of the established sacred and secular order which runs alongside the Reformation. He is also indebted to the Enlightenment of the eighteenth century, to figures such as Lessing and Moses Mendelssohn, to that intellectual enterprise that dismantles dogma in order to find not a valueless world but one informed by the moral dignity and humane passion of critical reflectivity as a form of this-worldly salvation. This strand of Zeitblom's humanism is particularly evident and important, as we shall see, in his analysis of the ideological currents operative in the Kridwiß circle.

I have thus far been concerned to summarize those elements from the German past that endow the Leverkühn and Zeitblom figures with a significant measure of representativeness. I want now to turn to the present of their historical and political experience; to their embeddedness in the social, cultural and political currents and counter-currents of twentieth-century Germany. At one level, it is possible to find parallels between certain events in the lives of both characters and the course of German history in the twentieth century. The first German intervention in Morocco (Tangier) occurs in 1905, the year of Adrian's visit to the brothel. A year later, Germany extracts concessions at the Algeciras conference, and Adrian, at his second meeting with Hetaera Esmeralda, contracts syphilis. In 1911 there is the Agadir crisis, and the Devil appears to Leverkühn. Germany is defeated at the end of the First World War in 1918, and Adrian's health collapses. The Treaty of Locarno and the attempted wooing of Marie Godeau both occur in 1925. In 1930 there is the dissolution of Germany's parliament, and Adrian loses his sanity. Zeitblom's last visit to his friend is in 1939, at the outbreak of war; and Adrian dies in 1940, the year in which the Western Front is opened.[2] Intriguing though these pointers are, however, one cannot help feeling that they do not take us very far. Much more significant are the moments of overlap between the climate of artistic and intellectual debate in Germany in the first half of the twentieth century and the slide into political disaster. To that climate both Leverkühn and Zeitblom are grudging witnesses, sometimes sceptical, even on occasion downright critical, yet ultimately implicated. By this token *Doktor Faustus* offers remarkable insights into the ideologies of high-bourgeois and intellectual circles, and into their complicity in the destruction of civil society in Germany. I shall comment later on Zeitblom's account of the Winfried and Kridwiß groups. But I want at this stage to invoke briefly J. P. Stern's notion of the 'Dear Purchase', because it is one that makes a link between on the one hand an artistic and philosophical endeavour of (potentially, at any rate) the highest distinction and on the other the politics of Nazism.[3] The crucial mediating factor is that particular cast of mind that, in a post-theological world, sees spiritual strenuousness and attrition to be the supreme value, replacing all notions of communality and human warmth. The key notion is 'Schwere', difficulty as distinction. Kretzschmar describes Beethoven's quest to master the fugue as one informed by 'der heiligen Schwere dieses Kampfes' (p. 80);[4] Schwerdtfeger and Institoris discuss notions of achievement as 'Erkämpftes, Errungenes, durch Willensanstrengung und Selbstüberwindung Geleistetes' (p. 385); Adrian in his confession insists 'daß alles zu schwer geworden ist' (p. 662), that he has 'Schweres vor mich gebracht' (p. 665), 'daß ich das Schwere gesucht und mir's habe sauer werden lassen' (p. 666). Stern shows how the discourse of authenticity, defined in terms of experiences of well-nigh intolerable difficulty, is an animating force in the culture of twentieth-century Germany – and also the catastrophic ideological centre of Nazism, in particular of Hitler's propaganda. This, Stern argues, is the point at which the gap truly closes between aesthetic-cultural discourse and the language of power-politics. He also suggests that, at this level of statement, Thomas Mann's *Doktor Faustus* is at one with the phenomena that it seeks to diagnose. It too derives totally from, and therefore validates, the ideology of the 'Dear Purchase'. Michael Beddow clearly has this argument in mind when he writes:

> The terms in which *Doktor Faustus* attempts to judge Fascism as a threat to modern societies imply a wish that is as chimerical as it is seductive: the longing for forms of assocation capable of securing not simply material prosperity but richness of experience; not only due process but integrity of being; not merely justice but justification. And since that longing is itself part of the totalitarian malady, this novel, a fascinating symptom rather than a telling diagnosis, offers little hope of a remedy.[5]

This is vigorously argued. But in this chapter I want to suggest that *Doktor Faustus* manages to thematize and explore – rather than simply to re-enact – the heavy cultural symptomatology of Germanness with which it is so centrally concerned. Perhaps, for clarity's sake, I may anticipate my argument here before passing on to sections of detailed illustration. *Doktor Faustus* is, by any standards, a fiercely – and manifestly – 'constructed' novel. Gunilla Bergsten refers to 'the extent and uncompromising coherence'[6] of its patterning, seeing it as in a sense fulfilling the compositional ethos of Leverkühn's greatest endeavours, which are grounded in that strictness of organization that means that no note is wasted, no note is free. Bergsten writes: 'All of Mann's works can be regarded as "good scores", but only *Doktor Faustus* realizes the ideal of "strict style".'[7] Yet, in the concluding phase of her argument, she resists the deterministic implications of this view, and suggests that the novel, like *Doktor Fausti Weheklag*, does offer a hope beyond despair, a redemption beyond dereliction, a freedom beyond pattern and symptomatology. I am not sure that I accept her theologically tinged argument, although I am far from sharing all Beddow's snootiness about the religious implications of Mann's novel.[8] But where I do agree with the thrust of Bergsten's thesis is that, at the end of our reading of *Doktor Faustus* (as at the end of Leverkühn's final oratorio), the novel becomes the object of our critique and reflection, and may indeed, in the process, change the final cadences of its statement. In my view, we register the constructedness of the construct; we hear that all-pervasive predisposition to symptomatology as the theme of the novel, and not as the sum total of its wisdom. In saying this, I am not simply arguing that at the end of the novel we can see more clearly than ever before the constituent strands of its total statement. That much is, of course, true of our relationship to any and every work of literature. My point in respect of *Doktor Faustus* is more specific than this: it is that certain key features of the text come into new prominence at the end of our reading of the novel. We subject the very constructedness of the text to historical diagnosis. And that diagnostic moment derives, in my view, predominatly from the figure of Zeitblom and from the kind of account he offers of his friend's life and work. To these issues I now turn.

In essence what I wish to explore is a governing dialectic in Zeitblom's narrative performance. On the one hand, in both the thematics and the stylistics of his account, Zeitblom is very much committed to a well-nigh claustrophobic, 'totalizing' symptomatology that unites Leverkühn and Germany in inextricable symbiosis. At that level of statement, he himself is not exempt from the patterns which he so zealously perceives and equally zealously delineates. On the other hand, and at another level, he does experience moments of unease, critique, dissent, moments in which the very mode and import of his own account is also called into question – in the service of historical scruple and diagnosis.

Let me begin by highlighting Zeitblom's rhetoric of connectedness. The opening few pages of his account illustrate what I mean. There is, in the exposition of the novel, very little sense of superabundance, contiguity, contingency – of what Roland Barthes calls the 'effect of the real', that narrative hymn in praise of material and experiential redundancy that is so central to the craft of realistic fiction.[9] By contrast, in Zeitblom's introduction of himself and his world there is no room for superfluity; rather, everything conspires to relevance, pattern, purpose, to intimations of destiny. He embarks on the 'Biographie des teuren, vom Schicksal so furchtbar heimgesuchten, erhobenen und gestürzten Mannes und genialen Musikers' (p. 9) – and already in this phrase from the first sentence of his account we hear the weighty invocation of Fate, of the rise and fall of a genius. Then, in the third

paragraph he reflects on the notion of genius; as a concept, it sounds radi-
antly positive – 'und doch ist nicht zu leugnen und ist nie geleugnet worden, daß an dieser strahlenden Sphäre das Dämonische und
Widervernünftige einen beunruhigen Anteil hat'(p. 11). One notes the
assertiveness – 'doch ist nicht zu leugnen und ist nie geleugnet worden' –
with which connections are established as axiomatic, unchallengeable, necessary. Time and time again, Zeitblom has recourse to categories of causal
implication; terms such as 'aufschlußreich für das Innenleben Leverkühns'
(p. 15), 'innere(r) und fast geheimnisvolle(r) Zusammenhang' (p. 16),
'Sphäre' (p. 16), 'Geisterwelt' (p. 17), 'geprägt von vergangenen Zeiten' (p.
22), 'Parallelbildungen' (p. 29), 'erfaßbare Genealogie' (p. 32) abound. Mention of the family and the childhood home is redolent with inescapable significance. Kaisersaschern is part of the portentous claustrophobia of setting
– as are Buchel and Pfeiffering, which are united by 'Parallelismus' (p. 40),
by 'der sonderbaren Entsprechung' (p. 273) that ensures not only a similarity of landscape, but a recurrence of such figures as the milkmaid with
the heavy breasts. The subtitle of *Doktor Faustus*, as we have seen, refers to
'Das Leben des deutschen Tonsetzers Adrian Leverkühn erzählt von einem
Freunde'. Yet frequently Zeitblom is not content to 'tell a life'; rather, he
bears witness to a destiny. And the linguistic mode can be very high-flown:

> Wir waren Kinder, – nicht aus Eigenempfindsamkeit, sondern um seinetwillen,
> beim Gedanken an sein Geschick, an den ihm bestimmten Aufstieg aus dem
> Tale der Unschuld in unwirtliche, ja schauerliche Höhen, bewegt mich der
> Rückblick. Es war ein Künstlerleben; und weil mir, dem schlichten Manne,
> beschieden war, es aus solcher Nähe zu sehen, hat sich alles Gefühl meiner
> Seele für Menschenleben und -los auf diese Sonderform menschlichen Daseins
> versammelt. Sie gilt mir, dank meiner Freunschaft mit Adrian, als das Para-
> digma aller Schicksalsgestaltung, als der klassische Anlaß zur Ergriffenheit von
> dem, was wir Werden, Entwicklung, Bestimmung nennen, – und das mag sie
> denn wirklich wohl sein. (p. 37)

This is biography in a very grand manner indeed.

Some of this grandiloquent, 'totalizing' tendency rubs off on the very tex-
ture of Zeitblom's cultural, historical, political commentary. There is, for
example, a crucial dialogue between himself and Adrian in which the topic
is Germany's need to break out of her inward-looking provincialism and spirituality in order to make contact with the world outside. Four key areas
interact in baleful interconnectedness – spirituality, culture, destiny, politics.
And the novel does not allows us to forget that the particularity at issue
behind these grandiose generalities is the outbreak of the First World War:

> 'Bei einem Volk von der Art des unsrigen', trug ich vor, 'ist das Seelische
> immer das Primäre und eigentlich Motivierende; die politische Aktion ist
> zweiter Ordnung, Reflex, Ausdruck, Instrument. Was mit dem Durchbruch zur
> Weltmacht, zu dem das Schicksal uns beruft, im tiefsten gemeint ist, das ist der
> Durchbruch zur Welt – aus einer Einsamkeit, deren wir uns leidend bewußt

sind, und die durch keine robuste Verflechtung ins Welt-Wirtschaftliche seit der Reichsgründung hat gesprengt werden können. Das Bittere ist, daß die empirische Erscheinung des Kriegszuges annimmt, was in Wahrheit Sehnsucht ist, Durst nach Vereinigung.' (pp. 408–9)

The voice we hear reported at this point shares fully in the ideological sleight-of-hand that conspires to invest territorial rivalry between the major powers with delphic spiritual significance. Zeitblom recalls the waves of patriotic emotion that sweep through the school at which he is teaching, and he admits that even his fastidious scepticism is overcome by a sense of the sheer greatness of the existential energies in play: 'Hier tritt aber das Moment der Opfer-, der Todesbereitschft ein, das über vieles hinweghilft und sozusagen ein leeres Wort ist, gegen welches sich nichts mehr sagen läßt' (p. 399). Some of this rhetoric of greatness can still be heard when Zeitblom reflects on the Second World War. He refers to the destiny of his people and admits: 'ich bin nicht frei von der Neigung, für dieses Schicksal eine besondere, nie dagewesene Tragik in Anspruch zu nehmen' (p. 45). Later he cannot suppress feelings of pride at the technological creativity which gives Germany such superiority in submarine power:

> ich kann eine gewisse Genugtuung nicht unterdrücken über unseren immer regen Erfindungsgeist, die durch noch so viele Rückschläge nicht zu beugende nationale Tüchtigkeit, welche immer noch voll und ganz dem Regime zur Verfügung steht, das uns in diesen Krieg geführt hat und uns tatsächlich den Kontinent zu Füßen gelegt, den Intellektuellentraum von einem europäischen Deutschland durch die allerdings etwas beängstigende, etwas brüchige und, wie es scheint, der Welt unerträgliche Wirklichkeit eines deutschen Europa ersetzt hat. (p. 229)

One notes the prevarication here, the sense that world opinion is strangely obdurate in its inability to accept the spiritual dream of 'Mitteleuropa' as expressed in Nazi expansionism. My point at this juncture is not to attack Zeitblom as some kind of crypto-fascist. Rather, it is to insist that the novel text does oblige us to attend to certain of the political consequences of Zeitblom's grand narrative manner. Zeitblom, in the last phases of the war, has clearly come to recognize the monstrosity of Nazism. What he is less able to perceive is the ways in which and the extent to which Nazism issued from cultural and intellectual tendencies which were – and up to a point still are – part of his mentality, and which continue to colour his narrative performance. The fondness for spiritually totalizing discourse played – and play – Zeitblom false.

That Thomas Mann's novel is not simply a symptom of the totalizing cast of mind but also its critique is made apparent by the fact that Zeitblom on occasion does register moral and intellectual objections to the spiritual glibness of those around him. His analysis and denunciation of the climate of reactionary aesthetic-cum-political debate in intellectual circles both before and after the First World War are very impressive. The chapters dealing with the Kridwiß circle are particulary fine. He is, for example, scathing about the interrelationship of fastidious aestheticism on the one hand and the worship of bloodthirsty rampant life on the other. While Zeitblom is honest in his admission that Adrian too is not untouched by this unholy alliance of effete spirituality and crude barbarism, he insists both on the difference in quality – Adrian's creativity operates 'auf höherer schöpferischer Ebene' (p. 470) – and on the perniciousness of the tendency, particularly when it is manifested in the flaccid self-importance of a Daniel Zur Höhe:

> Dies alles war 'schön' und empfand sich selber sehr stark als 'schön': es war 'schön' auf eine grausam und absolut schönheitliche Weise, in dem unver-schämt bezuglosen, juxhaften und unverantwortlichen Geist, wie eben Dichter ihn sich erlauben, – der steilste ästhetische Unfug, der mir vorgekommen. (p. 483)

One hears Zeitblonm's outrage here in the thrice-repeated 'schön'. Time and time again he criticizes – and at such moments we hear the voice of the humanist and moralist – the Kridwiß *habitués* for the irresponsibility of their diagnosis of cultural crisis. Their analysis of tendencies at work in the con-temporary world is alarmingly bereft of judgement, critique, outrage. All their sophistication is deployed in the service of doctrines of voluptuously articulated historical inevitablility:

> 'Recht wohl! Recht wohl! O freilich doch, man kann es sagen!' versicherte Zur Höhe und schlug dringlich mit dem Fuße auf. Natürlich konnte man es sagen, nur hätte man es, da es sich schließlich um die Beschreibung einer her-aufziehenden Barbarei handelte, für mein Gefühl mit etwas mehr Bangen und Grauen sagen sollen und nicht mit jener heiteren Genugtuung, von der man allenfalls gerade noch hoffen konnte, daß sie der Erkennntnis der Dinge und nicht den Dingen selber galt. (p. 486)

Such comments, in my view, serve to alert us to the dangers of a totalizing discourse of inevitable destiny – a discourse to which Zeitblom himself is no stranger.

Similarly, in respect of the immediate political context within which he pens his account, Zeitblom can be both equivocal (as we have seen – in, for example, his reflections on Germany's superiority in submarine warfare) and fiercely critical. In an unforgettable passage late in the novel he denounces the monstrosity of the concentration camps which is revealed in the news-reel reportage. Zeitblom's tendency to see language, thought, culture and politcs in some kind of necessary continuum discharges itself in accents of utter despair:

> Ich sage: unsere Schmach. Denn ist es bloße Hypochondrie, sich zu sagen, daß alles Deutschtum, auch der deutsche Geist, der deutsche Gedanke, das deutsche Wort von dieser entehrenden Bloßstellung mitbetroffen und in tiefe Fragwürdigkeit gestürzt worden ist? Ist es krankhafte Zerknirschung, die Frage

sich vorzulegen, wie überhaupt noch in Zukunft 'Deutschland' in irgendeiner seiner Erscheinungen es sich soll herausnehmen dürfen, in menschlichen Angelegenheiten den Mund aufzutun? (p. 638)

Clearly, in one sense Zeitblom's anguish leads him to overstate the extent to which all things German are for ever and a day compromised by the the the Holocaust. Even here, then, the totalizing statement is questionable. Yet at another level the universalizing grief has a measure of justification, because it recognizes that it was the totalizing culturo-political tendency that helped to produce a totalitarian regime. To that tendency and to that regime *Doktor Faustus* bears complex – part complicit, part critical – witness.

Zeitblom's role, then, is crucially to be both a symptom and a critic of certain characteristic discourses that seek to unite culture and politics in an overarching symbiosis. Precisely because he is writing at a time (1943–45) when the political consequences of that longing for symbiosis are all too disfiguringly apparent, Zeitblom is made to recognize his, and Adrian's, complicity in the disaster, although neither of them is in any sense responsible for it. I want, then, to insist that there is a measure of historical diagnosis built into the text, that it invites us to reflect on its own governing mode. In this context it is, I think, all-important to attend to those moments of narrative self-consciousness (in both senses of the word – embarrassment and self-reflexivity) which recur constantly in Zeitblom's account. A few examples must suffice. At the beginning of Chapter IX he worries if the preceding chapter, which summarizes Wendell Kretschmar's lectures on music, is too long. He defends himself by saying that the coherence and unity of Kretschmar's insights justifies the lengthy chapter, in defiance of all appeals to notions of brevity and user-friendliness:

> Die Gewissensfrage, ob ... ich jedem einzelnen der Vorträge Kretschmars ein besonderes Hauptstück zugewiesen hätte, muß ich verneinen. Jede gesonderte Teil-Einheit eines Werkes bedarf eines gewissen Schwergehaltes, eines bestimmten Maßes förderlicher Bedeutung für das Ganze, und dieses Gewicht, dieses Bedeutungsmaß kommt den Vorträgen nur in ihrer Gesamtheit (soweit ich sie referiert habe), – sie kommt nicht dem einzelnen zu. (p. 96)

Later, at the beginning of Chapter XIV, he comments on the fact that the preceding chapter has dealt with Schleppfuß's lectures on sin, witchcraft and demonology. Once again, Zeitblom is exercised by the relationship between parts and whole:

> Zahlenmystik ist nicht meine Sache, und immer nur mit Beklemmung habe ich diese Neigung an Adrian, bei dem sie sich von jeher still, aber deutlich hervortat, wahrgenommen. Daß aber auf das vorige Kapitel gerade die allegemein mit Scheu betrachtete und für unheilvoll geltende Ziffer XIII gefallen ist, hat denn doch meinen unwillkürlichen Beifall, und fast bin ich versucht, es für mehr als Zufall zu halten. Um einen Zufall allerdings handelt es sich, vernünftig gesprochen, dennoch, und zwar weil im Grunde dieser ganze Komplex von

Hallenser Universitätserfahrungen, so gut wie weiter oben die Vorträge Kretschmars, eine natürliche Einheit bildet, und weil ich nur aus Rücksicht auf den Leser, welcher immer nach Ruhepunkten, Zäsuren und Neubeginn ausschaut, in mehrere Kapitel aufgeteilt habe, was nach meiner, des Schriftstellers, wahrer Gewissensmeinung auf solche Gliederung gar keinen Anspruch hat. (p. 149–50)

In this passage, the issue of tact in respect of reader expectations interlocks with notions of chance versus necessity, to which I shall return shortly. My final example comes from Chapter XXI, where Zeitblom finds himself placing an asterisk to create a break in his account in order to allow the reader to catch his breath; but he then goes on to regret this concession to popular taste:

Ich kann nur wiederholen, daß Paragraphen und Sternchen in diesem Buche ein reines Zugeständnis an die Augen des Lesers sind, und daß ich, wenn es nach mir ginge, das Ganze in einem Zuge und Atem, ohne jede Einteilung, ja ohne Einrückung und Absatz herunterschreiben würde. Ich habe nur nicht den Mut, ein so rücksichtsloses Druckwerk der lesenden Welt vor Augen zu bringen. (p. 235)

(Perhaps, without knowing it, Zeitblom was waiting for the chance to join Thomas Bernhard in his love affair with single-minded prose.)

What, then, are we to make of Zeitblom's frequent exercises in redactional self-consciousness? At one level, we can register the fact that such moments serve to stress his ponderousness and pedantry. Yet it seems to me that more is at stake than a purely linguistic-cum-psychological tic. Zeitblom's digressions relate centrally to the issue – the totalizing tendency – we have been considering. The final quotation above establishes the notion that, conceivably, Adrian Leverkühn's life unfolds with no breaks, no discontinuities, no moments of harmless redundancy, of unaligned contingency; rather, that life, like that of the culture and nation to which it so inextricably belongs, is all of a piece – fiercely, claustrophobically welded into an inescapable symptomatology. While Zeitblom's account does, to be sure, have chapter divisions, there is, over long stretches, something monomanic about it. This is revealed by an intriguing comment which he makes early on. Zeitblom refers, in passing, to an acquaintance of his who tends, when he is ill, to regress to a pre-adult condition and to insist on being treated by a pediatrician. Zeitblom checks himself, and apologizes to his reader:

Es scheint mir ratsam, selbst festzustellen, daß diese Anekdote von dem Mann mit dem Kinderarzt insofern eine Abschweifung darstellt, als weder der eine noch der andere in diesen Aufzeichnungen überhaupt je wieder vorkommen wird, (p. 40–1)

The apology is intriguing and revelatory, because it implies that everything else in this narrative will recur, will establish itself as portentous, symptomatic, as part of the inescapablity of Leverkühn's destiny. If that is the case, then Zeitblom's account enshrines that ideology of which it is both the supreme exemplar and critique: the ideology that decrees total relevance, determinism, narrative totalization, political totalitarianism. The narrative self-consciousness of Zeitblom's account constantly reminds us of the textual, generic issue, which in its turn interlocks with the moral and historical issue. The Kridwiß circle is deeply enamoured of historical inevitability; and it is criticized for this by Zeitblom. Clearly, for much of his account, he does not realize how far he too is in love with discourses of inevitability, with a narrative of omnipresent relevance, from Kaisersaschern to 1945. But sometimes he does leap over his own shadow. And so too does Thomas Mann's text. The upshot is a work that, conceivably like many of Leverkühn's, is implicated in the phenomena which it tries to explore and against which, however imperfectly, it seeks to protest.

By way of conclusion I want to invoke a moment when Adrian and Zeitblom, towards the end of their school career, consider what subjects they should study at university. Initially, philosophy finds favour because it is the great Archimedean structure which houses every localized discipline in a total and totally intelligible world-view:

> Sie überblicke sie (=die Wissenschaften), fasse sie geistig zusammen, ordne und läutere die Ergebnisse aller Forschungsgebiete zum Weltbilde, zu einer überherrschendnen und maßgebenden, den Sinn des Lebens erschließende Synthese, zur schauenden Bestimmung der Stellung des Menschen im Kosmos. (p. 110)

Yet Zeitblom takes the argument a stage furhter and suggests that theology is the true meta-knowledge that transcends even philosophy:

> Wo die Weisheitsliebe sich zur Anschauung des höchsten Wesens, des Urquells des Seins, zur Lehre von Gott und den göttlichen Dingen erhebt, da, so könnte man sagen, ist der Gipfel wissenschaftlicher Würde, die höchste und vornehmste Sphäre der Erkenntnis, die Spitze des Denkens erreicht; dem beseelten Intellekt ist da sein erhabenstes Ziel gesetzt. (pp. 110–11)

Admittedly, this quest for the supreme mode of cognition is characteristic of the desire of the bright sixth-former to 'know everything'. But here, within the intellectual universe of Thomas Mann's novel, adolescent hybris is no simple moment of passing excess. Because the tendency – to perceive and conceive everything in necessary relation to everything else – is part and parcel of the culture that produces Leverkühn and Zeitblom and Hitler and Luther and Nietzsche and the *Faust* legend, and so forth. Thomas Mann's novel offers exemplification and historically diagnostic critique of these patterns of over-representation.

Doktor Faustus begins its symptomatology of Germanness with the Reformation. In terms of central doctrines of the Eucharist, the Reformation splits materiality and significance, outward, civic self and spiritually significant self. And thereby it sets up a disturbance of representation. In many ways the Reformation haunts the world inhabited by Leverkühn and Zeitblom, not least because their world – that of the first four decades of the twentieth century – is similarly marked by a sense of meaning fled, of significance forfeited. God is dead; the centre will not hold; one does not need to rehearse all the familiar tenets of European modernity here. But in Germany, perhaps more urgently, indeed frenetically, than anywhere else in Europe, the need to re-symbolize, to regenerate signification, to re-invest (in a whole number of senses) the material world with value made itself felt. *Doktor Faustus* is both a symptom of that need and its interrogation (in the spirit of Walter Benjamin's all-important defence of allegory in response to the post-Romantic prestige of the 'totalizing' symbol).[10]

Doktor Faustus, then, incarnates and probes the crisis of a nation and a culture desperately concerned to recuperate the representations that have lost all authority and slithered into mere contingency. It asks us to hear its own – and its characters' – constructions of meaning, and not simply to accept them as some all-encompassing encyclopaedia of German significances that lead to Nazism. It is, as we have seen, a highly foregrounded construct, remorselessly representational and representative; yet it also invites our reflection, critique, and – even – dissent. Just as, after the last note of Leverkühn's *Doktor Fausti Weheklag*, the high G on the cello, has died away, there is a countervailing voice to be heard in the silence, so we, Thomas Mann's readers, must hear the counter-indications set up by the text (and by our own historical retrospect as citizens of the late twentieth century).

We provide, then, the critical response: one that notes the analogies, correspondences, patterns, symptomatizations, symbolizations of the text – the massive army of German self-representations – and questions them. That questioning occurs in the name of an un-totalization of meaning. Put simply: Leverkühn is not Faust, nor is he Germany. And Thomas Mann's novel, miraculously, against all the odds, criticizes the temptation, in a context of acute cultural and political crisis, to succumb to the 'undisciplined squads of signification' (to borrow and modify a phrase of T. S. Eliot's). If the significations that scurry through Zeitblom's text work by a massive rhetoric of implication, then we can resist the implication; we can resist being implicated.

Doktor Faustus is, it has to be acknowledged, an un-lovely work – stressful, anguished, self-critical. But it is one to be cherished all the same, even more, perhaps, than that lovely product of German culture, Richard Strauss's *Vier letzte Gesänge*, a work exactly contemporary with *Doktor Faustus*, and one that betrays remarkably little self-consciousness or bad conscience at its musical and cultural intertextuality. To say this is not to denigrate Richard Strauss, but rather to suggest that certain works of the German tradition – and *Doktor Faustus* is a supreme example – are not only the object of our critique (in historical hindsight) but also engender that critique from within. Ultimately, although one would hardly guess it from looking at the criticism devoted to this great novel, *Doktor Faustus* relativizes, perhaps even rebuts, the notion that Nazism was the result of Lutheranism, or the Reformation, or German musicality, or whatever. Rather, it suggests that in the cultural climate of Germany during the first forty years or so of this century, representations (artistic, philosophical and political) were circulating, indeed copulating, indiscriminately in a conceptual Vanity Fair, littered with all manner of bric-à-brac, of cultural flotsam and jetsam; and that the attempt, in the spirit of Humpty Dumpty, to put the world together again, however understandable and well-meant and even honourable, was not the solution to the crisis, but rather the nemesis that flowed from it.

Notes

1 See John F. Fetzer, *Changing Perceptions of Thomas Mann's 'Doctor Faustus': Criticism 1947–1992*, (Columbia S.C.: Camden House, 1996).

2 See Osman Durrani, *Fictions of Germany: Images of the German Nation in the Modern Novel* (Edinburgh: Edinburgh University Press, 1994).

3 J. P. Stern, *The Dear Purchase*, (Cambridge: Cambridge University Press, 1995).

4 Page references throughout are to Thomas Mann, *Gesammelte Werke in dreizehn Bänden*, vol. VI (Frankfurt am Main: Fischer, 1974).

5 Michael Beddow, *Thomas Mann, 'Doctor Faustus'* (Cambridge: Cambridge University Press, 1994, p. 96).

6 Gunilla Bergsten, *Thomas Mann's 'Doctor Faustus': The Sources Structure of the Novel* (Chicago: University of Chicago Press, 1969, p. 173).

7 Ibid, p. 173.

8 See Beddow, *Thomas Mann*, pp. 67ff.

9 Roland Barthes, 'L'effet de réel', in Gerard Genette and Tzvetan Todorov (eds), *Littérature et Réalité*, (Paris, 1982), pp. 81–90.

10 See Günter Reiss, *'Allegorisierung' und moderne Erzählkunst: eine Studie zum Werk Thomas Manns* (Munich: Fink, 1970).

5

'Unzulänglichkeit gegenüber der Geschichte': Hochhuth's *Der Stellvertreter* and Weiss's *Die Ermittlung*

Judith Beniston

It is one of the more surprising features of postwar German history that, after the first wave of horrific revelations about Nazi concentration camps, and once the Nuremberg trials were over, the Holocaust seemed to fade from public consciousness until the successor trials began in 1958. In particular, the trial of Adolf Eichmann in Jerusalem (1961) and the Auschwitz war crimes trials held in Frankfurt (1963–65) returned the genocide to the fore-front of attention and forced people in both Germanies to reflect once again on the issues of individual and collective guilt. A substantial contribution to this somewhat belated confrontation with the legacy of Auschwitz was made by two controversial dramas, Rolf Hochhuth's *Der Stellvertreter* (1963) and Peter Weiss's *Die Ermittlung* (1965). The aim of this chapter is to examine the contentious, hard-hitting interpretations of the Holocaust put forward by Hochhuth and Weiss in the light of its official representation in the two Germanies and of contemporary trends in East and West German historiography. For, in the highly charged atmosphere of the Cold War, coming to terms with the past was inescapably a political process, tied in with the identities of the two German states and their desire for historical legitimation. The juxtaposition of Hochhuth, a West German citizen who until 1966 refused permission for *Der Stellvertreter* to be performed in the GDR, and Weiss, a German-Jewish exile who had made his home in Sweden and was increasingly critical of the Federal Republic (FRG), is particularly rewarding because their work and its early reception at once reflect and challenge key historiographical paradigms of the Cold War era.

Der Stellvertreter, which was first staged on 20 February 1963, in a production by Erwin Piscator at the Freie Volksbühne in West Berlin, centres on an exploration of the moral issues that were raised by the failure of Pope Pius XII to speak out against Nazism in general and the Holocaust in particular. In a plot dominated by tense dramatic confrontations, the Pope's refusal to intervene is contrasted with the courage of Kurt Gerstein, an SS officer and member of the Protestant 'Bekennende Kirche' who repeatedly risked his life to make known the facts of the genocide, and with the heroic self-sacrifice of fictional Jesuit Riccardo Fontana who, having failed to spur Christ's representative into action, resolves to redeem the honour of the Roman Catholic Church by joining a transport to Auschwitz. What validates the comparison with Weiss's *Die Ermittlung* is, however, that Hochhuth's indictment of Pius XII takes place within the framework of, and indeed contributes to, a much broader depiction of the Holocaust – one which attempts, like Weiss's play, to characterize the perpetrators, to assess the culpability of ordinary Germans, and to explore the experience of the victims.

Der Stellvertreter enjoyed a *succès de scandale* throughout the western world. In suggesting that the Vatican could have done more to prevent the genocide, Hochhuth not only broke a major taboo, but also implicitly questioned the moral authority of the postwar Church. Although, as the various volumes of response to *Der Stellvertreter* testify,[1] critical attention focused primarily on the religious issue, the play was also innovative in other respects. In the 1950s, Holocaust drama had barely gone beyond accounts of individual suffering and heroism, such as *Das Tagebuch der Anne Frank* (adapted for the theatre in 1956) and Erwin Sylvanus's *Korczak und die Kinder* (1957); Hochhuth, and subsequently Weiss, offered a broader, more analytical perspective on the question of German guilt and did so using documentary material rather than the more abstract, parabolic approach typified by Frisch's *Andorra* (1961) and Walser's *Eiche und Angora* (1962). Furthermore, Hochhuth dared to set the fifth act of *Der Stellvertreter* in Auschwitz itself.[2] As he implicitly acknowledged in rewriting the ending for a production mounted in Basel in October 1963, this was extremely problematic; and it was in part by demonstrating the difficulties of mimetic representation that Hochhuth paved the way for *Die Ermittlung*. Premièred on 19 October 1965, in an elaborate *Ringaufführung* which took in numerous locations in both Germanies, Weiss's spoken oratorio builds up a detailed and harrowing account of camp life from the evidence given at the Frankfurt trials, but puts on stage a representation of the courtroom rather than of Auschwitz itself. At first this tended to be contrasted favourably with Hochhuth's more direct, mimetic approach; however, here too scandal ensued as it became clear that the play was very different from the politically neutral memorial to the victims of the Holocaust for which it had initially been taken.

Even if one believes that it is theoretically possible for the historian or documentary dramatist to represent the past 'as it really was', this was a naive expectation when dealing with the issue of the Holocaust during the Cold War. Firstly, the sheer horror and magnitude of the events seemed uniquely to demand an ethically founded response: putting aside questions of innocence and culpability in favour of attempting to understand the Third Reich on its own terms was not in the 1960s a serious option. Secondly, the process of selecting and ordering material, which is invariably underpinned by theoretical paradigms, also came to be informed by the determination to ensure that such atrocities never happened again and by the need to legitimize the successor states on that basis. Hence, historians, writers and politicians on both sides of the inner-German divide competed to define particular groups and individuals as deserving to be censured, lauded or mourned, doing so in ways that had profound political and psychological implications for the postwar situation. Although academic history was always a more pluralistic discipline in the West than in the GDR, and although the literary community had a great deal more freedom in the Federal Republic, the Cold War displaced the issues in such a way that in both Germanies the historiographical models favoured in the political sphere tended also to find support amongst professional historians and to be reflected, at least to a certain extent, in contemporary literature.

It is barely an exaggeration to say that in the 1960s accounts of the Nazi era were, on both sides of the inner-German divide, relatively simple tales of villains and heroes, victims and dupes.[3] In the GDR Marxist doctrine identified the villains as 'imperialist monopoly capitalist fascists', while the heroes were those who had actively opposed fascism – most notably members of the organized communist resistance. By defining fascism as a product of late capitalism, the socialist state was able to claim that in rejecting the latter it (unlike the FRG) had automatically eradicated the former. In marked contrast to this, the dominant tendency in West German historiography was to view Hitler's Germany as a totalitarian dictatorship. Whereas the GDR viewed individual perpetrators as products of an intrinsically evil system, the totalitarian model demonized the handful of individuals at the centre of power – the likes of Hitler, Himmler, and Heydrich – and the asocial thugs (SS and *Einsatzgruppen*) who had done their bidding. As well as being favoured by many West German historians, this narrative underpinned Adenauer's approach to the issue of German guilt: through Nuremberg and the successor trials his government conceded that a small group of perpetrators deserved punishment but shied away from condemning the regime's many fellow travellers and *Schreibtischtäter*. Collective guilt was rejected in favour of collective shame that such crimes had been committed not by but 'in the name of' the German people. In the West German schema, those most likely to be cast as heroes were not the communist resistance but individuals who had opposed Hitler's regime on religious or moral grounds, and the 'conservative resisters' of the Stauffenberg plot. By blaming a small minority the West German model implicitly exculpated the majority of the population who had, at worst, been dupes, accessories to their crimes. Following this reasoning, the *Wirtschaftswunder* was a heartening sign that fascism had only shallow roots in the national psyche: as soon as the malign Nazi influence had been removed, ordinary Germans had rightly picked up their everyday lives and begun the process of rebuilding with exemplary diligence. Interestingly, the founding myth of the GDR – that the villains had gone west, allowing the erstwhile heroes to seize power – likewise assumed the innocence of peasants and workers and allowed for reconstruction without lengthy soul-searching. Finally, the two Germanies also defined the victims of the Nazi regime in different ways. While the official philo-Semitism of the Federal Republic ensured that the Jewish Holocaust came to the fore, East German accounts played down the racial issue, focusing instead on those victims who had actively opposed Nazism – in other words, the victims who could also be depicted as heroes.

By examining Hochhuth's *Der Stellvertreter* and Weiss's *Die Ermittlung* against this background, and by considering their early reception in the German-speaking world, it will be possible to explore the ways in which each drew on but also, and crucially, subverted the prevailing historiographical paradigms, thereby helping to bring into the process of *Vergangenheitsbewältigung* a vital element of critical self-consciousness.

Der Stellvertreter is in many respects the more complex and ambitious of the two dramas. Hochhuth tackles a wide range of issues – the culpability of the Pope, and by extension of ordinary Catholics, the extent to which individual Nazi perpetrators were responsible for their crimes and should have been brought to justice, the treatment and identity of the victims, and the nature and significance of German resistance to Nazism – and, especially when dealing with issues of culpability, offers a variety of alternative perspectives.[4] Attention is particularly drawn to this facet of the work in the published text of *Der Stellvertreter*, where frequent excursions into methodological reflection and inordinately lengthy stage directions accompany Hochhuth's dialogue, and the text proper is followed by an appendix headed 'Historische Streiflichter'. That the reader has access to so much additional information of course has implications for analyses of the play's reception: since the text only went on sale on the day of the première, one must expect the earliest responses to Piscator's production to differ radically from those which were also informed by a reading of the published text. In practice this difference is all the greater because the complete text of *Der Stellvertreter* would take approximately seven hours to perform. Although Hochhuth advised against attempting this feat, he has never produced an authoritative stage version.[5] Instead, every director preparing a production has been obliged, as Piscator put it, 'aus diesem "totalen" Stück eine Bühnenfassung herzustellen, ein Stück aus dem Stück zu schneiden'.[6] Consequently, the play is particularly susceptible to political instrumentalization. In examining the reception of productions one must be aware that the cuts made by a particular director may have been informed by a political agenda and will inevitably have simplified Hochhuth's historiography.

One can illustrate the interpretative openness of *Der Stellvertreter* by considering the relationship between Hochhuth's depiction of Pius XII and his treatment of German guilt. The dramatic crux of the play is undeniably the

Pope's refusal to condemn explicitly the Nazis' treatment of the Jews, even when in October 1943 they were being rounded up from within sight of the Vatican. The triangular relationship between the Pope, Riccardo Fontana and Kurt Gerstein is indeed the stuff of traditional (and especially Schillerian) dramaturgy, in which history is shaped by the personal decisions taken by essentially free individuals. According to Piscator's foreword, the emphasis on individual responsibility points to a freedom which every individual still possessed under the Nazi regime and consequently to 'die Schuld ..., die jeder auf sich genommen hat, der seine Freiheit nicht dazu benutzte, sich *gegen* die Unmenschlichkeit zu entscheiden' (*Stellvertreter*, p. 7). Piscator hopes that the audience will see in the Pope's failure to act a reflection of the guilt incurred by everyone who looked the other way as their neighbours were being rounded up and sent to their deaths.

Demanding that ordinary people should identify with Christ's representative on earth is, however, deeply problematic. Firstly, it assumes that the man in the street is endowed with similar spiritual and moral resources; and, secondly, it takes no account of the fact that the ordinary citizen could achieve far less by protesting. Instead, there is the real risk that the issue of German guilt will be submerged when such emphasis is placed on the Pope's failure to exploit his unique authority – that Germans will find in the play a comforting alibi. As Hellmuth Karasek put it: 'Wenn selbst der Heilige Vater, der es doch ohne Gefahr hätte tun können, dem Unrecht nicht gewehrt hat, wie hätte ich es als gefährdeter einzelner tun können?'[7] Challenged about this in a television interview, Hochhuth reluctantly agreed that the argument was admissible but countered:

> Es [dieses Argument] wird aber aufgewogen, glaube ich, dadurch, daß der Deutsche im Parkett ja auf der Bühne durch mein Stück ich glaube in diesem Ausmaß zum erstenmal die Deutschen am Werke der Judenvernichtung sieht. Es gibt ja sonst, glaube ich, kein Stück, wo also beispielsweise Eichmann und Hirt und diese ganzen Gangster auftreten. Ich glaube, es treten in meinem Stück wesentlich mehr Nazis auf, als etwa klerikale Würdenträger. Denken Sie nur an die Kegelbahnszene oder an die Auschwitzszene.[8]

This is a valid point, but for the fact that most productions (including Piscator's West German première, and the representative East German production at Berlin's Deutsches Theater) omitted the former scene because it is primarily illustrative and does nothing to further the dramatic conflict between the three central figures, and reduced the final act to a brief, almost expressionistic *Nachspiel* – few directors liking either Hochhuth's mimetic representation of Auschwitz or the melodramatic finale he imagined being played out there. In any production which offers few other candidates for the role of villain, the Pope, an icy diplomat who literally washes his hands of the Holocaust, could easily serve: no longer a symbol of German guilt but a means of diverting attention from it.

Although rarely staged, what Hochhuth calls the 'Kegelbahnszene', an evening of bowling and alcohol-induced conviviality at which Adolf Eichmann plays host to figures representing almost every aspect of Hitler's Jewish policy, is clearly central to his analysis of German guilt. Here one glimpses the fateful alliance between science, industry and institutionalized anti-Semitism. In line with the decidedly banal image of Eichmann which had emerged during his trial two years earlier, the administrative coordinator (one hesitates to use the grandiose term 'mastermind') of the Final Solution appears as 'ein freundlicher Pedant' (*Stellvertreter*, p. 28), a diligent host who sets up the skittles tournament and keeps it running with predictable efficiency. Of his guests, Eichmann seems to interact most easily with the Rhineland industrialist Baron Rutta, helping to defend him against the accusation that companies such as Krupp are ill-treating their slave labourers and sharing the private joke that things will be better regulated once the Auschwitz factory is operational. The Catholic Rutta not only typifies the sort of callousness and moral complacency that was legitimized by the Pope's refusal to rescind the Concordat between Berlin and Rome (which he, as Cardinal Pacelli, had negotiated in 1933); Rutta's easy-going relationship with Eichmann is also suggestive of that 'segensreiche Freundschaft' between capitalist greed and fascist dictatorship which Weiss castigates in *Die Ermittlung*.[9] The idea of leading industrialists and prominent SS men as friends and accomplices was not popular amongst conservative West Germans but was compatible with one of the more moderate strands of contemporary East German historiography.[10]

The Nazi alliance with industry is complemented in the 'Kegelbahnszene' by that with academia as August Hirt, the anatomy professor from Strasbourg who collects human brains 'mit der Habgier eines Philatelisten' (*Stellvertreter*, p. 44) and prefers to have them delivered live, combines viciousness with vanity, hoping that his researches will demonstrate 'warom die Endlösung der Judefrog auch wissenschaftlich / einwandfrei natur-gegeben ond notwendig war' (*Stellvertreter*, p. 46). Alongside science and industry, every stage of the Final Solution is represented at this gathering: the transportation expert Eichmann, the Doctor who separates those prisoners who are fit for work from those to be gassed immediately, the secretary-to-be Helga, the camp guard Fritsche, and finally the chemicals expert Gerstein. Although some of Eichmann's guests are determined careerists portrayed with a cold realism, others are clearly meant to be seen as caricatures – the assimilation-bent '"Beute"-Deutscher' Dr Pryzilla, and the Austrian 'Humanitätskarikatur' Oberst Serge, whose sentimental concern for the slave labourers in Rutta's factories parodies the intensity of Gerstein's conviction.

The initial atmosphere is indeed one of harmless amusement as the young pilot Rutta, practically the only character not linked with Auschwitz or with Germany's eastward expansion, is teased about fastening his newly won

Knight's Cross with a woman's garter. The ordinariness of Eichmann, who appears as neither a caricature nor a sinister figure and is sober enough to hold a businesslike conversation with Gerstein when the latter arrives at the very end, makes it tempting to view this scene, together with the exchanges in Helga's Auschwitz office in Act V, as demonstrating what the Eichmann trial prompted Hannah Arendt to call 'the banality of evil'.[11] Hochhuth's notes also indicate (albeit less forcefully than *Die Ermittlung*) that many of those involved with the running and the industrial exploitation of the death camps returned to ordinary civilian lives after the war, a transition that is only conceivable if one assumes that the perpetrators of heinous crimes might in other respects be peaceable, law-abiding citizens.

This essentially rational interpretation of the Holocaust which highlights the enormous human potential for evil and chides West Germany for not punishing the perpetrators more harshly is, however, severely undermined by the fact that, as the alcohol flows, the atmosphere of the 'Kegelbahnszene' becomes increasingly sinister and grotesque. The discrepancy between the different forms of relaxed, at times cosily accented speech and the euphemistic jargon of the extermination process is chilling and goes together with the macabre bowling terminology (such as 'Sarg' and 'tot') to create the impression of a satanic *Totentanz*. This is reinforced by the presence of the Doctor, who casts an eerie shadow over the whole scene. A *Spielverderber* who refuses to play skittles and deliberately sabotages the atmosphere, he is clearly out of place in such convivial company. Whereas Hochhuth's notes indicate that the others present are either *bona fide* historical figures (Eichmann, Gerstein) or recurring types (the SS-bride who will become a GI-bride, the unscrupulous capitalist, the young doctors and lawyers who will become pillars of the West German establishment), the Doctor exists on an entirely different plane. Although details of his 'medical' experiments are clearly based on the notorious Josef Mengele, whose whereabouts were uncertain in 1963, Hochhuth pointedly avoids mentioning that name or identifying the Doctor with any specific individual. Rather than being a human type he is conceived as evil incarnate; the models for the character are literary rather than historical. Hochhuth suggests 'daß hier eine uralte Figur des Theaters und des christlichen Mysterienspieles die Bühne wieder betreten habe' (*Stellvertreter*, p. 30), and there is also more than passing resemblance to Goethe's Mephistopheles in the Doctor's cold lasciviousness, his love of provoking the pious and the way in which he sets himself up as the antagonist of heaven, cynically destroying human life and human idealism at every opportunity. According to Hochhuth's notes, the Doctor appears in this scene as 'der geheime Regisseur', manipulating the other figures (*Stellvertreter*, p. 29).

Perhaps thinking back to the way in which works such as Zuckmayer's *Des Teufels General* (1944) had demonized Hitler in order to present Nazism as an aberration in an otherwise laudable German tradition, Egon Schwarz has suggested that 'nur in der Figur des dämonsichen Doktors bleibt Hochhuth der älteren Auffassung des Nationalsozialismus verhaftet'.[12] The issue is not, however, that the conception is outmoded; rather, Hochhuth's left-liberal critique, the ostensibly rational interpretation of the Holocaust that pilloried capitalism and would have been so unpalatable to West German readers, is overlaid with a metaphysical one. In a manner consonant with West German historiography of the 1960s, the unsuspecting skittles-players become puppets controlled by an unseen hand. Although this loss of autonomy devalues their humanity, it also goes some way towards exonerating them. The difficulty of resisting the demonic is exemplified, somewhat unsubtly, in the figure of Helga, who, despite finding the Doctor repulsive, is nevertheless seduced by him and, almost without realizing, becomes part of the Auschwitz operation. That Hochhuth was critical of such exculpatory narratives becomes clear in Act V, when he suggests that after 1945 Helga will be seduced just as easily by the occupying forces, admitting 'daß es "nicht schön" war, was man mit den Juden gemacht hat' (*Stellvertreter*, p. 184) but, as the use of 'man' implies, not concerning herself unduly with issues of responsibility.

Hochhuth's demonization of the Doctor is most obviously a response to the overwhelming magnitude of the Holocaust and the enormity of the crimes committed. Whereas Weiss in *Die Ermittlung* urges his audience to abandon 'die erhabene Haltung ... / daß uns diese Lagerwelt unverständlich ist' (*Ermittlung*, p. 85), for Hochhuth it remains barely credible that such events took place in our world, a surreal happening only explicable in metaphysical terms. Furthermore, in juxtaposing a personification of Nazi evil with Christ's representative on earth, Hochhuth goes beyond the comforting fiction of seduction by demonic forces, using it as the starting-point for a theological interpretation of the Holocaust in which Auschwitz becomes not merely a product of otherworldly evil but a satanic experiment, set up in order to prove that God is indeed dead. Although Hochhuth claims in his notes at the beginning of Act V that he is doing his utmost not to present the terrible reality of Auschwitz 'als Legende, als apokalyptisches Märchen' (*Stellvertreter*, p. 179), on one level he does precisely that: *Geschichte* becomes *Heilsgeschichte*, the historical drama a Christian *Legendenspiel*. The one early commentator who perceived this tendency was Willy Haas. He wrote:

> denn warum sollte man nicht eine christliche Legende erzählen dürfen, daß unter irgendeinem legendären Papst der Teufel die irdische Macht fast über die ganze sichtbare Welt an sich gerissen hat, und doch dieser Papst, in weltliche Probleme verstrickt, ihn nicht erkannt und nicht in den Bann getan, sondern sich in irgendwelche Diskussionen mit ihm eingelassen hat, um seine eigene Macht und die des Teufels gegeneinander abzugrenzen und den Besitz der Kirche zu wahren? Warum nicht? Es ist ein echt legendärer Stoff, man spürt förmlich seine innere legendäre Wahrheit.[13]

Finally appearing in person in the fourth act, Pope Pius XII is indeed presented in a critical light: his first words express concern about the Vatican's financial assets; in refusing to protest explicitly against the treatment of the Jews, his behaviour is not Christ-like but that of a diplomat, for whom *Staatsräson* is the most important consideration. Echoing the opinions of his oleaginous Cardinal, the Pope takes an extremely long-range, theological view of history in which Jews are clearly set apart from Gentiles (just as West German politicians tended to draw a line between Jews and Germans), and Hitler, whatever his crimes, remains an instrument of the divine plan, defending the Catholic cultural heritage against the godless Bolshevik hordes.

This view of the political situation, which refuses to empathize with the victims and falsely casts Russia as the aggressor, is of course vigorously contested by Riccardo Fontana and by Gerstein, for whom the human cost far outweighs any diplomatic or material considerations. If the Pope's failings are intended to remind the German audience of their own indifference, then Riccardo and Gerstein offer a rather more uplifting prospect; ritual shame is admixed with a memory of heroic resistance and a promise of atonement. Kurt Gerstein, the SS officer and member of the 'Bekennende Kirche' who told foreign diplomats and prominent churchmen the awful truth about the extermination camps while at the same time being instrumental in the development of Cyclon B for use in the gas chambers, is typical of what Klemens von Klemperer has called 'the solitary witness', making an ethically laudable but tragically ineffectual gesture of resistance.[14] Gerstein's memoirs, written shortly before his death in a Paris prison in 1945, had been published in an academic journal in 1953 and reproduced in Poliakov and Wulf's *Das dritte Reich und die Juden* two years later.[15] As well as details of his career, Hochhuth takes from Gerstein's text the harrowing account of gassings in Belzec reproduced almost verbatim in the opening scene of *Der Stellvertreter*. Although Gerstein had been the subject of a radio programme in 1957, his name was not widely known prior to the appearance of *Der Stellvertreter*. In bringing him to public attention, Hochhuth can indeed be said to have contributed to that popular historiography of resistance which, ever since 1945, has been used to counter notions of collective guilt.[16]

As an *Identifikationsfigur* Gerstein is, however, problematic in two senses. Firstly, just as Willy Brandt's wartime involvement with the Norwegian resistance led him to be accused of betraying his country, so Hochhuth feels obliged to defend Gerstein against the charge of treason, arguing that: 'Die Verräter sind es, sie allein, / die heute Deutschlands Ehre retten' (*Stellvertreter*, p. 65). Secondly, Gerstein's story is far from typical. In the words of Karena Niehoff: 'Mag der Mann noch so authentisch, noch so verbürgt sein – er bleibt immer eine unerhörte Begebenheit, ein schönes Wildpferd ohne das Zaumzeug der Wahrheit.'[17] In a curious sense Gerstein's double life makes him a similar figure to the Doctor – *unheimlich* in his psychological inaccessibility and, like the satanic intruder, a stranger, an outsider amongst his own people.

Notwithstanding these limitations, Gerstein is the only German character in *Der Stellvertreter* who possesses sufficient moral authority to speak up in defence of his countrymen, to argue that Hitler is not Germany. He does this with particular vigour when Riccardo brings up the old chestnut of the *Land der Dichter und Denker*:

> Warum das deutsche Volk,
> die Nation Goethes, Mozarts, Menzels ...
> Warum die Deutschen so verrohen konnten. (*Stellvertreter*, p. 66)

Gerstein responds firstly by asserting that the majority of the German public knew nothing about what happened to the Jews after deportation; secondly, he cites the many thousands of Germans who risked their lives by hiding Jews in their homes – a form of resistance in which he too participates by sheltering Jacobson. Gerstein also argues that 'Schweine gibt es überall' (*Stellvertreter*, p. 66): the Germans as a whole were no more morally reprehensible than other nationalities. Within the play Hochhuth's depiction of the Italian militia provides support for this thesis, and Gerstein also cites the willingness of Dutch and French police to assist in rounding up the Jews, and the fact that, in countries such as the Ukraine, Hungary and Poland, the local population were willing to deal with the matter themselves.

The Protestant resister Gerstein is complemented in *Der Stellvertreter* by the Catholic Riccardo Fontana, whose heroics owe a debt to the Polish priest Maximilian Kolbe, martyred in Auschwitz, and to Bernhard Lichtenberg, Dean of St Hedwig's in Berlin, who publicly prayed for the Jews and died in a transport to Dachau. Gerstein and Riccardo differ in the important respect that in the latter part of the play Riccardo is no longer trying to save Jewish lives; rather, his objective in going to Auschwitz is to redeem the honour of the Roman Catholic Church. Riccardo's despairing gesture of self-sacrifice is clearly in vain, and the final words of the play focus on the continuing escalation of the killing: '"So arbeiteten die Gaskammern noch ein volles Jahr. Erst im Sommer 1944 erreichte die sogenannte Tagesquote der Ermordungen ihren Höhepunkt ..."' (*Stellvertreter*, p. 227). But one might nevertheless argue that, in making Riccardo's act of atonement the finale of *Der Stellvertreter*, Hochhuth is not further compromising the authority of the Church but offering the Catholic spectator the play itself as a form of cathartic redemption.

If Hochhuth's portrayal of his play's heroes appears to contain relatively little to offend West German sensibilities, this also holds for his depiction of the victims of the Holocaust. All of those who appear on stage are explicitly identified as Jews – there is no mention of groups such as Sinti and Roma, homosexuals, Jehovah's Witnesses, or political opponents of the regime. This is a typically West German bias (reflected, for example, in the official philo-Semitism of Adenauer's government) and contrasts sharply with Weiss's *Die Ermittlung* where the racial dimension is almost entirely excluded. Hochhuth is, however, extremely selective in his representation of the Jewish victims. Firstly, all but one of those named in *Der Stellvertreter* are Italian rather than German Jews; only in the figure of Jacobson, the son of a German First World War veteran (to be considered more closely in the following section), does Hochhuth briefly abandon the principle of the Jew as 'other'. Secondly, Hochhuth focuses exclusively on assimilated Jews and Catholic converts, presumably in the belief that these 'special cases' will most readily arouse the sympathy of the spectator. Even more surprising, however, is that, in a play which attempts to provide an overview of the fourteen months leading up to October 1943, and which is packed with (not always terribly helpful) snippets of cultural and political information, one can find no reasoned explanation for the persecution of the Jews. Are they merely the unfortunate victims of the Doctor's experiment in theodicy? Rather than providing a basis for rational analysis, Hochhuth encourages an emotional response to the enormity of the crime by focusing on the anxious minutes leading up to the arrest of a single family in the third act and then beginning the fifth with tear-jerking monologues by three generational representatives. That two of these castigate or appeal explicitly to a Christian God further supports the view that this is an extremely partial representation of the victims of the Holocaust which does not stand up well to close scrutiny.

In a 1979 interview Hochhuth confessed that a feeling of 'Unzuläng-lichkeit gegenüber der Geschichte' was one of the motors of his creativity – in the sense of seeking both to overcome the inadequacy of his own histor-ical understanding and to combat that 'Gefühl hilfloser Unzulänglichkeit' which he considered typical of the German people as a whole.[18] The diffuse, ill-defined sense of shame which Hochhuth's portrayal of the victims seems designed to provoke is, at least in the view of this commentator, the most unfortunate product of a defective understanding.

The feeling that Hochhuth is all but overwhelmed by his subject matter indeed comes across repeatedly in *Der Stellvertreter*, not only in his failure to explain the Holocaust, but also in the lack of a coherent historiographical approach to the issue of culpability, in the almost encyclopaedic fullness of text and commentaries, and in the extent to which he thematizes the diffi-culties of the endeavour within the dialogue – for example having Gerstein warn Riccardo against demonizing 'einen Verbrecher von Rang' (*Stell-vertreter*, p. 65) since that distracts attention from those who brought him to power, and having Fontana senior remind his son of the 'alte Weisheit' that history only has meaning 'wenn die Historiker ihr einen geben' (*Stell-vertreter*, p. 85). However, these latter features of the play can also be viewed as strengths, insofar as they repeatedly remind the reader not only of the pit-falls but also of the necessary process of historical emplotment. That a good deal of this self-consciousness is inevitably lost in performance is therefore unfortunate.

If one examines the full printed text of *Der Stellvertreter*, Hochhuth's historiography can be said to be broadly in line with conventional West German interpretations: the play ultimately mythologizes Nazi crimes as the work of satanic forces, it focuses on individual rather than organized resistance, it offers a number of potential alibis for German guilt and provides, in the figure of Gerstein, a heartening reminder of that putative 'other' Germany, in which Christian moral imperatives never ceased to be obeyed. As the foregoing discussion has suggested, it was as much for dramaturgical as for political reasons that the first West German productions of *Der Stellvertreter* tended to subordinate the issue of German guilt, all too often explored in illustrative scenes and schoolmasterly speeches, to a depiction of the more dynamic interaction between Gerstein, Riccardo and the Pope, and the moral questions which that posed. Similar dramaturgical considerations came into play when Hochhuth's work was staged in the GDR – with the result that the essentially static 'Kegelbahnszene' featured in only one of the first four productions – but East German directors and commentators nevertheless tended to offer a very different reading of *Der Stellvertreter*, foregrounding Hochhuth's left-liberal critique of capitalist complicity with fascism, playing down the otherworldliness of Nazi evil and hinting at the senselessness of individual resistance in such a way as to bring his play into line with the founding myths of the GDR.

Although Hochhuth initially refused permission for *Der Stellvertreter* to be performed in the eastern bloc, for fear that it would be used as anticlerical propaganda, he relented in 1966, after which productions were quickly mounted in a number of East German cities, the first four being Greifswald, Rostock, Berlin and Leipzig.[19] Public interest had already been whetted by a radio play and a television documentary on the subject, and in 1965 a *Lizenzausgabe* of *Der Stellvertreter* had appeared, complete with an additional forty-six pages of documentation, put together by the Marxist historian Klaus Drobisch. In largely Protestant East Germany there was no equivalent to the storm of Catholic protest which the play had provoked in the West – a phenomenon which East German commentators most frequently attributed to the fury of the Christian Democratic Union (CDU) and the Christian Social Union (CSU) at finding their myth of the Catholic Church as a focus of anti-fascist resistance so severely undermined. East German responses were in general more sober and analytical, and concentrated less narrowly on the religious issue. This is reflected in the fourteen documents assembled by Drobisch. With the exception of one, a Soviet account of the murder of Polish officers at Katyn, which blames the Germans for the long-disputed atrocity and has no obvious connection to *Der Stellvertreter*, they either concern specific historical figures – Kolbe, Lichtenberg, Hirt, Gerstein – or provide further information on Auschwitz and the Final Solution. Excerpts from the Wannsee Protocol and from the testimony of Rudolf Höss (the Commandant of Auschwitz) are followed by accounts of 'Die nichtärztliche Tätigkeit der SS-Ärzte im KZ Auschwitz' and of the liberation of the camp. That this took place 'durch russische Soldaten' is, of course, the closing line of *Der Stellvertreter*. Whereas Piscator, and possibly other West German directors, pointedly omitted these words, they were firmly reinstated in East German productions, underlining, as Carl Amery put it, 'daß die schauerlichste Form der Unmenschlichkeit seit vielen tausend Jahren eben nicht von Christen, sondern von den "roten Horden" beendet wurde'.[20]

Hochhuth released *Der Stellvertreter* for performance in the GDR on the condition that the première would take place at the Deutsches Theater in East Berlin, under the direction of Erich Engel. As Engel fell ill during preparations and was replaced by Hans-Dieter Meves and Friedo Solter, the Deutsches Theater was overtaken by Greifswald and Rostock, but the Berlin production remained probably the most widely noticed East German interpretation of the play. The way in which Engel saw his task is clear from a letter to Hochhuth, in which he explains the nature of GDR audiences and the sort of historiographical approach to which they are most receptive:

> Sie ... stehen hier in der DDR vor einem Publikum, das von den dunklen Entstehungsgründen jener grauenvollen Geschichtsphase zusätzlich ein präzises Wissen erworben hat. Darum wird es gerade gegenüber solchen Ausführungen besonders hellhörig, die durch die religiösen, psychologischen, metaphysischen und seelischen Zwischenschichten hindurchgreifen und die realen gesellschaftlichen Kausalzusammenhänge vor den Blick bringen.[21]

Whereas it has been argued in this chapter that, despite his awareness of other perspectives, Hochhuth ultimately interprets the Holocaust in metaphysical terms, Engel insists on the primacy of social causalities; the 'präzises Wissen' with which he credits his audience is clearly the Marxist theory of fascism as an intrinsic product of the bourgeois capitalist system which, as its collapse becomes imminent, attempts to destroy the revolutionary working class by manipulating an alternative, more reactionary mass movement. Although no principles as doctrinaire as these can readily be derived from *Der Stellvertreter*, Hochhuth does suggest causal links between the Pope's concern for his financial assets, his anti-communism, and his acceptance of fascism.

The most substantial obstacle in the way of the Marxist interpretation Engel proposed was the demonic figure of the Doctor. Dramaturgical materials held in the Stiftung Archiv der Akademie der Künste in Berlin reveal not only that the dialogue between Gerstein and the Doctor in Act I, scene 3 and much of the final act were omitted but also that the characterization of the Doctor was entirely rethought:

> Der Doktor ist ein Glied aus der Kette der Mörder von Hitler über Eichmann
> bis hin zu Kaduk oder Boger. Sein Intellekt gestattet ihm eine Distanzierung
> von der Primitivität der nazistischen Ideologie und die [*sic*] meisten ihrer
> repräsentativen Vertreter. Aber gerade dadurch wird er zu einer besonders typ-
> ischen Gestalt innerhalb des faschistischen Systems.[22]

Here satanic provocation is replaced by cynical but all too human sadism.
Conceived thus, the Doctor ceases to be the 'geheimer Regisseur' of the Holo-
caust and becomes one more criminal who deserves to be brought to justice.
This reading of the play is clearly influenced by the Auschwitz trial (at which
Boger and Kaduk both received life sentences) and that of Adolf Eichmann.
Significantly, Boger and Kaduk also feature in Weiss's *Die Ermittlung*, the
première of which took place in October 1965.

The 'Aufführungskonzeption' which underpinned the Deutsches Theater
production of *Der Stellvertreter* maintained that the play was founded not
only, as West German critics had complained, on a hypothesis that could
neither be conclusively proven or refuted, but also on a 'historical error' –
the erroneous belief that a Papal protest was the best and possibly the only
means of halting the killing. This 'historical error' had implications for two
areas of the production. Firstly, and somewhat ironically given Hochhuth's
anxieties about East German anticlericalism, it meant that there was less
inclination than in most West German productions to question the moral
integrity and political acumen of the Pope and his entourage. Rather than
lacking compassion for his fellow men, Pacelli, or more precisely the
institution of the Papacy, was simply trapped in the imperialist system. The
'Aufführungskonzeption' stresses that, even though Hochhuth makes the
Cardinal something of a caricature, he should still come over as a first-
class political mind rather than a near senile one, and that the Abbot's
courage in offering sanctuary to individual Jews should be portrayed as
the admirable product of a deep and sincerely held faith rather than a token
gesture.

Secondly, the 'Aufführungskonzeption' argued that the two heroes of *Der
Stellvertreter*, Riccardo and Gerstein, made the same 'historical error' of
which Hochhuth himself was guilty, insofar as they persisted in the mis-
taken belief that only a Papal protest could halt the genocide and that the
Pope was in a position to take such a step. Consequently, a GDR production
could not regard the idealism of these two characters as entirely exemplary:

> Ohne die bedeutende humanistische Haltung der beiden Helden des hochhuth-
> schen Stückes einschränken oder gar eliminieren zu wollen, sehen wir es als
> wesentlich an, die im Stück notierten Möglichkeiten einer im guten Sinne kri-
> tischen Sicht deutlich sichtbar zu machen.[23]

Whereas Piscator drew approving parallels between the documentary drama
of the 1960s and Schiller's notion of the theatre as a place of moral education, the prominent East German commentator Werner Mittenzwei was to

see Riccardo as 'ein moderner Marquis Posa', a flawed hero living in a world of illusion.[24] This critique of the lone resister – who, in pragmatic terms, achieves very little – was not only typical of East German Schiller reception, it also reflects the far greater attention paid in GDR historiography and propaganda to the impact of organized (mainly communist) resistance. In performance, this dimension of *Der Stellvertreter* could be stressed by giving particular prominence to the Jew Jacobson. Having planned, if he could get out of Nazi-held territory, to fight on the side of the Allies, he is reunited with Riccardo and Gerstein in Auschwitz in the final act. In a tone of despairing incredulity he asks, 'Wo bleibt denn euer Widerstand?', and the stage direction reads '*Leise, inständig, verzweifelt*' as he continues, 'Oder sind Sie noch immer – Einzelgänger?' (*Stellvertreter*, p. 214).

That this critical moment was already there in the play is a further example of the almost obsessive self-consciousness and awareness of complexity which characterizes *Der Stellvertreter* and is perhaps the greatest strength of Hochhuth's historiography. However, the play's reception in the GDR also shows up a more unfortunate characteristic of his gargantuan composition: the opportunities it provided for radically different forms of political instrumentalization, for teasing out acting versions which privileged a coherent but ideologically limited reading of events.

If, in the theatre at least, Hochhuth's *Der Stellvertreter* seemed, by dint of its malleability, to underline the divisions of the Cold War era, then Weiss's *Die Ermittlung* appears at first glance to have overcome them. As part of the *Ringaufführung* which took place on 19 October 1965, readings and performances were held simultaneously in London and in numerous German towns and cities, including Cologne, Erfurt, Essen, Munich, Rostock, Weimar and both parts of Berlin (the precise number is unclear but was at least fifteen); soon afterwards the play was broadcast on all major radio stations, and a television film was produced in 1966. Whereas it was never in doubt that *Der Stellvertreter* was an essentially fictional *Thesenstück* inviting a critical response, the form of Weiss's play and its reliance on the transcripts of evidence given at the Frankfurt trial, which had closed less than two months before the première, seems to have led to the almost universal assumption that *Die Ermittlung* was a commemorative text and could not possibly be a challenging, politically contentious drama. Theatre directors and previewers were initially unanimous in viewing the *Ringaufführung* as a unique 'Wiedergutmachungs- und Aufklärungsaktion',[25] a ritual act of remembrance which would also inform the younger generation and anyone who had not followed press coverage of the Frankfurt trials about the nature of Auschwitz and the atrocities committed there. Given that notions of collective guilt were part of public consciousness and official rhetoric in West Germany, and had been rekindled by the trials, it is not surprising that theatres there should have been keen to take part; and, as will be discussed shortly, the particular way in which Weiss explained the Holocaust ensured that his work was welcomed in the GDR.

In certain respects *Die Ermittlung*, which is subtitled 'Oratorium in 11 Gesängen', is a very suitable work for a solemn act of remembrance. Like Celan's poem 'Todesfuge', it draws on a dignified musical form that is associated with some of the icons of the German cultural tradition – in this case they include Bach, Handel and Haydn. The epic-lyrical quality of the oratorio, in which different voices are juxtaposed rather than brought into direct conflict, helped Weiss to wrest aesthetic control of a supremely emotive subject and reduce the confrontational character of the courtroom scenario. Although the form of the oratorio has most famously been used to treat religious themes, secular oratorios are far from unknown (for example, Haydn's *Four Seasons*), and *Die Ermittlung* differs markedly from *Der Stellvertreter* in that it does not have a metaphysical or theological dimension – the Holocaust is explained in rational, purely human terms. Notwithstanding this, the structure of the play strikingly resembles that of a Bach *Passion*, as the successive *Gesänge* lead the spectator from the periphery of the concentration camp to its centre, progressing from the arrival of the prisoners on the selection ramp and an assessment of their chances of survival, via accounts of camp life, of punishment, torture and execution, through to the horror of the gas chambers and crematoria. Within this structure the basic principle of the play is iterative. This means that Weiss's text, which like *Der Stellvertreter* would take approximately seven hours to perform in its entirety, can be abridged relatively easily and without the inevitable shifts in emphasis which result in stage versions of *Der Stellvertreter*. By omitting or shortening a few of the accounts of suffering and brutality, one spares the spectator a little pain, without necessarily travestying Weiss's intentions. What he termed his 'Konzentrat' (*Ermittlung*, p. 9) of evidence given at the Frankfurt trial is simply boiled down a little further.

Although, in the weeks leading up to the première, there was lively discussion of *Die Ermittlung* in the West German press, the possibility that the play might be both a ritual act of remembrance seeking universal emotional assent and a documentary drama endeavouring to engage the critical faculties of the spectator was not initially considered – even though commentators were familiar with the political nature of documentary drama. In one of the earliest articles, Joachim Kaiser, writing in the *Süddeutsche Zeitung*, demonstrated his knowledge of the genre but argued that *Die Ermittlung* should not be classified thus because Weiss was presenting the incontrovertible facts about Auschwitz rather than putting forward a thesis with which the spectator was at liberty to agree or disagree.

> Das Publikum muß den Fakten parieren. Es hat keine Freiheit, weil sich auch der Autor keine Freiheit nahm. Und während sogar die guten 'Dokumentationsstücke' des modernen Theaters dem Zuschauer eine Alternative bieten, ein Problem, eine Mitdenk-Freiheit, muß der Parkettbesucher sich in der

'Ermittlung' ducken unter der Gewalt des Faktischen. Er wird um genau jene
Freiheit betrogen, die Bühne und Kunst versprechen.[26]

Kaiser's claim that the audience has no freedom of opinion because Weiss
has allowed himself none is quite astounding in its naivety and makes one
wonder how much of the text he had actually read. The article gives no consideration whatever to the fact that Weiss selected his material from a mass
of documentary data, transformed it into blank verse, and in so doing necessarily arranged and interpreted it. Like several other early commentators,
Kaiser seems to have accepted without question Weiss's claim to have produced a 'Konzentrat' and consequently feels uneasy about treating *Die
Ermittlung* as a play and making conventional aesthetic judgements – potentially along the lines of 'the Lili Tofler scene falls flat' or 'Kaduk was mis-
cast'.

A more sophisticated response came from Erasmus Schöfer, who pointed
out in the *Rheinische Post* that there is an element of play-acting in all forms
of ritual remembrance or celebration and went on: 'es gibt keinen Zeitungs-
bericht, keinen Film, keine Fernsehdokumentation, keinen Roman oder
Erlebnisbericht, der nicht auf Auswahl, Interpretation, Arrangement beruht.
Selbst die Fotos in Hiroshimas Friedensmuseum sind in diesem Sinne unecht,
weil gestellt.' Curiously anticipating the charge of trivialization which was
to be levelled, almost fifteen years later, at the American serial *Holocaust*,
Schöfer also answers Kaiser's concern that audiences might not treat a *play*
about Auschwitz with sufficient respect, pointing out that, as with any other
representation of the past, audience responses cannot be controlled. 'So wie
jene Fotos und auch die "echten" Relikte der Explosion Attraktion für
amerikanische Touristen wurden, so liegt jede Fernsehdokumentation über
die Konzentrationslager, auch wenn sie von etwas Beethoven abgeschirmt
wird, prinzipiell zwischen Krimi und Revue und hindert den Zuschauer
nicht, seine Würstchen weiterzuessen.'[27] An extreme example of what over-
familiarity might breed was indeed given in Thomas Schulte-Michels's 1979
adaptation of *Die Ermittlung*, in which drunken cabaret artistes, who know
Weiss's play only too well, act out sections of it in an atmosphere of
grotesque nonchalance.[28]

Early West German responses to *Die Ermittlung*, such as the above, have
in common that they deal almost exclusively with theoretical issues and
show little evidence of close textual analysis. Instead, worries about the
appropriateness of the medium are underpinned by the assumption that the
play is a ritual act of remembrance rather than a potentially tendentious
interpretation of the Holocaust. There was indeed a consensus amongst theatre directors and critics that *Die Ermittlung* should not be integrated into
the run-of-the-mill repertoire, as Siegfried Melchinger feared, between *The
Merry Widow* and *A Midsummer Night's Dream*. Indeed, Melchinger went so
far as to suggest that it should be staged in halls rather than commercial

theatres and that the actors, rather than being costumed, should simply come in off the street 'ohne in der Garderobe einen Blick in den Spiegel geworfen zu haben'.[29] This not only reveals an unease with the whole notion of representing the Holocaust on stage but may also be seen to mirror the enduring disinclination of West German politicians and historians to integrate the Nazi era, and especially the Holocaust, into the broader development of German history.[30]

Strikingly, the first West German commentators to accuse Weiss of partiality also did so with only perfunctory reference to the play itself. H. D. Sander, whose article in *Die Welt* was probably the first overtly to politicize the reception of *Die Ermittlung*, instead quoted at length the political opinions which Weiss had recently expressed in a number of speeches, interviews and articles. Always in the left-liberal camp and, as a Swedish citizen, previously quite even-handed in his treatment of the two German states, Weiss had indeed abandoned the liberal 'third way' in the summer of 1965 and come down on the side of socialism, telling an interviewer that it was 'das einzige System ..., das sich entwickeln wird' and proffering a standard East German critique of the Federal Republic: 'Der Haß gegen den Bolschewismus ist in der Bundesrepublik die Nachfolge des Judenhasses'.[31] Sander also gives a summary of Weiss's recently published '10 Arbeitspunkte eines Autors in der geteilten Welt', quoting his confession that 'die Richtlinien des Sozialismus enthalten für mich die gültige Wahrheit' and crudely paraphrasing his critique of western imperialism as 'Der Westen kämpft für eine verlorene Sache; er kann sie nur mit Terror, Brutalität und finanzielle Bestechungen aufrechterhalten'. Weiss's comment in a speech given in Weimar in May 1965, that writers in the western world are obliged to work subversively, 'als Partisanen', in order to disseminate truth, gave Sander his cue to dub *Die Ermittlung* 'die erste Partisanenaktion des Peter Weiss', written 'um, synchron mit der permanenten Propagandakampagne des Ostblocks, die Bundesrepublik anzugreifen'.[32] In order to investigate the validity of such claims, one must look closely at the text of *Die Ermittlung*, searching for omissions and emphases which might mirror those which were characteristic of contemporary GDR historiography and propaganda.

If the way in which Hochhuth allots the roles of victim, hero and villain in *Der Stellvertreter* both reflects how the West German establishment attempted to come to terms with the Nazi legacy and, especially as far as the villains are concerned, questions those narratives, then it may be argued that Weiss's *Die Ermittlung* stands in similar relation to the dominant paradigms of GDR historiography. Considering the victims first, it is perhaps the most remarkable feature of *Die Ermittlung* that, despite Weiss's own Jewish heritage (Weiss's father was Jewish, making him, in Nazi terms, a *Halbjude*), the word 'Jude' is to be found nowhere in the play. Although the '6 Millionen / aus rassischen Gründen Getöteten' (*Ermittlung*, pp. 195–6) are recorded at the end, earlier references to Jewish victims are extremely veiled: one guard allegedly yelled 'Los an die Wand Sarah' (*Ermittlung*, p. 113) before shooting a woman prisoner (Sarah being the name added to the passports of all Jewish women after 1939); the term 'Bunkerjakob' is used; and Defendant 8 (Hofmann) offers the illogical defence that, although he selected prisoners for the gas chambers, he personally was not anti-Semitic:

> Ich persönlich hatte gar nichts
> gegen diese Leute
> Die gab es ja auch bei uns zuhause
> Ehe sie abgeholt wurden
> habe ich immer zu meiner Familie gesagt
> Kauft nur weiter bei dem Krämer
> das sind ja auch Menschen (*Ermittlung*, p. 21)

In contrast to this, it is explicitly stated that the gas Cyclon B was first tested on Russian prisoners of war and that at least some of those held were left-wing political prisoners. This fading out of the Jews is very different from typical West German accounts of the Holocaust, which, like *Der Stellvertreter*, tended to dwell almost exclusively on that group. It is, however, broadly in line with the GDR approach, which was prone, in historiographical writings and in documents such as the brochures produced for those former camps which were on its soil, to make only passing reference to the massive Jewish death-toll and to celebrate instead the heroism of the communist resistance.[33]

Witness 3, who admits that he was imprisoned on political rather than racial grounds, introduces the subject of heroism when he tells of resistance within Auschwitz – something which GDR writing frequently stressed, most notably in the case of the supposed self-liberation of Buchenwald. In *Die Ermittlung* resistance is depicted as the preserve of the political prisoners, and consists of ensuring that written records of atrocities are kept and trying to uphold that solidarity which in a desperate situation is the last form of resistance – helping each other to stay alive in the hope that someone will survive to tell the story. This heroic determination is played off against the passivity which supposedly characterized the (implicitly Jewish) majority:

> Verstört und stumm
> gingen sie den letzten Weg
> und ließen sich töten
> weil sie nichts verstanden
> Wir nennen sie Helden
> doch ihr Tod war sinnlos (*Ermittlung*, p. 86)

The political prisoners' support of each other also contrasts starkly with the selfishness of Witness 5, who proclaims that one had to be crafty to survive, who admits to taking food from those who were too weak to eat, and adapted without remorse to the inhumanity of the camp regime (*Ermittlung*, pp. 37–9).

Whereas Hochhuth makes no attempt whatever to explain why the Holocaust came about, Weiss allows Witness 3 to do so in a surprising, somewhat unorthodox manner which ultimately overlaps with but is far from homologous with the standard Marxist interpretation and is certainly not based on evidence given at the Frankfurt trial. Describing the awkward moral position of the *Funktionshäftlinge* (such as himself) who effectively helped to run the camp, Witness 3 observes, 'Der Unterschied zwischen uns / und dem Lagerpersonal war geringer / als unsere Verschiedenheit von denen / die draußen waren'. Asked to elucidate further, he continues:

> Viele von denen die dazu bestimmt wurden
> Häftlinge darzustellen
> waren aufgewachsen unter den selben Begriffen
> wie diejenigen
> die in die Rolle der Bewacher gerieten
> Sie hatten sich eingesetzt für die gleiche Nation
> und für den gleichen Aufschwung und Gewinn
> und wären sie nicht zum Häftling ernannt worden
> hätten auch sie einen Bewacher abgeben können (*Ermittlung*, p. 85)

This is a deeply problematic speech, above all because the use of the passive voice and of verbs such as 'geraten' suggests the primacy of an impersonal system over the character and volition of the individuals within it, thereby seemingly shelving the issue of complicity and shifting the focus away from the investigation of criminal guilt, with which the Auschwitz trial was centrally concerned. It could be argued that the sense of arbitrariness reflects Weiss's own experience of growing up outside the Jewish community because of his non-Jewish mother but then being 'cast' as a *Halbjude* as a result of the Nuremberg Race Laws. However, the issue is more complex than this. On the one hand, the references to profit and expansion anticipate the Marxist explanation of the Holocaust which indeed follows this speech; on the other hand, the extended theatrical metaphor focuses attention on a socio-psychological dynamic that has no essential connection with capitalism and hints in the last two lines at possibly universal human characteristics.

The emphasis on role-play echoes an emblematic incident in Weiss's strongly autobiographical novel *Fluchtpunkt* (1962) in which the narrator recalls being amongst a group of boys acting out parts inspired by the film *Ben Hur*. He and another Jewish boy played the galley-slaves:

> War saßen auf einem Brett und bewegten uns vor und zurück an imaginären Rudern. Das Leiden meines Freundes begann, als er mich zum Aufseher ernannte und ich die Peitsche über ihm schwingen mußte. Als die Verfolger zu uns eindrangen, war ich schon bereit, auf ihre Seite überzugehen, und der Galeerensklave wurde unser Opfer. Aus Dankbarkeit, daß man mich verschonte, daß man diesmal einen anderen gewählt hatte, ergriff ich die Partei der Stärkeren und überbot sie an Grausamkeit.

From this the narrator concludes 'daß ich auf der Seite der Verfolger und Henker stehen konnte. Ich hatte das Zeug in mir, an einer Exekution teilzunehmen.'[34] This passage, like the above excerpt from *Die Ermittlung*, suggests a universal capacity for brutality and registers that the Jews invariably seem to be cast as victims, but does not explain why. In other words, Weiss, like Hochhuth, seems at a loss to explain the specificity of the Jewish Holocaust.

By reproducing the trial situation in *Die Ermittlung*, Weiss ostensibly creates an emphasis on individual responsibility akin to that which is at issue in *Der Stellvertreter*. In *Die Ermittlung*, as in Frankfurt, the plea of *Befehlsnotstand* is firmly rejected, as is the argument, put forward in the 'Gesang vom Phenol', that the doctors and orderlies who carried out 'Abspritzungen' were no more reprehensible than the *Häftlingsärzte* forced to work alongside them. However, this insistence on a distinction between the two groups stands in contradiction to the argument put forward by Witness 3, who proposes precisely that interchangeability of roles rejected in the 'Gesang vom Phenol' and considers not only agency but also structure.

According to Witness 3, it is the capitalist system which has allotted the roles in this brutal and volatile society. Using him as a mouthpiece, Weiss simplifies the Marxist theory of fascism as a product of late capitalism and makes it less historically specific by focusing on the principle of exploitation 'in der der Ausbeutende in bisher unbekanntem Grad / seine Herrschaft entwickeln durfte / und der Ausgebeutete / noch sein eigenes Knochenmehl / liefern mußte' (*Ermittlung*, p. 86). Shorn of their hair and robbed of every possession, those prisoners not immediately gassed were worked to death by German industrial concerns, only then to have their teeth removed, their fat used for soap, and their ashes spread on icy roads. Immediately condemned by the defence counsel in *Die Ermittlung* as 'ein schiefes ideologisches Bild', this is nevertheless the only explanation offered in the play. That the word 'Auschwitz', like the word 'Jude', is never explicitly used further facilitates the generalization that 'das Lager besteht weiter' (*Ermittlung*, p. 88) and the implicit indictment of the Federal Republic.

Just as Weiss uses juxtaposition in order to show up the political prisoners in a good light, so his indictment of capitalism is strengthened by being set alongside the immense courage of Lili Tofler, the only victim to be named in *Die Ermittlung* and for Weiss the epitome of 'das Anständig-Menschliche'.[35] As one of the few individual murders to which there were sufficient witnesses for a defendant (Boger) to be found guilty, the case of Lili Tofler is mentioned on at least six occasions in Bernd Naumann's account of the Frankfurt trial, from which Weiss drew much of his material.[36] There too she acquires emblematic status, having been caught smuggling a letter to a male prisoner and refused to reveal his name, even under torture. In *Die Ermittlung* Weiss highlights her humanity in two ways: firstly, by juxtaposing her story at the centre of the play with that of Unterscharführer Stark, the pathetic product of SS indoctrination who claims he was robbed of the ability to think for himself; and secondly, by including in the 'Gesang vom Ende der Lili Tofler' practically all the information which is given about Auschwitz as an industrial site. The testimony of the head of the IG Farben 'Pflanzenstation' in which she worked, including the chilling 'Lili Tofler war keine von den Spitzenkräften' (*Ermittlung*, p. 103), is to be found at the same point in Naumann's account; but the cross-examination of a former leading industrialist which is included in the middle section of the 'Gesang' is only connected with the fate of Lili Tofler insofar as the spectator is willing to view her as the victim of a system in which economics had primacy over politics. In the Frankfurt trial this particular exchange was part of an unrelated investigation into conditions at the Monowitz labour camp which, significantly, was instigated by the East German *Nebenkläger* Kaul. It is indicative of the extent to which the trial itself was affected by the antagonisms of the Cold War that Kaul's conclusions provoked what Naumann calls 'stereotyper Widerspruch' from the West German defence counsel, Laternser.[37]

Although, in writing about the exploitation of slave labour in Auschwitz, Weiss was essentially only reproducing evidence that had been adduced during the trial in Frankfurt, West German commentators were incensed by the connections he made, the conclusions he suggested, and the fact that he raised such contentious issues within a play which had all the trappings of a requiem. To cite but one of many furious responses, Günther Zehm protested in *Die Welt* that 'das klebrige oratorienhafte Ritual' combined with the incontrovertible nature of most of the evidence to make *Die Ermittlung* 'kein Prozeß, sondern – eine Gehirnwäsche'.[38] Although commentators have occasionally suggested that, if the play is insufficiently abridged, receptivity can give way to boredom, there can, I think, be little doubt that, as a solemn representation of the Holocaust, *Die Ermittlung* is enormously successful. By putting the trial rather than the camp itself on stage, Weiss avoids the *Theaterkitsch* to which the final act of *Der Stellvertreter* falls victim; he achieves a form of emplotment which conveys the anonymity of the victims and underlines their suffering discreetly and without sentimentality; the bare, unadorned verse of the witnesses displays dignity and restraint, while the defendants are condemned not only by the factual evidence against them but also by their more colourful, less controlled linguistic idiom and unthinking use of euphemistic jargon.

Whereas many West German critics felt that the moral and empathetic responses of the audience were being abused, from the GDR point of view *Die Ermittlung* was the perfect requiem for the victims of the Holocaust: it defined them appropriately, commemorated their sufferings in a dignified manner, and presented the causes in a way that also pointed to the dubious foundations on which the West German *Wirtschaftswunder* was built. It is a sign of official approval that the reading of the play held in the Deutsche

Akademie der Künste in East Berlin on 19 October 1965 was accorded the status of a *Staatsakt*: the cast included not only Helene Weigel but also the historian and *Kulturpolitiker* Alexander Abusch, the theatre director Ernst Busch, and the writers Stephan Hermlin and Bruno Apitz. That several of those who participated had been victims of Nazi persecution, either as Jews or on political grounds, added to the poignancy of the occasion, legitimizing it in the same way as the anti-fascist credentials of the political elites in the GDR could be cited to legitimize the claim that it, rather than the Federal Republic, was the genuinely anti-fascist state.

For East German commentators, the solemn act of remembrance in *Die Ermittlung* was inseparable from its current political relevance. This is nowhere clearer than in a review by Ernst Schuhmacher:

> Mir will scheinen, das Stück kann nicht oft genug aufgeführt werden, besonders in der Bundesrepublik.... Wenn die Bürger der DDR sich sagen können: *Die Opfer leben unter uns*, so muß den Bürgern Westdeutschlands zu Bewußtsein kommen: *die Mörder leben unter ihnen.*[39]

By internalizing the victim and externalizing the perpetrator in this way, Schuhmacher offers GDR audiences a guilt-free interpretation of the past which coincides with key tenets of the socialist state – that the ordinary people (in Marxist terminology the workers and peasants) knew nothing of the crimes perpetrated in their name, and that some of those responsible were still at large in the West. In so doing he exploits that fact that the Federal Republic was only able to try suspects living under its jurisdiction and wilfully misinterprets *Die Ermittlung*. For, rather than confirming the myth of innocence, Weiss allows Witness 3 to enumerate the many levels of popular complicity: from camp personnel and railway workers, secretaries and administrators, down to the many bystanders who watched the evictions and deportations. Whereas GDR historians did not begin to abandon the myth of innocence until Kurt Pätzold highlighted public indifference to the fate of the Jews in the early 1980s,[40] Weiss genuinely problematized the issue in 1965. Indeed, it is here and in his tentative exploration of mentalities that Weiss most clearly rejects the monumental simplicity of the Marxist paradigm and opens up more complex perspectives.

An indication of the extent to which both *Der Stellvertreter* and *Die Ermittlung* won official approval in the GDR can be found in Walter Ulbricht's speech to the Eleventh Plenum of the Central Committee of the SED, held in December 1965. At a time when GDR cultural policy was becoming more hardline and the malign influence of western youth culture was harshly condemned, he told delegates: 'Die Schriftsteller Weiss und Hochhuth haben sich mit dem Volk verbunden. Sie verkündeten von der Bühne die große Wahrheit unseres Zeitalters.'[41] In singling out Hochhuth (whose play was then still to be premièred in the GDR) and Weiss (whose *Marat/Sade* had also been well received there), Ulbricht both gloried in the fact that an anti-capitalist message was being proclaimed on the West German stage and implicitly castigated GDR writers for failing to produce works of similar calibre.

This lionization returns us to the question whether *Der Stellvertreter* and *Die Ermittlung*, by dint of being performed in both Germanies, succeeded in overcoming the divisions of the Cold War era or merely underlined them: did the theatre make a positive contribution to the process of *Vergangenheitsbewältigung*, or were both plays simply susceptible to various forms of political instrumentalization? Certainly, it was possible for *Bühnenfassungen* of *Der Stellvertreter* to be very different: if the role of the Doctor was reduced and his character rendered more human, Hochhuth's metaphysical interpretation of the Holocaust, which was in many respects consonant with West German historiography, gave way, at the very least, to a more pragmatic view of human brutality and institutional complicity. In a thoroughgoing Marxist reading of the play, the focus of criticism partially shifted from the Pope to the heroic but isolated resisters who mistakenly pinned their hopes on him. The abridged version of *Die Ermittlung* produced by Burkhardt Lindner in 1988 and performed in the Paulskirche in Frankfurt on the fiftieth anniversary of Reichskristallnacht demonstrated likewise that it was very possible to create out of Weiss's political drama the ritual act of remembrance inducing ill-defined feelings of shame which many West German commentators would have liked it to be from the outset.[42]

While it is clear that in certain respects both *Der Stellvertreter* and *Die Ermittlung* reflected prevailing historiographical paradigms and therefore had a potential to confirm preconceived ideas, they also pointedly challenged them. The trial setting of *Die Ermittlung* automatically ensured that the Nazi past was presented as an issue in the present and enabled Weiss to explore the relationship between the two. Although he did so in such a way as to make anti-Semitism little more than a by-product of capitalist exploitation, thereby allowing his audience to see the victims neither as Jews nor, with the sole exception of Lili Tofler, as individuals, *Die Ermittlung* nevertheless conveys the horror and magnitude of the crimes committed at Auschwitz with a unique immediacy. Furthermore, Weiss deviated substantially from the monumental simplicity of 1960s GDR propaganda in his presentation of individual and popular complicity, his play demonstrating beyond dispute that a wide-ranging, analytical treatment of the Holocaust is not beyond the scope of the theatre.

If one accepts the theological reading of *Der Stellvertreter* as dominant, Hochhuth makes the events of 1942–43 into a *Legende*, far in the past; he can suggest its connection with the present only in his notes and stage directions – information which is unfortunately not accessible to the theatregoer. However, the self-reflexivity of Hochhuth's historiography and the composite nature of the historical perspective – in particular, the variety of potential villains on offer in *Der Stellvertreter* – provocatively highlight the element of emplotment within the text, thus encouraging both spectator and reader to reflect on the very process of representing the past. Although one might object that, despite attempting to offer a comprehensive overview of the situation, Hochhuth depicts largely unrepresentative victims of the Holocaust in such a way as to provoke an empathetic rather than an analytical response, this does not negate the value of empathy *per se*; in his choice of method if not of subjects, Hochhuth indeed anticipates the techniques that were to be used to great effect in the American television series *Holocaust*.

Notes

1 Fritz. J. Raddatz (ed.), *Summa iniuria oder Durfte der Papst schweigen? Hochhuths 'Stellvertreter' in der öffentlichen Kritik* (Reinbek bei Hamburg: Rowohlt, 1963); Reinhold Grimm, Willy Jäggi and Hans Oesch (eds), *Der Streit um Hochhuths 'Stellvertreter'* (Basel and Stuttgart: Basilius Presse, 1963); Eric Bentley (ed.) *The Storm over the Deputy: Essays and Articles about Hochhuth's Explosive Drama* (New York: Grove Press, 1964); Hans Rudolf Tschopp-Brunner, *Kritische Bemerkungen zum 'Stellvertreter': Theater und Verantwortung* (Basel: the author, 1963); Josef-Matthias Görgen, *Pius XII: Katholische Kirche in Hochhuths 'Stellvertreter'* (Buxheim: Martin Verlag, 1964).

2 To my knowledge, the only earlier depiction of a concentration camp on the German stage was Hedda Zinner's *Ravensbrücker Ballade*, a somewhat melodramatic account of solidarity and resistance amongst women (especially political) prisoners, premièred at the Volksbühne in East Berlin on 6 October 1961.

3 For a detailed historiographical overview see Ian Kershaw, *The Nazi Dictatorship: Problems and Perspectives of Interpretation*, 3rd edn (London: Edward Arnold, 1993); and Mary Fulbrook, *German National Identity after the Holocaust* (Cambridge: Polity Press, 1999).

4 For a briefer study of the play see Judith Beniston, 'History and the Holocaust in Hochhuth's *Der Stellvertreter*', in Steve Giles and Peter Graves (eds), *From Classical Shades to Vickers Victorious: Shifting Perspectives in British German Studies* (Berne: Lang, 1999), pp. 111–22.

5 In the 1972 edition of his *Dramen*, Hochhuth put square brackets around non-essential lines but these cuts save minutes rather than hours; every production has been obliged to omit whole scenes.

6 Erwin Piscator, 'Vorwort' to Rolf Hochhuth, *Der Stellvertreter* (Reinbek bei Hamburg: Rowohlt, 1963), pp. 7–10 (p. 10). References to this volume will henceforth be given in the text as (*Stellvertreter*, page).

7 Hellmuth Karasek, 'Hintertreppe zum Vatikan: Hochhuths "Stellvertreter" bei Piscator in Berlin', *Deutsche Zeitung*, 23 February 1963, p. 24.

8 Rolf Hochhuth, interview with Friedrich Luft, 'Das Profil', *Fernsehen I*, 21 March 1965; transcript included in Inszenierungsdokumentation *Der Stellvertreter* am Deutschen Theater, Berlin 1966, Stiftung Archiv der Akademie der Künste Berlin, Arbeitsbereich Theaterdokumentation, 16 pages (p. 7).

9 Peter Weiss, *Die Ermittlung* (Frankfurt am Main: Suhrkamp, 1965), p. 101. References to this work will henceforth be given in the text as (*Ermittlung*, page).

10 See Andreas Dorpalen, *German History in Marxist Perspective: The East German Approach* (London: I. B. Tauris, 1985), pp. 394–5.

11 Hannah Arendt, *Eichmann in Jerusalem: A Report on the Banality of Evil* (Harmondsworth: Penguin, 1994; first pub. 1963).

12 Egon Schwarz, 'Rolf Hochhuths "Der Stellvertreter"', in Walter Hinck (ed.), *Rolf Hochhuth – Eingriff in die Zeitgeschichte: Essays zum Werk* (Reinbek bei Hamburg: Rowohlt, 1981), pp. 117–47 (p. 137).

13 Willy Haas, 'Hochhuths "Stellvertreter" – Legende und Historie', in Grimm, Jäggi and Oesch (eds), *Der Streit um Hochhuths 'Stellvertreter'*, pp. 23–33 (pp. 28–9).

14 Klemens von Klemperer, 'The Solitary Witness: No Mere Footnote to Resistance Studies', in David Clay Large (ed.), *Contending with Hitler: Varieties of German Resistance in the Third Reich* (Cambridge: Cambridge University Press, 1991), pp. 129–39 (p. 130); on resistance more generally see Kershaw, *Nazi Dictatorship*, pp. 150–79.

15 Kurt Gerstein, 'Augenzeugenbericht zu den Massenvergasungen', ed. Hans Rothfels, *Vierteljahreshefte für Zeitgeschichte*, vol. 1 (1953), pp. 177–94; reproduced in Léon Poliakov and Josef Wulf, *Das dritte Reich und die Juden. Dokumente und Aufsätze* (Berlin-Grunewald: Arani, 1955), pp. 101–15.

16 Prompted by *Der Stellvertreter*, a biography of Gerstein appeared in an 'Evangelische Zeitbuchreihe' soon after the première: Helmut Franz, *Kurt Gerstein: Außenseiter des Widerstandes der Kirche gegen Hitler* (Zurich: EVZ-Verlag, 1964).

17 Karena Niehoff, 'Papst Pius XII als Schauspielfigur', *Stuttgarter Nachrichten*, 25 February 1963, p. 7.

18 Rolf Hochhuth, 'Herr oder Knecht der Geschichte? Ein Interview', in Hinck (ed.), *Rolf Hochhuth – Eingriff in die Zeitgeschichte*, pp. 9–17 (p. 10).

19 For an overview of GDR reception see Hetty Burgers, 'Die "Stellvertreter"-Rezeption in der DDR: Zur Rezeption der einen Literatur im anderen Deutschland', in Jos Hoogeveen and Hans Würzner (eds), *Ideologie und Literatur(wissenschaft)* (Amsterdam: Rodopi, 1986), pp. 167–207. The first four productions are reviewed in Rainer Kerndl, 'Wider die Gleichgültigen. Zu vier Inszenierungen von Rolf Hochhuths "Stellvertreter" in der DDR', *Neues Deutschland*, 11 March 1966; and Horst Gebhardt, 'Nur Auseinandersetzung mit der Vergangenheit?', *Theater der Zeit*, 1966/8, pp. 16–19, 31.

20 Carl Amery, 'Der bedrängte Papst', *Süddeutsche Zeitung*, 2/3 March 1963; in Raddatz (ed.), *Summa*, pp. 84–91 (p. 90).

21 Erich Engel, *Schriften. Über Theater und Film* (Berlin: Henschelverlag Kunst und Gesellschaft, 1971), p. 112.

22 'Zur Aufführungskonzeption *Der Stellvertreter*', Inszenierungsdokumentation *Der Stellvertreter* am Deutschen Theater, Berlin 1966, Stiftung Archiv der Akademie der Künste Berlin, Arbeitsbereich Theaterdokumentation, p. 12. The documentation also reveals that the GDR theatres which mounted early productions of the play exchanged such dramaturgical materials.

23 'Aufführungskonzeption', p. 14.

24 Werner Mittenzwei, 'Die vereinsamte Position eines Erfolgreichen: Der Weg des Dramatikers Rolf Hochhuth', *Sinn und Form*, vol. 6 (1974), pp. 1248–72 (p. 1250); the essay was reprinted in the Reclam (Leipzig) edition of *Der Stellvertreter* in 1975. For a comparison of *Der Stellvertreter* and Schiller's *Don Carlos* see R. C. Perry, 'Historical Authenticity and Dramatic Form: Hochhuth's *Der Stellvertreter* and Weiss's *Die Ermittlung*', *Modern Language Review*, vol. 64 (1969), pp. 828–39 (pp. 830–1).

25 Joachim Kaiser, 'Plädoyer gegen das Theater-Auschwitz', *Süddeutche Zeitung*, 4/5 September 1965.

26 Ibid.

27 Erasmus Schöfer, 'Plädoyer für eine ungewöhnliche Gelegenheit', *Rheinische Post*, 9 October 1965.

28 For reviews of this production see Gerd Weinrich, *Peter Weiss: 'Die Ermittlung'* (Frankfurt am Main: Diesterweg, 1983), pp. 58–60.

29 Siegfried Melchinger, 'Auschwitz auf dem Theater?', *Stuttgarter Zeitung*, 11 September 1965.

30 As late as 1985, Martin Broszat's plea for a 'historicization' of the Nazi era was extremely controversial. See Kershaw, *Nazi Dictatorship*, pp. 180–7.

31 Thomas von Vegesack, 'Die Unmöglichkeit der Neutralität. Interview mit Peter Weiss. Ende Mai/Anfang Juni 1965', in Rainer Gerlach and Matthias Richter (eds), *Peter Weiss im Gespräch* (Frankfurt am Main: Suhrkamp, 1986), pp. 77–81 (p. 78).

32 H. D. Sander, 'Das Ende eines "dritten Weges": Peter Weiss und seine politischen Metamorphosen', *Die Welt*, 18 September 1965. Peter Weiss, '10 Arbeitspunkte eines Autors in der geteilten Welt', is included in Weiss, *Rapporte 2* (Frankfurt am Main: Suhrkamp, 1971), pp. 14–23; his speech 'Partisanen der Wahrheit' appeared in *Neues Deutschland*, 21 May 1965.

33 See Fulbrook, *German National Identity after the Holocaust*, pp. 28–35.

34 Peter Weiss, *Fluchtpunkt* (Frankfurt am Main: Suhrkamp, 1962), pp. 16–17.

35 'Gespräch mit Peter Weiss, August 1965', in Karlheinz Braun (ed.), *Materialien zu Peter Weiss' 'Marat/Sade'* (Frankfurt am Main: Suhrkamp, 1967), pp. 102–11 (p. 106).

36 Bernd Naumann, *Auschwitz: Bericht über die Strafsache gegen Mulka und andere vor dem Schwurgericht Frankfurt* (Frankfurt am Main: Athenäum, 1965). The book was based on reports published in the *Frankfurter Allgemeine Zeitung*. On Weiss's use of source material see Erika Salloch, *Peter Weiss' 'Die Ermittlung': Zur Struktur des Dokumentartheaters* (Frankfurt am Main: Athenäum, 1972), pp. 87–126. Another detailed analysis of the play, which includes a section on '"Die Ermittlung" im geteilten Deutschland' is Karl-Heinz Hartmann, 'Peter Weiss: "Die Ermittlung"', in *Deutsche Dramen: Interpretationen zu Werken von der Aufklärung bis zur Gegenwart*, 2 vols (Königstein/Ts: Athenäum, 1981), vol. II, pp. 163–83.

37 Naumann, *Auschwitz*, p. 448.

38 Günther Zehm, 'Gehirnwäsche auf der Bühne', *Die Welt*, 25 October 1965.

39 Ernst Schuhmacher, 'Die Opfer sind unter uns – die Mörder unter ihnen', (East) *Berliner Zeitung*, 21 October 1965, p. 6; italics in original. In the Suhrkamp edition of *Die Ermittlung* a retitled version of this article appears (without this section) as a representative East German response (*Ermittlung*, pp. 211–33).

40 Fulbrook, *German National Identity after the Holocaust*, pp. 133, 136–7.

41 Elimar Schubbe (ed.), *Dokumente zur Kunst-, Literatur- und Kulturkritik der SED* (Stuttgart: Seewald, 1972), p. 1087.

42 See Burkhardt Lindner, *Im Inferno: 'Die Ermittlung' von Peter Weiss* (Badenweiler: Oase Verlag, 1988).

6

'Du bist in einem Mörderhaus': representing German history through the *Märchen* of 'Blaubart' and 'Der Räuberbräutigam, in works by Dieter Hildebrandt and Helma Sanders-Brahms

Mererid Puw Davies

The stories so far

In the tale of 'Bluebeard', a young woman, under persuasion or coercion, and most often with misgivings or reluctance, marries a wealthy older man. He has a mysterious blue beard and in some versions an enigmatic marital history too, in that many of his young wives have inexplicably disappeared. After the wedding, Bluebeard's bride lives in his well-appointed home, and soon Bluebeard announces that he must go away, leaving his wife with the keys and freedom to look in every room but one. However, the bride succumbs to the temptation of looking into that forbidden room, to find it filled with the decapitated or dismembered corpses of Bluebeard's previous wives. In her horror, she drops the key to the room in the blood on the floor. That bloodstain on the key is evidence of the woman's disobedience, so that on Bluebeard's disconcertingly sudden return, he prepares to murder her. Happily however, the bride is usually saved by the intervention of her siblings and the summary execution of Bluebeard at their hands.

In the closely related, variant tale 'Der Räuberbräutigam', a miller promises his daughter's hand to a rich suitor, but she feels 'ein Grauen in ihrem Herzen' at the thought of her prospective bridegroom. The stranger invites his fiancée to visit his home in the dark woods and strews ashes along the path so that she may find her way. When the young woman follows the path, she too marks the path by scattering peas and lentils behind her. When she arrives at her bridegroom's house, a bird warns her to turn back, saying: 'du bist in einem Mörderhaus'. The bride nonetheless enters the house to find it deserted, but for an old woman, who informs her that this is the home of cannibal robbers. However, the old woman takes pity on the heroine and hides her. When the robber bridegroom and his gang return, the heroine observes them poisoning a captive girl, and stripping, dismembering, salting and eating her. During this process, one of the victim's fingers, with a golden ring on it, flies off into the hidden bride's lap. However, the old woman dissuades the robbers from searching for the finger and serves them a sleeping potion. The two women then escape and follow the sprouting peas and lentils back to the mill. On the wedding day, each guest is asked to tell a story and the bride recounts what happened, with repeated assurances that: 'Mein Schatz, das träumte mir nur'. This dissembling strategy enables the woman to tell the whole story without awakening the robber's suspicions, so that as soon as she produces evidence in the form of the incriminating finger, he can be apprehended, handed over to the authorities and executed. The earliest known 'Bluebeard' tale emerged not in Germany but in France, in Charles Perrault's fairy-tale collection *Histoires ou contes du tems [sic] passe* (1697). Nonetheless, these tales have long had a place in German culture of the modern period too. The *Blaubartmärchen*'s popularity in Germany was reflected by its inclusion in the first edition of Jacob and Wilhelm Grimm's *Kinder- und Hausmärchen* (*KHM*) (1812) as an authentic German story. However, the Grimms later found that their 'Blaubart' resembled Perrault's 'La Barbe bleue' too closely for their taste and omitted it in all later editions in favour of the variants 'Fitchers Vogel' (*KHM* 46) and 'Der Räuberbräutigam' (*KHM* 40) (I, pp. 219–23), which they believed to be more German.[1]

Therefore, 'Blaubart' and 'Der Räuberbräutigam' are generally perceived by scholars to belong to the same category of tale, that of the *Blaubartmärchen*, since they share the motif of a murderous man and an innocent woman who narrowly escapes disaster in his house before returning to her family. Like all *Märchen*, these tales have been used throughout the modern period to reflect contemporary issues; and most prominently, the 'Bluebeard' tales with their emphasis on marriage have been used to address changing issues in gender politics.[2] However, these tales have also been used most strikingly to explore issues of German history and identity in the postwar period. A series of texts using the *Blaubartmärchen* and its variants includes Ingeborg Bachmann's fragmentary novel *Das Buch Franza*; Dieter Hildebrandt's thriller, *Blaubart Mitte 40* (1977); Helma Sanders-Brahms's film *Deutschland, bleiche Mutter* (1979); Helga Schubert's essayistic short story 'Das verbotene Zimmer' (1982); Karin Struck's novel *Blaubarts Schatten* (1991); Elisabeth Reichart's short story 'Die Kammer' (1992); Gunter Grass's novel *Ein weites Feld* (1995); Wolfgang Rohner-Radegast's prose fragment *Vetter Blaubart oder wie die wohl drüben* (1995) and Ingo Schramm's novel *Fitchers Blau* (1996).[3] These texts and films have otherwise little in common, and it cannot be assumed that their authors wrote with knowledge of one another. Therefore, the similar ways in which they use the *Blaubartmärchen* to reflect on national history and identity provide compelling evidence both that the *Märchen* is a privileged medium for representing such issues; and that the grisly *Blaubartmärchen* and its variants in particular appear to be especially useful in that regard in the postwar period.

Here, I shall examine two of these documents, *Blaubart Mitte 40* and *Deutschland, bleiche Mutter*, to assess why this might be so. These two texts provide good material for a comparative reading in that they were produced contemporaneously in West Germany; and in that each presents an emblematic West German biography, which is on one level individual, but on another symbolic.

Dieter Hildebrandt, *Blaubart Mitte 40* (1977)

Hildebrandt's apparently lightweight thriller tells the story of one Alexander Falck, a successful architectural engineer specializing in bridges and involved in a prestigious Franco-German bridge-building project. The plot concerns Falck's fantastical private life and his six girlfriends who co-exist uneasily. Falck's relationships are of stereotypical character, for instance with Annette, a GDR citizen who is involved in Stasi (East German secret police) intrigue, and Hülya, a Turkish *Gastarbeiterin* who speaks broken German and does menial work. These arrangements lead to a journalist lightheartedly identifying Falck with the *Märchen* character of Bluebeard, who was popularly thought to have had six wives, before being destroyed by a seventh. But this flippant identification takes on a more sinister character when, one by one, Falck's lovers meet unnatural deaths. However, the lady-killer Falck is not the murderer, and the novel ends dramatically with his own murder at the hands of his ex-wife Julia, whom he had planned to murder himself ten years previously. While Falck had believed that his plan of shooting Julia in a railway tunnel as she travelled by motorrail to Italy had been carried out on his behalf by his psychiatrist and lover Sarah, Julia is alive, and murders Falck using the same method.

There is a second level of narrative too in that Falck's biography emerges as flashbacks in the course of the novel, beginning in 1944 when he was conscripted into the *Wehrmacht* at the age of sixteen. The text emphasizes that Falck was not involved in fighting, let alone war crimes, but that rather, thanks to his mathematical talents, he was sent to France to help calculate the systematic destruction of bridges during the German retreat. Following his demobilization, the eighteen-year-old Falck was travelling to relatives through the Soviet-controlled zone of Germany, when his papers were stolen at a railway station. Looking back, Falck describes that event as follows:

> Ich hätte ja weitergehen ... können, aber nein: ich dachte auf gut deutsch, ohne Papiere kannst du nicht dastehn, ohne Papiere bist du nichts wert, und der einzige Kontakt mit deiner Identität ist dieser Bahnhof hier, wo man von dem Überfall weiß. Ich dachte nicht mal, daß ich sie wiederkriege; ich dachte nur: die wissen, was eben passiert ist, die müssen dir weiterhelfen mit irgendeiner Bescheinigung, einem Stempel, einem Zettel, wo mein Name draufsteht und was Russisches. (p. 156)

But this innocent request he made to officials led him straight to a Soviet prison camp, from which he was only released three years later.

These experiences account for Falck's chosen profession. He reflects retrospectively of his *Wehrmacht* duties:

> damals, er hätte es eher für unmöglich gehalten, daß er je danach aus Zahlen seinen Beruf machen könnte, aus Zahlen, die er doch nur als Destruktionschiffren kennengelernt hatte, als Zerstörungsmittel; aber dann, als er zu studieren anfing, gab es keine Frage, was. Und als er zu bauen anfing, gab es ... keine Unentschiedenheit: Brücken. Hochgespannt, weit, leicht, frei. Ein Akt des Wiedergutmachens? Bauen, um ein Trauma abzubauen? Konstruktionen gegen die früheren Ohnmächte? Brückenbau als Individualpolitik? (pp. 177–8)

Falck's love life is accounted for by the years of imprisonment, sexual deprivation and attendant trauma, but while he claims that in general: 'Man wurde krank vor Entbehrung', of himself he insists that:

> Ich war nicht kaputt wie manche. Ich hatte schwer arbeiten müssen, aber nach den ersten Monaten merkte ich, daß einem da was zuwächst an Zähigkeit. Nein, kaputt war ich nicht, nur wütend vor aufgestauter Lebensgier. (p. 157)

Thus driven by these two key events in his past, Falck was highly successful with his twin passions, bridges and women. He was offered academic posts in Germany and the US, but instead established himself independently. But after meeting Julia, he gave up polygamy and developed a relationship with her so obsessive that, when she left him, he suffered a breakdown and planned her murder, believing that he could only survive if she died. Since then, Falck embarked on his six simultaneous relationships as a compromise between promiscuity and emotional commitment.

There are many homologies with the *Blaubartmärchen* in *Blaubart Mitte 40*. Both narratives are sinister murder mysteries involving a male protagonist who has multiple relationships with women who are killed and in which an initial murder (or in Falck's case, attempted murder) provokes the deaths of a series of innocent women and ultimately the male protagonist's own summary execution through the agency of a fatal, seventh woman. Furthermore, each male protagonist has a blue beard, since Falck too has a dark beard which he shaves with a Bluebeard-type cut-throat razor, producing bluish stubble. Each protagonist is wealthy and successful, and in both narratives the interior of his house is described in detail. Finally, the texts also share the motif of journeys and travel.

On the face of it, this novel is a flimsy, extravagant account of masculine mid-life crisis, accompanied by clichéd fantasies like the harem of six highly attractive, intelligent and submissive women. That fantasy goes hand in hand with the expression of a subliminal, profound fear of the feminine and Woman. The novel stresses that women are irrational, destructive creatures, especially when not under the firm control of men, since they are described as having tentacles in their vaginas; plotting Falck's murder; resorting to scandalous lesbianism as soon as his back is turned; and so forth. As such, Hildebrandt's novel belongs in an important twentieth-century trend in Bluebeard writing by male authors, in which Bluebeard is not an ogre, but both sexually masterful hero and victim, usually of monstrous women against whom suspicion and aggression are directed.[4] But in addition, *Blaubart Mitte 40* is an interesting representation of recent national history, and Falck's biography evokes an emblematic West German identity characterized by outward success and inner complexes, thus taking on symbolic dimensions, as I shall now show.

Falck is old enough to have been traumatized by the results of the war and Soviet occupation, but too young to bear any responsibility for National Socialism, the war or its aftermath. Thus, he is an innocent German victim of war, and even more unjustly, of persecution by the Soviet Union due to his explicitly German virtue of bureaucratic 'Ordnungsliebe', expressed in his fatal desire to fill in a form. Therefore the true catastrophe he suffers is less that of National Socialism itself and its consequences, than the consequences of the defeat of Nazi Germany in 1945 and the arrival of the Allies, who make Falck into a victim – a beloved and widespread self-stylization in postwar West Germany. Furthermore, Falck's loss of his papers and its consequences echoes the West German founding myth of the *Stunde Null*, where all past identity and hence responsibility were lost.

However, just as the devastation of the *Stunde Null* preceded the spectacular reconstruction of West German identity and society, so too does Alexander Falck overcome this unjust start to his adulthood and become involved in heroic projects of reconstruction, conquest (*nomen est omen*) and the domination of his environment.[5] Falck stresses that 'schwer arbeiten müssen' in the prison camp was a formative experience, just as the ability to work hard became a fundamental virtue in the reconstruction of West German identity. In studying in the early postwar years, Falck is part of the (re-)construction of a West German generation of intellectuals supposedly unburdened by the ideology of the past; and in setting up in business, he stands too for a brave new generation of equally unburdened capitalists. Falck receives academic support in the US in an intellectual variant on the historical Marshall Plan, showing where West German intellectual and geopolitical alleigances lay. And as an engineer, Falck is literally involved in the *Wiederaufbau* of the state's architectural and logistical fabric. He is involved in the reconstruction of relationships with France in particular, since his major project is a Franco-German bridge, just as diplomatic relations with France were a keystone of West German state policy.

Finally, Falck's prodigious love life too is linked to such confident projects of reconstruction, since it correlates with his other successes and stands for a sexualized self-assertion towards 'others', in terms of gender (women); other countries (his foreign girlfriends); 'others' within Germany (Hülya);

and East Germany (Annette and her Stasi contacts). In other words, Falck's amorous success is symbolic of West Germany's reassertion of its status in international 'affairs'. It is no coincidence that, just like the bridges he builds on which one can travel, Falck's relationships permit 'Verkehr' in more than one sense of the word – not only sexually, but in terms of physical mobility and social intercourse too, both inside and outside Germany. Thus, Falck's sexual and concomitant social and physical mobility appear to be attempted compensation for the years of deprivation and immobility in the Soviet camp, which began at the end of the war when Falck's freedom of movement was symbolically halted at the railway station where his papers were stolen. Just like the bridges he builds, then, 'Verkehr' with his partners symbolizes Falck's desire to overcome his past.

In short, therefore, the emblematic, idealized West German self-image for which Falck stands begins with a clean slate in 1945, is predicated on an assertive, mobile and emphatically masculine subject, and is youthful, confident and energetic in both moral and architectural reconstruction. However, the novel does not stop at this anodyne, exculpatory fantasy of national identity and history. Rather, it problematizes it, demonstrating where its fissures lie.

In fact, the novel shows that Falck is in no way consistently invincible or innocent, but rather that he is haunted by his past and its consequences. These pressures destroy others, and finally him. After Soviet captivity, the second catastrophic turning point in Falck's biography is the end of his marriage in breakdown and attempted murder so that his apparently brilliant history masks psychological disturbance and profound, unresolved aggression. That aggression is directed not only at Julia, but more obliquely too at the women who die by violence as a result of associating with Falck, and ultimately leads to his own (self-)destruction at Julia's hands. Because of Falck's once-symbiotic relationship link to Julia, we can interpret her as an image of his past self, so that in the last analysis Falck's amorous schemes are ultimately destructive and frustrated by his own past. Or in other words, Julia's re-emergence in the plot embodies a return of the repressed: that is, of Falck's own vengeful, murderous fantasies, since she carries out precisely the murder he had planned for her.

If we understand Falck as a personification of the West German dream, then these dark elements in the plot must also symbolize more nightmarish elements in West German history and identity. As was acknowledged in the late 1960s by Alexander and Margarete Mitscherlich, the bright West German success story personified here by Alexander Falck indeed had a dark obverse.[6] The Mitscherlichs analysed Germany's crippling collapse of identity at the end of the war, with the loss of the National Socialist ideal and of the identificatory figure of the Führer himself.[7] The Mitscherlichs argued that the trauma of that unacknowledged loss and guilt drove the massive efforts underpinning the *Wirtschaftswunder*, yet generated an underlying collective depression and neurosis. Similarly, Falck himself admits that his sexual and professional ambitions are driven by trauma – a trauma which began not with Nazism, but rather with the defeat and symbolic loss of identity which he suffers at the railway station. There, with the loss of his papers, Falck loses the guarantee of his irreproachable national identity, and the Soviet authorities fail to compensate him for that loss. Indeed, they inflict on him the stigma of German crimes which he did not commit, and punish him for them. Despite this traumatic foundation, Falck denies all responsibility, or that he was 'kaputt' after his experiences. Given the Mitscherlich's arguments, it is therefore unsurprising that Falck's activities have an obsessive tinge and end in breakdown and disaster. Precisely his obsessive 'Verkehr', in all senses, his fatal sexual and professional hyperactivity, can be understood as a compulsive denial of his trauma.

Given this, it is most interesting that Falck's plans for freedom of movement by means of bridges and sophisticated transport should be consistently frustrated, since most frequently it is while or after travelling that mishaps occur to him and his girlfriends. Indeed, it is in trying to reach Italy, that traditional locus of escape from Germany, German identity and the German past (and through a symbolic masterpiece of engineering, the Alpine tunnel, to boot) that Falck is killed. That is, the legacy of his past, German self literally prevents him from leaving Germany and reaching Italy; and ultimately destroys him, just as Bluebeard is finally destroyed.

So if Falck is a personification of West German success, the novel reveals the dark side of that apparently successfully reconstructed identity and the intertext of the *Blaubartmärchen* plays a key role in that deconstruction, since that dark side is highlighted by the references to Bluebeard, a wealthy, powerful man with skeletons in his closet which threaten his outward success. Much the same might be said of the West German self-image analysed by the Mitscherlichs. While West German history did not live up to the apocalyptic prophecy of the *Märchen*, the identification of Falck not only with Alexander the Great but also with Bluebeard, a man with a history of aggression and a haunting past, nonetheless stresses that in 1977 the German past was an unresolved, uncanny and disruptive presence.

Helma Sanders-Brahms, *Deutschland, bleiche Mutter* (1980)

More explicitly than *Blaubart Mitte 40*, *Deutschland, bleiche Mutter* is part of that trend of the 1970s and 1980s in which a new generation of Germans examined both the National Socialist past and their relationships with their parents.[8] In this film Sanders-Brahms creates a fictionalized account of her mother Lene's life from around 1933 onwards. Lene shows interest neither in Party membership nor in the deportation of her Jewish neighbours, and marries the equally apolitical Hans. However, history intervenes when Hans is sent to the Polish front in 1939. Lene and her young daughter Anna learn independence during the war, but with the return of peace and Hans, Lene's life becomes unbearable, partly because her formerly gentle husband has become hardened and authoritarian. Lene's suffering is marked by severe psychosomatic facial paralysis and deterioration in her family relationships, and the film ends with her attempted suicide, from which she is dissuaded by Anna. Anna is particularly important in the film because she is also its adult narrator, intervening in voice-overs. That device stresses that she, as Sanders-Brahm's own fictional persona, is self-consciously constructing and reconstructing her parents' story, rather than merely reproducing it naively.[9]

It has been argued that the film makes classic use of the topos of a bourgeois woman to represent the nation, and that Lene thus becomes an allegory of Germany itself.[10] Indeed, Lene has an emblematic West German biography which resembles Alexander Falck's in many ways. In each case, the significant segment of the biography begins in the National Socialist period, with a particular emphasis on the Second World War. While each figure is an 'Aryan' German, their involvement in National Socialism is portrayed as reluctant, minimal or passive. Therefore, they seem to have little involvement in the historical events of 1933–45; and in both cases too, those Germans who did bear serious historical responsibility are absent from the texts, thus locating such moral responsibility beyond the individual spheres in which Lene and Falck live. Indeed, these two protagonists come close to being stylized as victims both of the German political class which provoked those events, and of the Allied forces which later occupied Germany. And both figures after 1945 embody certain founding myths of West German reconstruction in quite literal ways: Lene is a *Trümmerfrau* and Falck a successful, Western-oriented engineer. However, Sanders-Brahms's text differs from Hildebrandt's in that it exposes more explicitly and critically the way in which the film-maker believed that women paid a higher price than men for the Economic Miracle. Thus Lene's story too reveals the fissures in the apparently miraculous reconstruction of West Germany, and, like Falck's, does so partly by using a *Blaubartmärchen,* in this case 'Der Räuberbräutigam'.

In the central section of the film, Lene and Anna are bombed out of their home, becoming itinerant refugees in Pomerania. During this section, while they are wandering through a forest, Lene tells Anna 'Der Räuberbräutigam' practically verbatim from the *KHM.* While Lene tells the tale, mother and daughter find in the forest a deserted, industrial building with a tall chimney and ovens where they take shelter and the tale is continued. While Lene cannot identify this site, to the viewer its features may recall a ruined extermination camp. Lene and Anna then move on and the *Märchen* is continued after Lene is raped by two American soldiers. The tale is finally completed as mother and daughter ride illicitly on a train, and these scenes are interpolated with documentary footage of the wartime destruction of German cities.

Sanders-Brahms has called the *Märchen* 'dies verrückte Umgetüm mitten im Film', and commented:

> Ich weiß, das geht eigentlich nicht, mitten im Film so die Form wechseln. Aber das Märchen leistet eine Menge – es beschreibt ziemlich präzise Lenes Geschichte und die deutsche Geschichte in einer sehr durchsichtigen Metapher. Außerdem hat es alle pyrotechnische Kunststückchen überflüssig gemacht. Außerdem sind Lene und Anna da auf merkwürdig intensive Weise zusammen und getrennt zugleich. Lene erzählt und erzählt, und das Kind ist zugleich verschreckt und skeptisch.[11]

In this quotation, first, Sanders-Brahms is claiming that the *Märchen* makes a statement about the historical plight of women under patriarchy. Just as the *Märchen* heroine discovers that her betrothed has a secret, murderous life, patriarchy reveals its darker side to Lene in the form of war, after which she is raped by the peacemakers and trapped in an unhappy marriage. Thus, the adult narrator Anna comments of the onset of peace: 'Das war die Wiederkehr der Wohnstuben. Da ging der Krieg innen los, als draussen Frieden war.' In short, the feminist statement is that to reinstate peace without dismantling the society which engendered war in the first place makes little or no difference to a woman who is condemned to an oppressive home.

Second, in the quotation given above, Sanders-Brahms is suggesting that the *Märchen* makes a statement about what she refers to as other aspects of 'German history': that is, among other things, the Holocaust. The scene in the *Märchen* in which the unknown young woman is captured and murdered by the robbers, while being observed by another young woman who does not intervene, resonates with one of only two other references which the film makes to the Holocaust: the deportation of Rahel, Lene's neighbour, which Lene insists on ignoring. The clothes and the gold ring plundered by the robbers from the woman's body in the *Märchen* recall the plundering of Jewish property and bodies, as highlighted by the film's other Holocaust reference, where Lene loots a deserted shop owned by Jews. Above all, however, this dimension is emphasized by the *Märchen*'s appearance in tandem with the extermination camp if we interpret that site as such. The murderer's house (the camp) is deserted in both the *Märchen* and the film, and in both narratives the female protagonist is unaware of what has happened there. Just as ashes lead the Grimms' heroine to the murderer's house, in the film too, the motif of the chimney and the cold ovens are emphasized and we can imagine the chimney blowing out ashes as a visible sign of its location while it was still in use. The sprouting peas and lentils in the *Märchen* echo the green spring landscape into which Lene and Anna depart from the camp. And in both narratives, the act of narrative itself is significant. Just as the Grimms' heroine tells what she saw and produces incriminating evidence, so too does the film's narrator, by retelling German history and producing documentary footage of wartime destruction. Effectively then, the *Märchen* reveals that

Germany itself is a 'Mörderhaus' in which not only women are silently oppressed, but the shameful secret of genocide is hidden too.

Thus, there are compelling parallels and connections not only between the *Märchen* and Lene's experiences as a woman under patriarchy, but also between the *Märchen* and the history of the Holocaust.[12] It seems to me that there are two possible ways of understanding this use of the 'Der Räuberbräutigam' in the film and the moral implications of that usage, and I shall now discuss these two readings in turn.

On an immediate viewing, the way in which the *Märchen* condenses the fate of Lene as a woman under patriarchy with that of Jews and other persecuted groups under National Socialism appears problematic for three major reasons. First, this condensation blurs issues of moral responsibility, since the victims in the *Märchen* are innocent women, and Woman/Lene thus comes to stand in metonymically for another group of victims, the Jews. But one effect of this condensation and concomitant identification of Lene with the victim of the *Märchen* appears to be the symbolic exculpation of 'Aryan' German women like Lene; and since Lene stands also for the German nation, all ordinary Germans thus come to be implicitly exculpated, or even stylized as victims, to an unjustifiable degree.[13] Of course Lene's position in the history of the Holocaust is more ambivalent than this condensation in the *Märchen* suggests. In fact, she is also to be aligned with the murderers and robbers in the tale, since it is with her passive support that the Holocaust was carried out, and more actively, too, she is guilty of looting a shop owned by the deported or fugitive Jewish Duckstein family.

Second, by making the history of the Holocaust ancillary to a narrative about women's suffering under patriarchy, as the *Märchen* seems to do, it effectively serves to erase the history of the historical victims of the Holocaust and obliquely to deny their suffering, while sympathetically stressing the suffering of a woman complicit in their persecution. And due to the structure of equation and reciprocity inherent in metaphor (saying that one thing 'is' another, or that one thing *is the same as* another), a narrative which uses suffering Woman in order to represent the Holocaust might seem to imply another, subtextual and reversed narrative in which the Holocaust, in turn, might also represent the suffering of Woman. If such a reading of Sanders-Brahms's *Märchen* is possible, then we are confronted with George Steiner's uncomfortable question as to whether using the Holocaust as a metaphor for the misfortunes of others (for example, bourgeois women) is not a 'subtle larceny', a moral crime against the victims of Auschwitz?[14]

Third, Sanders-Brahms's use of 'Der Räuberbräutigam' as a metaphor for the Holocaust runs up against what has been held by some thinkers to be one of the most profound difficulties involved in representing that series of events. This difficulty centres around the fact that representation can never be history itself, but must always be a metaphor standing in its stead. But Alvin Rosenfeld has suggested that:

> There are no metaphors for Auschwitz just as Auschwitz is not a metaphor for anything else.... Why is this the case? Because the flames were real flames, the ashes only ashes, the smoke always and only smoke.... the burnings do not lend themselves to metaphor, simile, or symbol – to likeness or association with anything else. They can only 'be' or 'mean' what in fact they were: the death of the Jews.[15]

That is to say that the use of metaphor always invests the events of the Holocaust with other, extraneous meanings, distracting from its reality. And with reference to Rosenfeld's remark, James E. Young adds that such a process of turning the Holocaust into metaphor, i.e. investing it with 'meaning', is also 'suggesting a meaning in the death of the Jews': whereas in fact, that event was devoid of anything as symbolically positive as 'meaning' (p. 90). If such arguments are followed, this objection appears to be an unsurmountable obstacle for any attempt at representing the Holocaust. However, I shall now move on to my second, alternative reading of the *Märchen* in *Deutschland, bleiche Mutter*, which indeed goes some way to addressing this problem inherent in representing the Holocaust.

At a less evident level, it seems to me that another, different reading of the *Märchen* is possible which goes beyond that which Sanders-Brahms herself suggests in her cursory explanation quoted above. On this alternative reading, moral responsibility is more clearly differentiated, and the Holocaust is referred to in a strikingly distinct way which does not confuse it with Lene's story and avoids at least some of the potential pitfalls of metaphor. In the rest of this section I shall examine how this alternative reading is produced, by (re-)exploring first the plot of the *Märchen* and what it may tell us about Lene's position in the history of the Holocaust; second, the way in which Lene herself chooses to represent the Holocaust; and finally, what I perceive to be the distinct narrative mode which the film adopts for referring to that event.

With reference to Lene's role in the *Märchen* plot, Barbara Hyams points out that, as well as the innocent victim, there is a further female figure in the *Märchen* whose role is more ambivalent (pp. 353–4). This is the old woman who lives with the robbers and knows of their crimes, yet never prevented them, raised the alarm or left. Hyams suggests that Lene need not be identified with the innocent, murdered woman in the *Märchen*, but with that old woman who is to some extent a victim of her domestic masters, but also at least passively complicit in their acts. In many ways Lene's position is closer to that of the old woman, and to identify Lene with that old woman in the *Märchen* is to account more satisfactorily for her more equivocal role in the Holocaust.

And it seems to me that Hyams's interpretation can be expanded as follows. Further evidence that Lene may be aligned most appropriately not with the innocent victim but with the murderers and robbers in the *Märchen* is her later facial paralysis. In 'Der Räuberbräutigam', the murderer scatters ashes on the path to his house and turns 'kreideweiß' when he is discovered.[16] That is, he is not only associated with ashes, a substance traditionally linked with death, but he also bears the evidence for his crimes in his face, which is likened to another lifeless, colourless substance. Just like the murderer, Lene too comes to bear the marks of history and responsibility on her face, in the form of her paralysis. This paralysis affects one side of her face only, thus becoming a literal representation of the Janus-faced psyche of many West Germans after the war, in that they were both aware of history and concerned to deny it as discussed above with reference to the Mitscherlichs' work. And if the heroine of 'Der Räuberbräutigam' cannot be fully identified with Lene, it may make more sense to identify that heroine with Anna, who is too young to be complicit like Lene is. In making the film, she recounts the story of what has happened, as the *Märchen* heroine does.

Furthermore, I argue that the way in which *Deutschland, bleiche Mutter* uses the *Märchen* also implicitly takes issue with the way Lene and her generation told history to their children. Indeed, in this reading Sanders-Brahms's *Märchen* is less of an attempt to represent the Holocaust itself than an account of the way in which the Holocaust was represented by Lene's generation. While on one level the *Märchen* told by Lene recalls the traditional topos of tale-telling as a subversive, proto-feminist activity among women, in which the mother shares important, illicit wisdom with her daughter,[17] on another level Lene's telling of the *Märchen* is as much a source of tension as it is of feminine or feminist solidarity. Unusually, there is distance and tension between Lene and Anna in the scene in the deserted industrial site, since Anna refuses to take bread from her mother, thus rejecting the usual nurturing relationship between them, and Sanders-Brahms points out that the attitude of the child in the film to what her mother tells her is both 'verschreckt und skeptisch'. And in that same 'Nachrede', Sanders-Brahms says of the way her mother told her *Märchen*: 'Meine Mutter hatte Spaß, wenn ich weinte, während sie mir Märchen erzählte. Mit der Zeit stumpfte ich ab und weinte nicht mehr, da steigerte sie die Gefühle und die Schrecken' (p. 116). This description is less positive than one might expect of a supportive community of tale-telling women (although not completely incompatible with it).

In other words, there are indications that the child takes a critical distance from the story her mother tells, just as many of the younger West German generation represented by the adult Anna tended, from the late 1960s onward, to take a critical distance from their parents' story of how National Socialism happened. Therefore, the film might be suggesting that the elder generation did with their children precisely what Lene is doing here with Anna: they told them *Märchen*, in the negative sense of lies or fantasies, about their past. In such accounts of the past, tellers like Lene could block out the fate of Jewish and other persecuted neighbours, in order to focus on their own problems, stylize themselves as victims and make their own history the dominant history of modern Germany. But the fact that the tale is

told against the background of what may be an extermination camp speci-
fies that the past in question includes National Socialism and the Holocaust,
so that by inserting that background so ostentatiously into the film's
Märchen sequence, the film-maker/narrator indicates that she knows and
can tell more than her parents' generation was prepared to admit.

It follows therefore that *Deutschland, bleiche Mutter* implicitly deals, too,
with the question of how the Holocaust may be adequately represented by
Anna's generation. In terms of plot, I have argued that the *Märchen* condenses two separate histories, that of Lene's fate as a wife and that of the
Holocaust. However, in rhetorical terms, the film differentiates sharply
between those two histories and that distinction is introduced by Anna, as
the narrator/film-maker of the next generation.

First, the *Märchen* gives us a *symbolic* account of Lene's life, if we understand a symbol to be a textual device which, like the *Märchen* here, has a
dual meaning. That is, a symbol has both immediate, specific referents in the
text, as well as pointing figuratively towards further meanings without such
immediately present refererents. Thus, Lene's life is present in the film on
two levels: as a realist, detailed narrative about her life, such as her marriage and rape; and as a *Märchen*, which symbolically recapitulates that realist narrative in the motifs of betrothal, dismemberment and so forth. So in
rhetorical terms, the *Märchen* is a symbol of Lene's life. However, the
account the film gives of the Holocaust is *allegorical*, if we understand an allegory to be a textual device which works on the figurative level alone, that
is, one which has no immediate, realistic referent in the text. In the film, the
Holocaust exists on one level only, that of the *Märchen*. That is, while Lene's
life is represented both realistically and through the symbolism of the
Märchen, the Holocaust is represented almost exclusively through the
Märchen alone, since with the exception of the brief scene where Rahel is
taken away, there is no parallel, realist narrative of the Holocaust. So, all we
see of the Holocaust is its prelude (Rahel's deportation) and its aftermath (the
Ducksteins' empty shop and the empty industrial site), but not the events
themselves. The events of the Holocaust are therefore an absence in the film
rather than a presence. Appropriately then, all the viewer sees is empty
interiors: the inside of a looted shop and the cavities of the ovens. We may
understand this conspicuous absence, highlighted by the rhetorical device of
allegory, as a representation not only of the emptiness which the Holocaust
left behind, but also of the way in which it became a blind spot in the
collective memory of West Germany.

Thus, I conclude that the alienation device of the *Märchen* allows the film
to refer to the Holocaust, without entering the fraught territory of how to
represent it by means of what the film-maker has critically called the
'pyrotechnische Kunststückchen' of realist narrative.[18] And so it seems to me
that this use of the *Märchen* goes some way to addressing the seemingly
insoluble problem highlighted by Rosenfeld and Young, that to represent the

Holocaust is always to invest it with inappropriate metaphor and meaning. In fact, the *Märchen* here does not represent the Holocaust, but points out for the viewer the *Leerstellen,* the empty spaces it left behind and in which it is to be located, both literally, in terms of the empty interiors, and figuratively, in the incomplete collective memory described by the film.

By doing this, the film goes beyond many of contemporaneous cultural documents in which Sanders-Brahms's generation sought to explore their parents' history, since commonly, such cultural production failed to address the history of the Holocaust adequately, if at all.[19] And in this regard, the film, whether intentionally or not, takes its place too in a postwar narrative tradition which dealt critically with the possibility of representing Auschwitz directly through art.[20]

Conclusion

Both Sanders-Brahms and Hildebrandt have recognized the Bluebeard group of tales as an important means of representing German history and identity of the National Socialist period and after. In this final section, I shall first examine why two such apparently different texts as these should have chosen *Märchen* in general to encode these issues; and second, why in particular the *Blaubartmärchen* should have been chosen.

First, the use of the *Märchen* genre is at least partly due to the nature of the history in question. Some aspects of the German history discussed in this chapter have often been unacknowledged or repressed, so that by encoding rather than narrating that history, the authors may, consciously or unconsciously, be reflecting its silencing. Alternatively, it may be that the history in question is so horrific that it is felt to defy direct expression, either from concern for a certain moral authenticity, or for the more pragmatic reason of plausibility. But in addition, I would adduce more local, specific reasons for such encoding of German history and identity in the *Märchen,* since an association between the *Märchen* and notions of German national identity has in fact long been familiar.

Recently, a prominent critic has written of a 'German obsession with fairy tales', and this national preoccupation dates back to the emergence of the *Märchen* as we know it in the eighteenth and nineteenth centuries in the hands of such writers as Herder and the Brothers Grimm, who believed the genre to be intimately, supremely German, and an expression of a specifically German sensibility.[21] That perception reached as far as Britain, where in 1828 a translator of the Grimms could describe tales like those in the *KHM* as epitomizing 'the genius of German romance'.[22] And the association between *Märchen* and German identity persisted in the twentieth century. After 1945, for example, the Allies banned the *KHM,* albeit briefly, for fear of its pernicious nationalistic influences.[23] And it is to this perception of the *Märchen* as a privileged vehicle for expressing national identity or history that *Märchen* are evoked in the film *Deutschland im Herbst* (1978). That film, contemporaneously with the texts discussed here, presented a psychogramme of West Germany, in which *Märchen* emerge in a sequence about a history teacher who finds conventional historiographies of Germany wanting, and searches for more truthful accounts in the *Märchen*.[24] The *Märchen*, then, is a privileged signifier for notions of German identity and it is no coincidence that these recent German texts resort to *Märchen* to encode emblematic, modern German identities and historical issues.

Second, why do these texts encode this recent history using, specifically, the *Blaubartmärchen* and its variants? This is due to the fact that there are clear and consistent correspondences between the *Märchen* motifs and the historical events in question, which indeed make the tale 'eine sehr durchsichtige Metapher'.

For instance, these *Märchen* thematize the ways in which certain aspects of the history in question (National Socialism; the ravages of the war; and the Holocaust) have often been repressed, for in Bluebeard's house there is a secret chamber whose contents testify to horrible aggression, are kept hidden, and whose existence both signal and perpetuates danger. Traditionally, German Bluebeard tales have often described the violent denial and suppression of difference or 'otherness', metonymically represented by Woman. The 'other' which is violently eliminated may be understood in these texts as the dark side of their fictional subjects' selves, their scandalous knowledge of their past, and their own traumatic experiences which may return in damaging ways. And in addition, Sanders-Brahms senses that these *Blaubartmärchen* are particularly apt for representing a period in German history characterized by an official, national ideology which involved the savage elimination of 'others' in a most Bluebeard-like way.

The murderer in the *Märchen* is a shadowy, powerful, masculine figure, who embodies social and symbolic authority and against whom his victims are helpless. Similarly, the two texts discussed here show protagonists whose relationship to a shadowy notion of (implicitly patriarchal) authority is passive and submissive. Thus the dominance of Bluebeard or the robber in these texts may symbolize what has been perceived as the traditionally passive relationship of many Germans to authority,[25] and which has been held to have been a contributory factor to the rise of authoritarian National Socialist ideology. And the motif of the murderer's house is important in the *Märchen*; similarly, Sanders-Brahms evokes the physical buildings in which the Holocaust crimes were committed, and whose very interior topographies (chambers, ovens, chimney) have become imprinted on the collective memory of the twentieth century. On a different level too, in the poem by Bertolt Brecht that gives Sanders-Brahms's film its title, the house of that 'pale mother' is a metaphor for the land in which crimes are committed. In turn, that image resonates with the constricting space which Germany proves to be for Alexander Falck.

Finally, I noted in my introduction that from one of its earliest appearances – and disappearances – in German, that is, in the Grimms' *KHM*, 'Blaubart' has been linked to issues of national identity. But given that the Grimms felt the tale told its readers little about a specifically German identity, and that many authors and critics, concerned to distance themselves from its disturbing content, have since followed their lead in suggesting that the tale is not German, it appears paradoxical that precisely this *Märchen* should be used to explore issues in German history and identity.[26] However, the use of a tale which has traditionally been denied national German character is on one hand an index of the way in which Hildebrandt senses that the events encoded in the *Märchen* must be distanced in order to be represented. 'Der Räuberbräutigam', on the other hand, was endorsed by the Grimms as being especially German, and it is therefore peculiarly appropriate that Sanders-Brahms selected this very tale to represent twentieth-century German history.

Notes

1 Jacob and Wilhelm Grimm, 'Blaubart', no. 62 in *Kinder- und Hausmärchen. Gesammelt durch die Brüder Grimm. Vergrößerter Nachdruck der zweibändigen Erstausgabe von 1812 und 1815*, ed. Heinz Rölleke and Ulrike Marquardt, 3 vols (Göttingen: Vandenhoeck & Ruprecht, 1986), vol. I, pp. 285–9; also in *Kinder- und Hausmärchen* (1857 edition), ed. Heinz Rölleke, 3 vols (Stuttgart: Reclam, 1980), vol. II, pp. 36–41. On the Grimms' 'Blaubart' and its history, see my D.Phil. thesis, 'The *Blaubartmärchen* and its Reception in German Literature of the Nineteenth and Twentieth Centuries' (Oxford, 1998), especially pp. 74–80 and pp. 158–66.

2 See Hartwig Suhrbier, 'Blaubart – Leitbild und Leidfigur', in Hartwig Suhrbier (ed.), *Blaubarts Geheimnis: Märchen und Erzählungen, Gedichte und Stücke* (Cologne and Düsseldorf: Diederichs, 1984), pp. 11–79; my thesis 'The *Blaubartmärchen*'; and my article '"In Blaubarts Schatten": Murder, *Märchen* and Memory', *German Life and Letters*, vol. 50 (1997), pp. 491–507.

3 On Struck's and Reichart's treatment of German history using the *Blaubartmärchen*, see my article '"In Blaubarts Schatten"'.

4 See my thesis 'The *Blaubartmärchen*', pp. 221-83.

5 Falck's name recalls not only the amorous connotations of the literary falcon motif, but also Alexander the Great. As Suhrbier's article and my thesis show, in German texts Bluebeard often embodies the masculine, heroic, conquering subject of modern civilization.

6 Alexander and Margarete Mitscherlich, *Die Unfähigkeit zu trauern: Grundlagen kollektiven Verhaltens* (Munich and Zurich: Piper, 1967).

7 Ibid., p. 30.

8 See Richard W. McCormick, *Politics of the Self: Feminism and the Postmodern in West German Literature and Film* (Princeton and Oxford: Princeton University Press, 1991), pp. 178–207.

9 Cf. Ibid., p. 197.

10 Barbara Hyams, 'Is the Apolitical Woman at Peace? A Reading of the Fairy Tale in *Deutschland, bleiche Mutter*', (1988), included in Terri Ginsberg and Kirsten Moana Thomson (eds) *Perspectives on German Cinema* (New York: G. K. Hall, 1996), pp. 346–60.

11 Helma Sanders-Brahms, 'Kleine Nachrede. Hinterher geschrieben, also 1979', in *Deutschland, bleiche Mutter. Film-Erzählung* (Reinbek bei Hamburg: Rowohlt, 1980), pp. 115–17 (p. 116).

12 Hyam's article 'Is the Apolitical Woman at Peace?' is just one instance of much interesting secondary writing on *Deutschland, bleiche Mutter* which explores critically questions of guilt and responsibility arising from the film's treatment of the relationship of women to National Socialism.

13 Cf. Anton Kaes, *From Hitler to Heimat: The Return of History as Film* (Cambridge, Mass.: Harvard University Press, 1989), p. 148.

14 Quoted by James E. Young in *Writing and Rewriting the Holocaust: Narrative and the Consequences of Interpretation* (Bloomington and Indianapolis: Indiana University Press, 1988), p. 130.

15 Quoted in ibid., p. 90.

16 Interestingly, Hyams points out that one English translation of the *Märchen* gives 'kreideweiß' as 'as pale as ashes' ('Is the Apolitical Woman at Peace?', p. 351).

17 Roger F. Cook, 'Melodrama or Cinematic Folktale? Story and History in Deutschland, bleiche Mutter', *The Germanic Review*, vol. 66 (1991), pp. 113–21 (p. 118).

18 In the piece quoted, Sanders-Brahms distinguishes between realism and authenticity, valorizing authenticity but treating traditional cinematic realism with suspicion. It could be argued that her account of the Holocaust through the *Märchen*, too, resonates with that commitment to a non-realist authenticity.

19 Just one instance of this omission is Bernward Vesper's 'Romanessay' *Die Reise* (posthumous, 1977), generally acknowledged to be a classic of so-called *Väterliteratur*, in which the principal victim of Nazism is the German son and protagonist.

20 See Petra Kiedaisch (ed.), *Lyrik nach Auschwitz: Adorno und die Dichter* (Stuttgart: Reclam, 1995).

21 Jack Zipes, 'The Grimms and the German Obsession with Fairy Tales', in Ruth B. Bottingheimer (ed.), *Fairy Tales and Society: Illusion, Allusion and Paradigm* (Philadelphia: University of Pennsylvania Press), pp. 271–85.

22 'Preface', in George Godfrey Cunningham, *Foreign Tales and Traditions Chiefly Selected from the Fugitive Literature of Germany* (1828), quoted in Martin Sutton, *The Sin-Complex: A Critical Study of English Versions of the Grimms' 'Kinder- und Hausmärchen' in the Nineteenth Century* (Kassel: Brüder Grimm-Gesellschaft, 1996), p. 60.

23 Jack Zipes, 'The Struggle for the Grimms' Throne: The Legacy of the Grimms' Tales in the FRG and GDR since 1945', in Donald Haase (ed.), *The Reception of Grimms' Fairy Tales: Responses, Reactions, Revisions* (Detroit: Wayne State University Press, 1993), pp. 167–207 (p. 167).

24 *Deutschland im Herbst*, directed by Alf Brustellin, Bernhard Sinkel, Rainer Werner Fassbinder, Alexander Kluge, Maximiliane Mainka, Edgar Reitz, Beate Mainka-Jellinghaus, Peter Schubert, Hans-Peter Cloos, Katja Rupé, Volker Schlöndorff, 1978.

25 Cf. Hyams, 'Is the Apolitical Woman at Peace?', p. 347.
26 See my thesis 'The *Blaubartmärchen*', p. 89.

7

The Holocaust and the representation of the female subject in Ingeborg Bachmann's *Malina* and Anne Duden's *Das Judasschaf*

Stephanie Bird

Ingeborg Bachmann's *Malina* and Anne Duden's *Das Judasschaf* are both novels in which the female first-person narrator makes her own suffering and anguish in a hostile society the central theme. In both, the female subject is depicted as divided: in *Malina* the female narrator is juxtaposed to her male alter-ego Malina, and in *Das Judasschaf* the narrator presents herself both as 'Ich' and 'Die Person'. Crucially, both books relate the anguish of the narrator to her female subjectivity and to her awareness of the atrocities of the past. The representation of female subjectivity is thus intricately bound up with the experience of history, the violence perpetrated by society, and specifically the Holocaust. It is this relationship which I shall attempt to explore by examining the function which references to the Holocaust perform for the narrators, the complex issues concerning identification which arise, and the implications for feminist criticism which result.

Malina

Malina is a text which lends itself to interpretations which are based on the dichotomy of male and female.[1] The book itself is structured around this opposition: the narrator is a woman, and the three chapters focus on her relationship to three male figures, her lover Ivan, her father and her companion and alter-ego Malina. The narrator expresses the suffering which these relationships cause her, finally describing her disappearance into a crack in the wall as 'murder', with Malina standing as the obvious perpetrator, but with Ivan and the father implicated as other men who have failed to understand her. Not surprisingly, *Malina* has become one of the major works of the women's writing canon. Written in 1967–70, it is the first part of a trilogy, which, however, remained unfinished at the time of Bachmann's death. Bachmann named the trilogy *Todesarten*, thus apparently emphasizing the books' thematization of the destruction of female subjectivity.

The confrontational structure of *Malina* has encouraged feminist criticism which emphasizes the oppression of the female narrator by the male figures. Her emotional stance, her difficulty in articulating her subjectivity and her debilitating relationships with the egoistic Ivan, her cruelly analytic alter-ego Malina, and the sadistic father-figure are seen as testifying to the impossibility of the existence of 'woman' in patriarchy. The narrator's suffering is conveyed with the greatest impact in the middle section of the book, 'Der dritte Mann'. Here, the narrator recounts a sequence of dreams in which oppression, violence, murder and terror are described and communicated with shocking vividness. It is as part of these dreams that references to the persecution of the Jews and the Holocaust are made.

The Holocaust is sometimes referred to directly, sometimes implicitly suggested by the descriptions of violent oppression. It is, however, the narrator who is the victim of brutality in these scenes, and thus her suffering becomes identified with that of the persecuted Jews. Furthermore, since references to the Holocaust form part of the narrator's wider dream-experience of being abused and persecuted by her father, the genocide is also effectively equated with the oppression of women. The figure of the tormenting father is not an individual, but, as Sigrid Weigel comments, the Name of the Father.[2] Patriarchy and the persecution of the Jews are thus always linked: 'Mein Vater nimmt ruhig einen ersten Schlauch von der Wand ab, ... und eh ich schreien kann, atme ich schon das Gas ein, immer mehr Gas. Ich bin in der Gaskammer, das ist sie, die größte Gaskammer der Welt.... Man wehrt sich nicht im Gas' (pp. 182–3). The narrator dreams that she is one of the Jews waiting to be transported: 'Ich habe den sibirischen Judenmantel an, wie alle anderen. Es ist tiefer Winter, ... wir [warten] alle auf den Abtransport.... [Mein Vater] sieht, daß ich abreise mit den anderen, und ich möchte noch einmal mit ihm reden, ihm endlich begreiflich machen, daß er nicht zu uns gehört' (p. 201).

While some references are not explicitly to the Holocaust, they are so by implication, following as they do from the preceding unmistakable descriptions: 'Aber jetzt kommt jemand, ... es ist mein Vater. Ich zeige auf Ivan, ich sage: Er ist es! Ich weiß nicht, ob ich deswegen die Todesstrafe zu erwarten habe oder nur in ein Lager komme' (p. 206). Like the Nazi concentration camps, the narrator's prison is surrounded by electric wire, and in the attempt to run away she gets caught on the wire: 'es ist Stacheldraht, es sind Stacheln, mit 1000 000 Volt geladen, die 100 000 Schläge, elektrisch, bekomme ich.... Ich bin an der Raserei meines Vaters verglüht und gestorben' (p. 229). And a dream in which the narrator is being turned into ice by her father is reminiscent of the 'Erwärmungsversuche' at Dachau: 'Wir stehen bei 50 Grad Kälte, entkleidet, ... müssen die befohlenen Positionen einnehmen.... Ich höre mich noch wimmern und eine Verwünschung ausstoßen' (p. 221).

References to the Holocaust are not extensive, but they perform an important function: the narrator is presenting the Holocaust as a metaphor for the suffering of women. Such a direct identification of the oppression of women in patriarchy with the persecution of the Jews is a worrying feature in the book. Not only is the oppression of women generalized in the process, with no account taken of socio-economic, ethnic or historical differences between women. But this fades into insignificance in the face of the generalization which obscures the fundamental difference between the narrator, a successful and acclaimed female writer, and the disenfranchised, disempowered and eventually gassed or brutally murdered Jew. Now certainly, the degree of generalization can at one level be explained, even excused, by the fact that the comparison is only ever drawn in the narrator's dreams; she never *consciously* compares her sense of oppression to Holocaust victims in the way that the narrator of *Das Judasschaf* does. Nevertheless, in terms of the status which the dream sequences have for expressing experiences of persecution which cannot adequately be articulated in the language of conventional discourse, the equation of women and Jews as common victims still stands.

The evaluation of such direct identification depends upon the way in which the figure of the narrator is viewed: whether she is seen to represent the suffering voice of oppressed femininity and therefore privileged in the text, or whether she is seen as part of a complex critique of gendered oppositions, where her perspective is as flawed as that of her male alter-ego, Malina. If, as has been the case with much feminist criticism of *Malina*, the narrator's perspective is privileged by virtue of her suffering as a woman, then there are basically two interpretative strategies with which to approach the complex issue of an identification which assumes shared victimhood.

The first of these is simply not to acknowledge the difficult issues which relate to identification of one person or group with another. The references to the Holocaust are not explicitly addressed or are seen as a variation on the narrator's emotional sensitivity. Her empathy is a positive characteristic, for it means that the suffering of others can be understood, will not be denied or forgotten and so also intensifies the political opposition against the oppressive patriarchy. However, this view of identification fails to recognize that the assimilation of another person's experience of suffering to one's own equalizes and ignores difference, and denies the other's specificity.

The second strategy open to critics who accept the narrator's perspective is to acknowledge the problems surrounding the shared victimhood, but to see them as problems at the authorial and not the diegetic level. According to this view, the naivety of the universalizing sentiment reflects the time in which the book was written and so reflects on Bachmann's own politics; the issues are not seen as being explored by the text itself, but as problems to which the text is blind. Thus the book as a whole may be treated as flawed, or as presenting a disjunction, but the narrator herself, as the character who makes the identification, escapes the brunt of the criticism.

In contrast to these interpretative strategies, if an attitude to the narrator is adopted which approaches her critically from the start, then the association of Woman and Jew as eternal victim is not a weakness of the book, but becomes thematized as part of the narrator's limited perspective. I shall argue that Bachmann's primary concern in *Malina* is not the privileging of the female perspective over that of the male, but is rather a study of the effects of different responses to historical experience, including that of the Holocaust, and how these different modes of responding are central to definitions of the female subject.

Experience

'Und wenn ich zum Beispiel in diesem Buch "Malina" kein Wort über den Vietnamkrieg sage, kein Wort über soundso viele katastrophale Zustände unserer Gesellschaft, dann weiß ich aber auf eine andere Weise etwas zu sagen – oder ich hoffe, daß ich es zu sagen weiß.'[3] Bachmann's novel is certainly no naturalistic exposition of global catastrophe; rather its central theme is a history of endured abuse, a history which cannot be treated by recounting events: 'Denn ich glaub' nicht, daß man, indem man zum hundertsten Mal wiederholt, was an Schrecklichem heute in der Welt geschieht, es geschieht ja immerzu Schreckliches, daß man das mit den Platitüden sagen kann, die jeder zu sagen versteht. In den Träumen weiß ich aber, wie ich es zu sagen hab.'[4] This book is very much about history and experience and its effect on the individual; more specifically it is about its effect on the female subject, how she is able to respond and how this response defines notions of subjectivity. The narrator reacts to experience emotionally, investing events with feeling and also with the desire to feel absolutely. She does not relativize through analysis and forms judgements based on the immediacy of the feeling which events provoke. In contrast, Malina remains emotionally distant and insists upon constant questioning of facts, causes, the meaning which might lie behind the appearance of an event. He insists on constant enquiry, she on the immediacy of the felt instant.

Far from removing *Malina* from the arena of feminist debate by seeing it as a text primarily concerned with interpretations of experience, I am concerned to pinpoint one of the most crucial and controversial issues of the feminist discourse: the status of experience. For many areas of feminist theory, women's experience is regarded as central to the claim for emancipation. The very existence of feminism as a political programme depends upon women's feeling of being oppressed and on founding an identity politics based on the generalized concept of Woman. Women's historical experience of oppression and exclusion is used to justify the existence of a female subject as different and as Other, with different modes of perception and response. Experience thus becomes the foundation of feminist ontology, whereby women's status as marginalized in patriarchal society is equated with a different subjectivity. So in the face of post-structuralist denials of the

subject, many feminists argue that it is only now that they are able to articulate the subjectivity which has hitherto been negated or denied, and assert
that subjectivity as different, and as equally valid.

In contrast to an insistence on the importance of experience, certain
strands of feminist philosophy refuse to accept it as an adequate basis for
identity. Deconstructionist feminists question the whole relationship of experience and female identity, arguing that women's experience tends to be
approached as though it is intrinsically significant, with the concomitant
assumption that merely recounting it must therefore be beneficial for
women. Instead, they see the emphasis on experience as a way of reinscrib-
ing existing structures of domination: experience in this process repeats the
pattern of all foundationalist myths, one in which primary premises and pre-
sumptions are not questioned. As Joan W. Scott argues: 'Experience is at
once always already an interpretation *and* is in need of interpretation. What
counts as experience is neither self-evident nor straightforward; it is always
contested, always therefore political.'[5] Any attempt to unite women on the
grounds of their common experience as 'women' is thus effectively to elevate
experience to the position of a new truth and so to impede the analysis of
what structures that experience in the first place.

The validity and inadequacies of these two very different approaches to
experience are held up for scrutiny in *Malina*. Each approach is exemplified
in the figures of the narrator and Malina: one in which the female subject
is defined by the immediately felt effect of experience on the self, and one
which persistently seeks to analyse what lies behind experience. However,
the contrast is not a simplistic one. For each type of response is shown to
entail both positive and negative aspects, and neither response is evaluated
as being superior to the other.

The first person narrator

The trouble with first-person narrators is that their perspective dominates,
identification and sympathy are facilitated, and it can be difficult to maintain critical distance. The desire to identify with the woman's voice in *Malina*
has often meant that rigorous scrutiny of the reliability of the narrator has
been neglected as a result of identification with her as the female element.
Yet there is ample evidence to suggest that the text invites the reader to
maintain distance from the perceptions of the narrator. Crucially it becomes
clear already in the prologue that her recollections are not always accurate.
At one point she states 'es war auf der Glanbrücke. Es war nicht die Seepromenade' (p. 22) and two paragraphs later: 'Es war nicht auf der Glanbrücke, nicht auf der Seepromenade, es war auch nicht auf dem Atlantik in
der Nacht' (p. 23). Her memories are often governed by what she would
have liked to have happened, so it is clear that what is important for her is
that memory is not limited to fact but that it is governed by present emotional perception. The past, experience, is felt; its reality is not to be accom-

modated within the dispassionate enquiry of science.

The world as felt experience reaches its apotheosis in her relationship to Ivan, and again it is significant that in the structure of the novel this episode should come first. For in the narrator's deification of Ivan, her clichéd behaviour in relation to him, and her self-deception that 'für Ivan habe ich nichts zum Schein' (p. 37), the reader is presented with evidence that the narrator is gullible, naive and dominated by feelings which can clearly have a negative effect. That her relationship to Ivan reduces the narrator to conventional images of the desperate mistress has been commented upon amply by critics, but it rarely results in a questioning of her perspective as a whole. However, it is crucial to see this episode as an important indication of the narrator's inadequate modes of perception, not just in relation to Ivan, but in relation to what follows with Malina. The fact that the prologue's thematization of the importance of emotion in reacting to experience is followed directly by an illustration of how the protagonist's feelings lead her into stereotypical patterns of behaviour is a textual invitation to be aware of the limitations of her viewpoint and not to privilege her perceptions in the book. For the text is concerned to explore two differing modes of responding to experience not simply by setting up a simple opposition, but by systematically exposing the devastating implications of remaining trapped within opposition.

For the narrator, the meaning of an experience lies in the immediacy of its emotional effect upon her and she seeks to comprehend the hidden truths of experience in this perceived effect. Her absolute involvement in emotion is coupled with an active resistance to questioning or analysing this involvement. The narrator elevates her feelings to the status of absolutes which she never challenges. Her relationship with Ivan takes on religious fervour, describing him as 'mein Mekka und mein Jerusalem!'. She does not reflect about her own perceptions, for this would detract from the immediacy which for her is life-enhancing. She constantly emphasizes her existence in the present, for to exist in the here and now precludes a reflexive stance, a distance from which to start analysing. She admits to Malina, 'Es muß einfach alles gleichzeitig aufkommen und auf mich Eindruck machen' (p. 307), and she suppresses knowledge in order to persist in a particular emotional reaction: 'nie wollte ich denken, wie es im Anfang war, nie, wie es vor einem Monat war ... Ehe gestern und morgen auftauchen, muß ich sie zum Schweigen bringen in mir. Es ist heute. Ich bin hier und heute' (p. 154–5). The narrator perceives the effect of Ivan upon her as life itself, so to relativize that experience or cast doubt upon it by questioning it would for her be life-threatening. This response to Ivan is typical of her perceptions generally, whereby she derives her identity from her emotional reaction to experience and is therefore fundamentally threatened by the concept of analytical thought and self-reflexivity.

The consequences of the narrator's refusal to reflect upon or question her absolute identification with feeling are shown to be destructive. Her behaviour is reduced to the enactment of clichés of Woman and for all that she is so devastated by different levels of experience, personal and political, she is so absorbed in her feeling of devastation that she becomes dominated by narcissism which results in the marginalization of whatever concern for victims she might feel. The Bulgarian with Morbus Buerger becomes an object of revulsion from whom she must escape, the personification of the disease itself: 'der Morbus ist da' (p. 117). And she finds contact difficult even with 'healthy' people: 'Warum habe ich bisher nie bemerkt, daß ich Leute fast nicht mehr ertragen kann?' (p. 175).

Although the narrator may wish to view her withdrawal into her personal love of Ivan as positive, with Washington, Moscow and Berlin described as 'bloß vorlaute Orte, die versuchen, sich wichtig zu machen' (p. 25), it is nevertheless revealed as intrinsically debilitating and self-destructive. She is rendered helpless by the impact of events upon her and is dependent on Malina for both maintaining the household and retrieving her from moments of extreme despair and collapse. She can do nothing to help herself because her identity is so utterly defined by the emotions of the moment which dictate her response. So although she can in one way be seen as passive, and her suffering as real, the narrator is nevertheless complicit in her own destruction precisely because she actively insists upon the supremacy of emotion.

Her complicity in destruction takes the form of enabling destruction to occur without offering effective opposition. There is a revealing exchange between the narrator and Malina in one of their dialogues in the central chapter, in which Malina asks her why she sought to protect her murderous father from the police. Her reasons are based on feelings of the moment: 'Meine Absicht war es ... das Schlimmste im Moment zu verhindern' (p. 217). This indicates that although the narrator figures in the dream sequences as a victim of the crimes of the father, she is not herself uninvolved in their perpetuation. Similarly, her emotional perception of past crimes means that although she is able to recall the crimes in dream images, she at the same time represses the implications of those images when they become emotionally overwhelming. In this way her mode of response functions both to expose the horror of the crime but also to resist examining her relationship to the perpetrators. So when Malina questions her about the four murderers, she gives the impression of refusing to recognize what she must know: 'Von dem vierten kann ich nicht reden, ich erinnere mich nicht an ihn, ich vergesse, ich erinnere mich nicht' (p. 297).

The negative aspects of the narrator's response to experience do not exist in isolation. They have been emphasized hitherto because they are often overlooked in order to privilege her perspective and draw attention to her suffering as a woman. These negative aspects are, though, inseparable from the empowering qualities of the narrator's identity as oppressed female subject. It is to these qualities that I shall now turn, albeit briefly.

Despite what has been described as her rejection of reflexive thought and her own admission that 'die Abstraktion ... ist vielleicht nicht meine Stärke' (p. 92), it is the immediacy with which she experiences events which enables her to adopt a critical stance towards society. Her attachment to absolute values gives her a yardstick with which to judge complacency and battle against silence. Relating to experience emotionally enables her to react with indignation to injustice, to recognize hypocrisy and to challenge the detachment and cynicism of contemporary society. Much comes under criticism: the high society of which she herself is part, the media's reporting of events, consumerism as an extension of the black market, and the commodification of values through advertising. She points to the silence surrounding the first postwar years in Austria: 'diese Zeit ist aber aus ihren Annalen getilgt worden, es gibt keine Leute mehr, die noch darüber sprechen. Verboten ist es nicht direkt, aber man spricht trotzdem nicht darüber' (p. 289).

The narrator concludes that 'die Gesellschaft ist der allergrößte Mordschauplatz. In der leichtesten Art sind in ihr seit jeher die Keime zu den unglaublichsten Verbrechen gelegt worden, die den Gerichten dieser Welt für immer unbekannt bleiben' (p. 290). This quotation serves as a neat example of the combination of the negative and positive aspects of the narrator's responses. On the one hand she is empowered to stand back and criticize the hypocricy of society, and the destructive and primitive relationships formed within it; on the other hand the comment is a universalizing condemnation behind which the narrator is able to ignore her own participation. Nevertheless, her criticism is a real one.

Finally, in relation to the past, and indeed to the continued violence of the present, it is the narrator's emotional perception of history that enables her to recount the horrors of war and murder in a manner which is unmediated and powerful. Through the medium of the narrator's dreams Bachmann starkly illustrates her comment 'In den Träumen weiß ich aber, wie ich [Schreckliches] zu sagen hab'. The dream sequences convey cruelty, fear, brutality and desperation, and, through the narrator's refusal to accept a distanced position, reveal the devastating effects of traumatic events on the psyche.

It may appear contradictory to stress the inadequacies of the narrator's mode of perception, its destructive aspects, narcissistic domination and involvement in perpetuating structures of oppression, while concurrently affirming the critical stance with which the narrator is empowered. But it is precisely this double aspect which the text is concerned to reveal and refuses to simplify. Her emotional response to experience is both positive and negative; it at once empowers her and continues to deform her. And in relation to Malina, whose response to experience is that of the questioning analyst, a similar ambivalence is depicted, one that is destructive and constructive.

Unfortunately pressure of space does not allow a detailed discussion of

Malina's position, but suffice it to say that he responds to experience by refusing to accept it as self-evident and constantly demanding that it be interpreted. For him, experience needs to be contested, as do the concepts with which experience is articulated, and herein lies the threat to the Ich. The negative effects of the unremitting refusal to accept a subject's experience as a basis for identity is taken to a logical extreme in this text when the narrator perceives herself as murdered by Malina. He denies her identity by denying her experience and the emotional importance to the narrator of that experience. He challenges normative values, is critical of assumptions and rejects absolutes, viewing the narrator's experience-related identity as a hurdle to change: 'Wenn man überlebt hat, ist Überleben dem Erkennen im Wege' (p. 233). Far from being complacent, he is concerned to disrupt the existing order and the unchallenged acceptance of concepts within it. As Malina says to the narrator: 'Du mußt nicht alles glauben, denk lieber selber nach' (p. 192).

Conflict and identification

Thus the two different modes of responding to experience each have negative and positive features, and the mode of response represented by the narrator is by no means privileged in the text. This carries important implications for feminist criticism, for it challenges any reading of the book based upon the narrator's perspective, one which then necessarily accepts and privileges the emotional and non-reflexive aspects of the narrator. We ignore at our cost the text's emphasis on these characteristics as *also* negative and as traits which can facilitate complicity with the oppressive structures. The text agitates against any acceptance of the male/female polarity at face value; rather, it presents that polarity as in fact the object of criticism: the destructive conclusion of the novel comes about precisely because of the maintenance of the male/female opposition. It becomes inevitable as a consequence of the rigidity with which the narrator and Malina are fixed within their static positions. But this polarity is not thereby being confirmed as inevitable and untransmutable. On the contrary, the opposition is thus exposed as spurious, as reductive, and not as a basis upon which change can be effected. The polarity is set up in order to reveal its inadequacy and its potency as a tool of oppression. Bachmann is pointing to the need for the interaction of both modes of responding to experience in the formation of identity. Neither mode is shown to be superior to the other, but it is the intransigent and ultimately inhibiting labelling in terms of gender which is the basis for (self-) destruction.

Yet here comes the final insoluble difficulty, a difficulty which the text neither shirks nor resolves. Each mode of response does necessarily remain irreconcilable with the other; a female subject defined by the experience of oppression cannot at the same time question the very notion of the subject and refuse the universalizing signifier 'Woman'. The narrator and Malina co-exist in one woman, but an exchange between them can always only be momentary, for each must deny the other. Yet Bachmann is not attempting to offer a utopia based on reconciliation. She is in this text acknowledging that conflict is part of the discourse surrounding the question of the female subject, while at the same time exposing the futility of fixed polarities. Furthermore, this conflict, if it is not reduced to fixed opposites by those themselves involved in it, can be a productive clash or tension, as suggested by brief moments of exchange between the narrator and Malina. As she says to him: 'was du und ich zusammenlegen können, das ist das Leben' (p. 308). Momentum for change is produced not by the triumph of one way of conceiving the subject over another, but by the acceptance of conflict which would itself then undermine the destructive efficacy of fixed polarities. As Butler rather cryptically writes: 'I would argue that the rifts among women over the content of the term ["woman"] ought to be safeguarded and prized, indeed, that this constant rifting ought to be affirmed as the ungrounded ground of feminist theory.'[6]

It is now that we can return to the discussion of the identification of the narrator with victims of the Holocaust. If, as I have argued, the complexity of identity and experience is itself being explored by the text, then the implicit equating of Woman as victim with the Jews also forms part of what the text is scrutinizing. In the figure of the narrator both the negative and positive qualities of identification are represented: on the one hand the political impetus it can provide, the power of the images which is evoked through the unmediated emotion, and the expression of horror which might otherwise be silenced; on the other hand the lack of specificity, the narcissistic placing of the self in the centre of others' suffering, and the political incapacitation caused by the generalization of oppression into a monolithic mass.

The narrator's identification with the Jews is one manifestation of a subject position which depends upon investing emotions with truth, rejecting analysis and reacting with immediacy to the instant. *Malina* shows this subject position to be wanting, despite the appearance of sympathy, just as it shows the inadequacy of the perpetually analytic subject Malina. The text is itself revealing the complex relationship of experience to identity and identification as part of the critique of rigid polarities; they do not just emerge by default. Thus the example of the Holocaust representation in *Malina* serves to emphasize and to problematize the ethical importance of the status of experience. It also points to the importance of the reader or critic themselves resisting quick identification with the protagonist on the basis of an identity politics – an issue which is also crucial in my reading of *Das Judasschaf*.

Das Judasschaf

Anne Duden is a writer who explores the complex interaction of female identity and national identity, confronting, indeed emphasizing, aspects that are often ignored or repressed: despair, horror, violence and death. It is this confrontation with violence and the resulting suffering of the female subject that has led to feminist interpretations of Duden's work that implicitly accept the female subject as a victim within patriarchy. The violence in her writing is accepted as an external ill inflicted upon her narrators. What has been inadequately acknowledged is that the texts manifest a fascination with violence and horror, an interest pursued to the point of indulgence. Violence is at once fantasized and suffered, and it is this relationship that must be explored before feminist interpretations of Duden can become convincing. For as Jacqueline Rose argues, 'there can be no analysis for women which sees violence solely as accident, imposition or external event. Only a rigid dualism pits fantasy against the real.'[7]

In *Das Judasschaf*, the tension between suffering and fascination is particularly complex.[8] The female narrator portrays her suffering with unremitting intensity, appealing to male/female polarities to justify her position as victim. She identifies with victims of atrocities, with male martyrs and Holocaust victims, without reflecting upon the appropriateness of this identification. The narrator is a woman who never gives the reader her name, who perceives herself as split into the narrative personas of 'Ich' and 'Die Person', and who defines her age in relation to the Wannsee Conference: 'Neunzehn Tage nach ihrer Geburt war im selben Wohnort während einer Konferenz der Beschluß gefaßt worden, elf Millionen Menschen zu beseitigen' (p. 43). The constant awareness of the German past makes her unremarkable daily existence one in which she sees violence, anguish and death lurking behind the veneer of the 'Alltag'. She finds moments of respite, of reflection and of escape from this oppressive awareness in the contemplation of Renaissance paintings.

The anguish of the narrator is ever-present in terms of both mental anguish and fear, and in the physical manifestation of this anguish. There are constant references to pain and nausea, and she perceives her life as a life of surviving horror: 'Immer, wenn wieder ein Moment vergangen war, hatte sie ihn mitüberlebt. Sie war ein Vehikel des Überdauerns' (p. 12). Her suffering is related both to the overwhelming knowledge and constant awareness of the Holocaust and to her femininity, and crucially, the two are related. Whereas she sees others able to live with the legacy of the atrocities, she, as a German woman, experiences memory as a perpetual torment. 'Schlimm waren nur die angehäuften Erinnerungen, die sich nie zersetzten und die ich Tag und Nacht allesamt aushalten mußte' (p. 48). And later she says 'Ihre Erinnerungen sind unheilbar krank. Wie immer schon' (p. 67). The narrator is not referring to personal memories, but rather to a cultural memory, to a 'Gedächtnis' that is usually repressed, but that is made immediate and shocking in this book by the inclusion of historical documents testifying to the cruelty and horror of the genocide. They include a quotation from Kitty Hart, a Holocaust survivor, from the commander of Auschwitz and from Himmler, and reports from Dachau concerning the use of victims' hair and the results of experiments on humans.

Her inability to concur with the general forgetfulness stems from the narrator's strong identity as a woman, that she is concerned to emphasize: 'Ich bin eine Frau, ein Mädchen, ein weibliches Kind' (p. 59). She is 'eine schlanke weibliche Person mittleren Alters' (p. 74). It is her femininity that is central to her suffering, and she asks herself the question: 'Seit wann hatte ich mich bloß so verändert? Vielleicht waren es auch nur die Auswirkungen eines zu langen weiblichen Lebens' (p. 54). Male and female economies do not overlap, and to ignore violence and atrocities, to repress the knowledge of death with which the narrator is confronted, is firmly defined by her as male: 'Männlichere Lebensaussichten konnte sie bei sich nicht anwenden. Denn es fehlte ihnen, was sie erst noch durch Zusammenstoß mit sich selbst und Versteinerung beseitigen mußte: Gedächtnis' (p. 45).

Clearly, this aspect of the text lends itself to interpretations that see the female subject marginalized within the patriarchal symbolic, seeking to express her suffering. Yet such readings do not address either the problem of the narrator's unreflected identification with victim figures or the textual fascination with violence. There is in this book an almost indulgent level of gruesome physicality which at once explains and exceeds the suffering. By drawing on Lacan's complex concept of desire and transgression the crucial links between suffering and violence can be explained.

Transgressive desire

The 'extraneous' material in the book, the paintings and the historical documents, signal the unexpected relationship between victims and violence. The images and the documents seem to illustrate opposites. On the one hand four of the five paintings depict individuals who have suffered torture as a direct result of their profound beliefs: St Mark, St Peter, Job and Christ. On the other hand there is the material relating to the Holocaust, which, with the exception of the quoted sentence from Kitty Hart, is all from the perspective of the perpetrators. Victims and oppressors are juxtaposed in the text as opposites within a violent world, they are linked as the active and passive constituents of the dominant order. But through the manner of their presentation in *Das Judasschaf* such a link becomes both stronger and questionable. For in terms of 'style', the representations of oppressor and victim are remarkably similar. They both convey a certain matter-of-factness, a calm despite the horrors they depict or that lie behind them. This similarity is most marked at the beginning of Chapter 2, 'Panorama Berlin'. Here, a document concerning the 'Verwertung der abgeschnittenen Haare' of concentration camp inmates is almost immediately followed by an extract from the Legenda aurea about St Peter, and then a description of the Carpaccio painting of him.

SS-Brigadeführer Glück could be reporting on the different sorts of bottles that can or cannot be recycled and sorted into the appropriate coloured glass: '*das Haar der männlichen Häftlinge [wird] erst dann abgeschnitten, wenn dieses nach dem Schnitt eine Länge von 20 mm besitzt ... Die Mengen der monatlich gesammelten Haare, getrennt nach Frauen- und Männerhaaren, sind jeweils zum 5. eines jeden Monats ... nach hier zu melden*' (p. 34). Soon afterwards the narrator introduces the painting of St Peter: 'Es ist ein Bild der abgebrühten Stille' (p. 35). Here too is an image of violence presented as though nothing is going on: 'Das Krummschwert, das ihm seitlich in den hinteren Schädelteil gekeilt worden ist, steckt noch an derselben Stelle – wie nach getaner Arbeit die Axt im Baumstumpf. Es scheint ihm nichts weiter auszumachen, mit gespaltenem Schädel herumzulaufen' (pp. 35–6). The narrator's description of St Peter, while depicting him as 'der Überlebende', concurrently acts as a commentary on the tone of Glück's letter as routine, as 'one of those things': 'Es ist wieder Alltag geworden', 'daß ein Dolch in seiner Herzgegend steckengeblieben ist, macht ihm nichts aus.... Na und. Das bringen die Kriege so mit sich, alle Arten von Kriegen' (p. 36).

St Peter and Glück are undoubtedly being differently morally evaluated here. The narrator goes on to identify herself directly with St Peter, comparing his actual physical injury with her own feelings of injury, thus situating herself with St Peter as a victim. However, there is undeniably a link being made, despite the different moral evaluation of St Peter as survivor and Glück as oppressor, a link that can be explained with reference to the Lacanian concept of transgressive desire.

Lacan's formulation of the concept of desire is central to his understanding of subjectivity. Separation of the child from its mother is what leads to existence within the symbolic order, for it is through the lack that is caused by separation that the subject is formed. A subject is always a desiring subject, seeking to regain a supposed lost unity. Lack and desire are coextensive, the subject desires to fill the lack in the Other, but the desire fully to satiate the Other's lack is structurally unfulfillable. This is because the Other's desire will always elude the control of the subject, just as the mother's desire eludes the control of the infant. It is this rift, the impossibility of the subject's desire and the desire of the Other to coincide, a rift intrinsic to the nature of desire, that leads to the formation of the object *a*.

The object *a* is the object-cause of desire; it can be seen as a trace of the hypothetical unity of mother/child once that unity has collapsed, both as a remainder and reminder of it, as Bruce Fink succinctly puts it.[9] It is by clinging to the object *a* that the split subject is able to deceive itself as to his or her wholeness, ignoring divisions and sustaining the illusion of completeness. It is in fantasy that the subject relates to the object *a*, through fantasy that the subject achieves an illusion of fulfilment. However, it is by no means a relationship that is always pleasurable. For desire is characterized by a twofold movement, the presence of both pleasure and enjoyment. With the 'pleasurable' pole of desire the subject takes into account what is good or bad for him or herself; the pursuit of pleasure, of wholeness, is guided by a self-regulation that is moral in kind. It is a form of desire that converges with the 'good' in the sense of justice or well-being. This pole of desire belongs to the realm of the signifiable, be it in the imaginary or the symbolic. The parallel movement of desire, enjoyment or *jouissance*, takes no account of what is satisfying for the individual; it is a pitiless desire, a desire that remains beyond signification. To quote Bruce Fink:

> Given ... that the subject casts the Other's desire in the role most exciting to the subject, that pleasure may turn to disgust and even to horror, there being no guarantee that what is most exciting to the subject is also most pleasurable.... This pleasure – this excitation due to sex, seeing, and/or violence, whether positively or negatively viewed by conscience, whether considered innocently pleasurable or disgustingly repulsive – is termed jouissance, and that is what the subject orchestrates for him or herself in fantasy.[10]

Jouissance is transgressive desire and it is such desire that can be located in Duden's text. In Seminar VII, *The Ethics of Psychoanalysis*, Lacan describes two forms of transgressive desire in relation to Kant's example in the *Kritik der reinen Vernunft*. Here, a man can enter a room where the woman he lusts after is and can satisfy his desire or need, but next to the door is the gallows on which he will be hanged if he does so. 'As far as Kant is concerned, it goes without saying that the gallows will be a sufficient deterrent; there's no question of an individual going to screw a woman when he knows he's to be hanged on the way out.'[11] Lacan's point, however, is that Kant has missed something in assuming the man will resist temptation. He argues:

> it is not impossible for a man to sleep with a woman knowing full well that he is to be bumped off on his way out, by the gallows or anything else ...; it is not impossible that this man coolly accepts such an eventuality on his leaving – for the pleasure of cutting up the lady concerned in small pieces, for example.

He then goes on to say: 'I have outlined then two cases that Kant doesn't envisage, two forms of transgression ..., namely, excessive object sublimation and what is commonly known as perversion'.[12] In Lacan's example, perversion manifests itself as the murder of the woman. In contrast, object sublimation, the over-evaluation of the object, conventionally the sublimation of the feminine object, means that the woman's value to the man exceeds that which he attributes to his own life.

To return to *Das Judasschaf* and the juxtaposition of St Peter and Glück, it is possible to see in each of them the signs of transgression. I would suggest that in St Peter we have a figure whose sublimation of the Christ figure has, so to speak, led to the gallows. His desire for Christ surpasses the value he puts on his own life. And whereas Lacan's pervert cuts up the woman, Glück is concerned with the cutting up of victims' hair.

However, what makes this whole issue of transgressive desire particularly acute is that the narrator is herself implicated; not only does she bring object sublimation and perversion together in the form of 'extraneous' material, but she herself is caught up in these desires. The narrator portrays herself as suffering, and there is certainly no reason to be sceptical of this. But there is a dimension to this suffering that is enjoyment, *jouissance*; it is not pleasurable, but causes excitement even though it is consciously perceived as horrific and repulsive. The text's constant emphasis on dismembered bodies and on physical cruelty reveals not just horror but an almost perverse fascination, a certain indulgence, that is also present in the descriptions of the wired-up jaw in Duden's short story 'Übergang'.[13] The violent tone is already established on the first page of *Das Judasschaf* when the narrator is dreaming (or daydreaming) on the aeroplane to Venice:

> Drei Männer ... sind sehr beschäftigt. Sie zersägen und zerlegen den toten Körper eines Schwarzen.... Sie spalten und zerhacken ihn, bereiten die einzelnen Teile zu. Saubere Schnittflächen, geglättete Knochentrennungen, wie für das Schaufenster eines Fleischerladens. (p. 7)

Or there is the ghastly description of animal slaughter:

> zwei bis drei Sekunden Schädelbeschuß [sind] die Regel. Danach wird eins der Hinterläufe an eine Oberleitung gekettet. Ein Stilett schlitzt die Kehle auf. Bisweilen geschieht das noch gerade während der zwei bis drei Sekunden andauernden Betäubung, meistens aber wird das Messer erst angesetzt, wenn die Betäubung wieder nachgelassen hat und das Bewußtsein zurückkehrt mit einem Schrei. Das meiste Fleisch blutet sich zu Tode, kopfüber durch den Schlund. (p. 55)

These scenes of violence provoke horror and repulsion on the part of the narrator and the reader, and are effective critical pointers to the violence of society. However, this horror is not undermined by a reading of the narrator's focus on violence as one that goes beyond conscious suffering and condemnation. While repulsed by violence, she is also fascinated by it and, crucially, is even dependent on it for assertions of her own subjectivity, a point that will be discussed shortly. First, though, to return to the other form of transgressive desire, that of object sublimation. The narrator's treatment of the Carpaccio paintings exemplifies the overinvestment of an object with significance. Her need to enter the paintings and to contemplate them at length offers her a release from suffering to such a degree that death becomes an enviable state; indeed the narrator herself relates the ability to enter the pictures to forms of death. She wishes to join the dead Christ in the *Meditation on Christ's Passion*, and at the end of the book she describes her only option as being able to join the spread-out Christ in the *Preparation for Christ's Entombment*: 'Alles andere führt zu nichts, ist mühselig und immer das gleiche' (p. 136). It is in the pictures that she is able to live by facing death.

Suffering as complicity

Hitherto I have argued that while the narrator holds up an apparent juxta-position of transgressor and victim, this opposition is not as simple as it initially seems, and that furthermore she is herself caught up in realms of desire that make her position questionable. The narrator identifies herself with the victims; she describes herself as a survivor, thus allying herself with the Christian martyrs and with the concentration camp victims. However much it stems from her very real suffering, such self-alignment is nevertheless questionable, and, coupled with a lurking fascination with violence, it must lead to a consideration of the issue of complicity. A discussion of complicity in relation to a suffering first-person narrator is not to suggest that her suffering is not felt, nor indeed that the narrator is actively contributing to forms of oppression in such a way that she could then herself be described as a perpetrator. Complicity is in this context tied in with personal identity and how the subject takes responsibility for its identity. In relation to this narrator the question of complicity involves the reader looking critically at how she uses her suffering as a means to constructing a certain identity, rather than being drawn into privileging her perceptions because she is suffering.

In order to explore this problem of complicity it is important to return to the notion of desire, central as it is to subject formation and identity. Implicit in what has been said about the importance of the Carpaccio paintings to the narrator is the textual emphasis on the importance of looking. In *Das Judasschaf* looking at paintings is crucial for the narrator for satisfying desire; in front of them she is able to achieve calm and temporary release from suffering. This fits in closely with the role of fantasy as a means for the subject to achieve an illusion of completeness, and leads specifically to the notion of the gaze. Lacan defines the gaze as object *a* – that trace of a subject's unattainable unity. As an object *a*, the gaze triggers desire, but is not an actual object, does not belong to a chain of signifiers within the symbolic. At the same time the gaze places the seeing subject within the symbolic as already given-to-be-seen. Crucial to the concept of the gaze is that it shows, as Rose puts it, 'the presence or insistence of desire inside those very forms which are designed to reproduce or guarantee the specular illusion itself (image, screen, spectator)'.[14]

Bound in with this concept, therefore, is the complex area of a subject's imaginary and symbolic identification. Imaginary identification is based on the subject's misrecognition of its mirror image as representing wholeness. The subject identifies with the mirror image, deriving narcissistic gratification from identification with an image that seems to guarantee completeness. Symbolic identification involves introjection from the field of the Other; it is no longer an identification limited to the one opposition of same/different, but involves language, morality, knowledge and authority. It is what the subject would 'like to be' in order to retain or regain that primary imaginary identification. To quote Rose again, it is 'necessary for the subject to be able to retain its narcissism while shifting its "perspective"'.[15] The difference between imaginary and symbolic identification is the difference between the ideal ego and the ego ideal, the former being the projected, constituting identification, the latter being the introjected, constituted identification.

It is with these concepts in mind that the issue of the narrator's complicity can usefully be addressed. The narrator presents herself in the form of a split between 'Ich' and 'Die Person', a split that does not simply represent her conscious sense of a lack of unity. For it seems to be closely related to the difference between ideal ego and ego ideal. The narrator identifies with the pictorial images, and importantly, all the descriptions of the pictures are presented from the perspective of the 'I'; the one exception is with the last description of the *Entombment* where the narrator specifically comments 'Ich komme an und werde wegen der herrschenden Lebensgefahr jetzt nicht mehr ich sagen' (p. 128). After this she is 'die Frau', and no longer 'die Person' until the very last line, 'es ist schön und ich habe Angst' (p. 138). The assertion of the 'I' in front of the paintings is suggestive of the reassuring imaginary identification of the subject with the specular image. It fulfils the desire of the subject to find a guarantor of subjectivity in a specular image, as Lacan describes it in seminar XI: '[The painter] gives something for the eye to feed on, but he invites the person to whom this picture is presented to lay down his gaze there as one lays down one's weapons. This is the pacifying, Apollonian effect of painting.'[16] It is such a pacifying effect that the narrator experiences when she contemplates the paintings. By identifying with the victims they depict she derives narcissistic gratification, a guarantee of her subjectivity.

In contrast, her reference to herself as 'Die Person' conveys a sense of distance, of how she is watching herself, how she sees herself when viewed from a different perspective. Overall, her position is surely not unlike that of Hegel's 'schöne Seele', which for Lacan offered an appropriate image for the human ego: 'the ego of modern man ... has taken on its form in the dialectical impasse of the *belle âme* who does not recognise his very own *raison d'être* in the disorder that he denounces in the world'.[17] Slavoj Zizek discusses Lacan's use of the term in relation to political examples, and sees certain sorts of dissidents in socialism fitting this definition. He also gives as an example the mother who sacrifices everything to be the pillar of the family:

> The mother's fault is therefore not simply in her 'inactivity' in silently enduring the role of exploited victim, but in actively sustaining the social-symbolic network in which she is reduced to playing such a role.... On the level of the ideal-imaginary ego, the 'beautiful soul' sees herself as a fragile, passive victim; she identifies with this role; in it she 'likes herself', she appears to herself likeable; this role gives her a narcissistic pleasure; but her real identification is with the formal structure of the intersubjective field which enables her to

assume this role. In other words, this structuring of the intersubjective space (the family network) is the point of her symbolic identification, the point from which she observes herself so that she appears to herself likeable in her imaginary role.[18]

In *Das Judasschaf*, the narrator's symbolic identification is with a point from which society is perceived only in terms of atrocities. The genocide of the Jews in particular enables her to adopt and sustain her role as victim, a position that is further justified by her reference to other instances of destruction and pain. Furthermore, her assertion that others' lack of 'Gedächtnis' is male, acts to bolster her role as victim in relation to her identity as a woman. It is in terms of this symbolic identification that the narrator's relationship to atrocities can be viewed as one of complicity. Her complicity does not reside in aiding and abetting the oppressors, or feeling sympathy for what they do; it resides in her dependence on the horror that violence provokes and a dependence on others' and her own suffering for structuring her identity.

Complicity and feminism

This critical interpretation of the narrator might be seen as tantamount to once again denying women the voice to express and denounce their own suffering. Is it not thus a deeply anti-feminist gesture? On the contrary. It is only by approaching the narrator critically that we can perceive the complexity of Duden's reckoning with female identity. For her exploration of female identity and desire is an analysis that refuses to simplify problems because they concern a female protagonist. Where many books depict female identity as complex, this book confronts the issue of women's own responsibility for that complex, even contradictory, identity. It forces the reader to question how women situate themselves in relation to their desires and this may well be an unpleasant exercise. *Das Judasschaf* does not let women off the hook and it is precisely this that makes it valuable for a feminist critique. The questions it asks about identification, fantasy and complicity may be disquieting, but this makes it all the more indispensable.

It is important finally to comment on the title of the book. The Judasschaf is described at the end of Chapter 2, following the description of animal slaughter quoted earlier. It is the sheep, or sometimes the goat, which meets the shipment of animals to be killed, and which leads them into the slaughterhouse. It does not itself get slaughtered, but returns to meet the next batch of condemned beasts. A powerful and unpalatable image, this treacherous beast is not explicitly related to a human equivalent. But there can be no stronger signal of the text's preoccupation than giving the book the name of this animal. For this image is about identification; the sheep comply with the smooth functioning of the slaughter because the Judasschaf appears to be like them. It vividly represents the danger of unreflected identification. The image functions as a figure of reading, whereby the narrator appeals to her readers to identify with her because she appears like one of them – with fatal consequences if we lay down our critical gaze. Identification is not always what it seems.

Notes

1 All references to *Malina* will be to the Suhrkamp Taschenbuch edition (Frankfurt am Main: Suhrkamp, 1991) and will be given in parenthesis.
2 Sigrid Weigel, '"Ein Ende mit der Schrift. Ein andrer Anfang." Zur Entwicklung von Ingeborg Bachmanns Schreibweise', in Heinz Ludwig Arnold (ed.), *Ingeborg Bachmann* (Munich: Text und Kritik Sonderband, 1984), pp. 58–92.
3 Ingeborg Bachmann, *Wir müssen wahre Sätze finden. Gespräche und Interviews*, ed. Christine Koschel and Inge von Weidenbaum (Munich: Piper, 1983), pp. 90–1.
4 Ibid., pp.69–70.
5 Joan W. Scott, '"Experience"', in Judith Butler and Joan W, Scott (eds), *Feminists Theorize the Political* (New York and London: Routledge, 1992), pp. 22–40 (p. 37).
6 Judith Butler, 'Contingent Foundations: Feminism and the Question of "Postmodernism"', in Butler and Scott (eds), *Feminists Theorize the Political*, pp. 3–21 (p. 16).
7 Jacqueline Rose, *Sexuality in the Field of Vision* (London and New York: Verso, 1986), p. 16.
8 Anne Duden, *Das Judasschaf* (Berlin: Rotbuch, 1985). All references will be to the 1994 edition.
9 Bruce Fink, *The Lacanian Subject. Between Language and Juissance* (Princeton: Princeton University Press, 1995), p. 59.
10 Ibid., p. 60.
11 Jacques Lacan, *The Ethics of Psychoanalysis* (London: Routledge, 1992), p. 108.
12 Ibid., p. 109.
13 Anne Duden, *Übergang* (Berlin: Rotbuch, 1982).
14 Rose, *Sexuality*, p. 190.
15 Ibid., p. 177.
16 Jacques Lacan, *The Four Fundamental Concepts of Psycho-Analysis* (London: Penguin, 1979), p. 101.
17 Jacques Lacan, *Écrits. A Selection* (London: Routledge, 1977), p. 70.
18 Slavoj Zizek, *The Sublime Object of Ideology* (London and New York: Verso, 1989), p. 216.

8

Staging the East German 'working class': representation and class identity in the 'workers' state'

Corey Ross

In a 1991 survey on 'subjective class categorization', 61 per cent of Germans in the new *Bundesländer* viewed themselves as belonging to the 'lower and working class', 37 per cent to the 'middle class' and only 2 per cent to the 'upper-middle and upper class'. By contrast, in the old Federal Republic only 25 per cent considered themselves 'lower and working class' compared to 62 per cent 'middle class' and 13 per cent 'upper-middle and upper class'.[1] Despite the slightly higher percentage of manual workers in the region of the former German Democratic Republic than in West Germany, it is clear that this massive East–West difference cannot be explained solely on the basis of the socio-economic structure of the East German populace. The official report on the survey thus explains the difference largely as a matter of East German feelings of being underprivileged in terms of pay and employment opportunities compared to West Germans. In this view it was therefore a feeling of relative deprivation, of being the 'underdog', that led so many former East Germans to count themselves among the 'lower and working class'.[2] Clearly, such resentments were extremely common in the new *Bundesländer* in the midst of widespread plant closures and massive reductions in the workforce. But does this interpretation, devoid of any reference to the East German past, really offer a sufficient explanation of the huge cleft between patterns of class identity among East and West Germans in the wake of reunification? If one casts a glance back at the history of the idea of the 'working class' in the GDR and how it was constantly staged throughout the history of the East German 'workers' state', post-*Wende* feelings of relative deprivation appear as only part of the puzzle.

Since the Second World War, one of the most fundamental social and structural changes in industrial societies has been the growth of the service sector and the related tendency towards de-industrialization, the shrinking of the industrial workforce and the decline of what might broadly be called the 'proletarian milieu'.[3] In 1989, only 19.4 per cent of the West German workforce was involved in the actual extraction of raw materials, the production of goods or construction, compared to 80.6 per cent working in the 'service sector' in the broadest sense of the term.[4] Such figures are more or less typical for North America and western Europe, where the concept of 'working class' in the traditional sense of the nominally class-conscious manual labourer is becoming increasingly confined to pensioners in flat-caps. In these 'post-industrial' societies, factories have been turned into art museums, and docks and warehouses have been converted into luxury flats and shopping centres. Smoke-stacks that once characterized urban skylines have largely given way to telecommunications towers. Leftist parties facing the decline of their traditional demographic base of support are either 'modernizing' or in various states of disarray. Mainstream cultural iconography in television, film, advertising and even political life is almost exclusively that of the middle-class-yet-classless consumer – the symbol of the postwar 'affluent society', or what in the 1950s and 1960s was often called the 'American way of life'.

In East Germany, like the other postwar socialist states, the situation was rather different. For a number of reasons, the 'working class' and 'proletarian milieu' survived much more intact in this self-styled 'workers' and peasants' state'. For one thing, the GDR started out with a higher percentage of industrial workers and a 'higher degree of proletarianization' than the Federal Republic as a result of industrialization during the interwar period.[5] In the 1939 census, 56 per cent of the working population in *Mitteldeutschland* were classified as 'workers' compared to 48 per cent in western Germany. Moreover, this trend of industrialization continued both during and after the war in the region of the GDR, especially with the expansion of raw materials industries in the 1950s. This general trend is visible even if one takes the official East German statistics with a pinch of salt: according to these statistics the percentage of 'workers and *Angestellten*' actually rose from 68.6 per cent in 1952 to 76 per cent in 1960.[6] This trend was further reinforced by the mass exodus to the West up until 1961, in which the educated and propertied were roughly doubly represented.[7] Whatever the problems with official East German statistics, the demographic divergence from West Germany was in any event unmistakable. According to the last official census statistics in the GDR in 1981, 37.1 per cent of all East Germans in employment were considered 'workers in production occupations' (as we will see below, this category is far more useful than merely 'worker') compared to only 20 per cent in West Germany in 1989.[8]

There were, then, a number of differences in the economic and social structure of the GDR that made it a more 'working-class' region than western Germany. But what was decisive was that *idea* of 'workers' and 'working class' survived relatively intact. Of course the maintenance of a relatively high percentage of workers itself underlay this, especially in the industrial conurbations in the south of the GDR. There were also certain region-specific factors at work: the industrial centres of Thuringia and especially Saxony – the so-called *'Werkstatt Deutschlands'* – were traditional bastions of 'working-class' life and culture and were also electoral strongholds for the workers' parties before 1933. Most importantly though, the 'worker' and 'working class' were constantly being staged and propagated as the central icons of political and cultural life in the GDR. Instead of the classless consumer, the official cultural icon in the GDR was the politically mobilized and class-conscious manual worker – above all engaged in industrial production. East German film, television and literature tended far more than in the West to be set in the industrial or working-class milieu, were far more apt to deal with class as a theme and were certainly more clearly couched in the language of class struggle. East German political imagery (in a narrower sense) was almost exclusively set in an industrial milieu, often with a stony-faced, confident and determined production worker as the central feature. Throughout the history of the GDR, representations of 'worker' and 'working class' took on a variety of different functions which – though this was not the only intention – no doubt contributed to the maintenance of a broad 'working-class' identity in the GDR. This chapter will focus on two aspects: the staging of the 'working class' as a source of political legitimation and as a means of mobilization for the economy.

The 'working class' as source of legitimation

In view of the permanently high percentage of 'workers' in the East German population and one of the highest rates of paid employment in the world, the fact that the SED leadership still considered a constant staging of the 'working class' necessary even after the official establishment of the 'dictatorship of the proletariat' tells much about the relationship between East German workers and 'their' state. The SED was a self-consciously 'workers' party'. It understood and presented itself as the historic culmination of the German workers' movement, and it claimed to rule on workers' behalf – in Marxist-Leninist theory as the communist avant-garde of the new dictatorship. In this view, the bond between the party leadership and the manual (above all, industrial) workforce was taken as axiomatic and questioned only insofar as one recognized certain 'ideogically backward' portions of the otherwise revolutionary working class. As unshakeable as this self-understanding appears to have been among the party leadership, it was still difficult to reconcile with the everyday experience of governing the *actual* working masses in the GDR. By June 1953 at the latest, when thousands of workers marched through the streets demanding a better living standard and the toppling of the communist-led government, the cleft between theory and practice was obvious to all. The problem was that the SED's entire legitimation was based on that theory. As Bertolt Brecht ironically commented in the wake of the June uprising, 'would it not be simpler if the government dissolved the people and elected another?'[9] In a sense, this is precisely what it did by staging a theatrical production of an East German working class that conformed to theory.

An important part of this stage production consisted of presenting the proletariat as legitimate dictators. Although the methods by which this was done changed over the forty years of the GDR's history, especially with the expansion of electronic media, the continuities far outweighted the changes. This reflected both the high level of personal continuity within the party leadership as well as the essentially unchanged understanding of its own right to rule. The lack of democratic legitimacy via open elections was compensated for by the notion of the historical mission of the working class, which was, again, conflated with the party itself. The SED consciously made use of the icons of the prewar and especially interwar workers' movement as a means of evoking a sense of anti-fascist moral authority after the horrors of Nazism.[10] Political placards in the GDR showed striking similarities with those of the 1920s and 1930s in both style and content. Although the socialist state was already established, the sense of movement and struggle was retained, as were the principal icons of the factory worker, miner and construction worker. Public rituals, such as the May Day parades, also fell back on the traditions of the prewar workers' (especially communist) movement. The annual commemoration of the murders of Rosa Luxemburg and Karl Liebknecht show even more clearly the attempt to evoke a sense of moral authority from the interwar workers' movement (although Luxemburg's defence of the 'Freiheit der Andersdenkenden' was conveniently left out of the celebrations). Although Soviet influence was becoming increasingly visible in the 1940s and 1950s in the form of the personality cult and commemoration of the October Revolution, even the new public rituals in the GDR such as the 'Day of Liberation' (8 May) and the anniversaries of the founding of the Republic were based in theme and format on these prewar precursors. Common to all of these carefully stage-managed public rituals was the effort to give form to the idea of an historic mission of the working class, to convey an impression of spontaneity while at same time to demonstrate the solidarity, single-mindedness and strength of the politically organized and class-conscious working masses.

Of course the staging of these mass public rituals took some time to perfect. Reports on marches and demonstrations in the early years of the GDR constantly complain of banners not being completed on time, of participants stealing out of the ranks and heading home, or of large numbers of workers who had agreed to participate failing to appear in the first place. The majority were simply uninterested in the SED's stage productions and had better things to do. Comments such as 'We're sick and tired of demonstrating'; 'We're not going to demonstrate any more if we have to remain standing for so long'; 'If we don't get paid on 1 May we're not going to demonstrate' are common in the reports.[11] But even by the end of the 1950s, these problems had largely been ironed out. Reports on the tenth anniversary of the founding of the GDR in 1959 speak of the highest number of participants to date, thousands of houses hanging out flags and generally attentive crowds – though most people simply played their part and left after what seemed a decent interval.[12]

In the SED's view, the difference between a 'people's democracy' and western 'bourgeois democracy' was that the former was governed in the interests of the working masses instead of the privileged few. In the absence of open elections, the claim that under 'real existing socialism' the working masses were in effect governing themselves could only be upheld insofar as the working class maintained a numerically dominant position in society. Despite the rapid expansion of heavy industry in the 1950s and the relatively slow mechanization of work processes compared to the West, this nonetheless presented a long-term problem. The result was a tendency to define social and demographic categories as generously as possible in favour of the 'working class', such that it always accounted for a significant majority of the populace.

A glance at the official Statistical Yearbooks shows how this worked. In the 1955 yearbook (based on 1950 census data), 'workers' comprised 52 per cent of the working populace, '*Angestellten*' 21 per cent, self-employed 14 per cent and 'assisting members of the family' 13 per cent. By 1966 (based on 1964 census data), 'workers and *Angestellten*' were lumped together and comprised 82 per cent of the working populace, compared to 13 per cent 'members of cooperatives' and only 4 per cent 'others'. This basic demographic formula of 'working-class, members of a cooperative, intelligentsia and others' grew more and more vague over time, as the pressures of growing service industries and increasing mechanization necessitated an ever-broader definition of 'workers'. In the 1989 statistics, 90.5 per cent were classified as 'workers and *Angestellten*' and 9.5 per cent as 'members of cooperatives and others'.[13] The following year, a sociologist estimated that only 32 per cent were in 'genuine worker occupations'. The fact that everyone from coal miners to hairdressers to nurses and shop attendants were subsumed under the category 'workers' was not merely an expression of the attempt to hide the continuing social and economic distinctions between different segments of society, it was a crucial component of the SED's self-legitimatory staging of the East German 'working-class'.[14]

Apart from demographic trends, another problem was that, whatever its size and composition, the 'working class' could only be posited as a ruling class insofar as the ruling SED could be presented as a 'party of the working class', and this meant above all being a party composed of workers. Guaranteeing a sufficiently high percentage of 'workers' in the party was a matter of constant concern and attention, and the SED's history was punctuated by periodic campaigns to recruit new members from the ranks of industrial workers. At first this was hardly a problem. During the 1940s and early

1950s a large proportion of the party rank-and-file could reasonably be called 'workers' in the traditional sense of manual wage labourers. But already by the latter half of the 1950s the rapidly declining percentage of industrial labourers in the party necessitated a looser definition of 'workers' as a means of upholding appearances. By then, the party had become far more 'professionalized', which resulted above all from the SED's own attempts in the 1950s to create a 'new intelligentsia' recruited primarily from among the working classes. Whereas 48.1 per cent of its members in 1947 could be classified as 'workers' compared to 22 per cent '*Angestellten* and intelligentsia', by 1957 these proportions had reversed to only 33.8 per cent 'workers' and 42.3 per cent '*Angestellten* and intelligentsia'. Since recruiters were finding it difficult to win actual industrial workers for the party, the problem required a more creative solution. At the Fifth Party Convention in 1958 it was suggested that functionaries of the party, state and mass organizations 'regularly participate in production work or in the *Nationalen Aufbauwerk*', and that all spend some time each year 'at the basis'.[15] In other words, if one could not get enough workers to join the SED, the next best thing was to make existing members more like workers.

But this quasi-'proletarianization' of regime functionaries could not solve the problem for long, and membership statistics eventually had to be massaged. In 1966, the official percentage of 'workers' in the SED once again rose to 45.6 per cent while '*Angestellten* and intelligentsia' fell to 28.4 per cent (19.6 per cent 'others'), which obviously amounted to little more than a considerable broadening of the definition of 'worker' at the time. In 1973 the percentage of 'workers' rose again to 56.6 per cent, this time at the expense of the category 'others', which fell to a mere 7 per cent, with '*Angestellten* and intelligentsia' remaining more or less level at 30.7 per cent. Thereafter the official percentage of 'workers' in the SED changed only slightly for the rest of its history. Yet it nonetheless remained a point of concern. At the Tenth Party Convention in 1981, Honecker felt obliged to emphasize that of the 263,920 'workers' recruited as members and candidates since the last convention, 241,423 were 'involved directly in the sphere of material production'. Such success reports were dubious, however, for at the Eleventh (and last) Party Convention in 1986 it was openly conceded that 58.1 per cent of party members and candidates were classified as workers 'in terms of their social background' – how far back and precisely what this meant was not mentioned.[16]

Although the doors of higher education were opened to workers on an unprecedented scale in the 1940s and 1950s, the declining percentage of workers studying at East German universities soon presented a similar problem in staging the 'working class' as ruling class. The percentage of 'workers' at the universities peaked in 1958 at 52.7 per cent, thereafter followed by a swift downward trend. By 1960 the proportion of 'workers' was already down to 39.2 per cent, only to fall further to 31.1 per cent in 1966 (over the same period the percentage of 'intelligentsia' at the universities rose from 17.8 per cent to 30.2 per cent). The solution to this problem was much more straightforward than the solution to the problem of dwindling numbers of 'workers' in the party ranks: after 1967 statistics on the social background of university students were no longer kept.[17]

The ideal worker as a means of mobilization

The staging of the East German 'working class' had more than just legitimatory functions, and was also periodically used as a means of mobilizing workers to raise productivity. Over the years it became more and more common to present individual workers or groups of workers as idealized representatives of the 'working class', as models for what the SED thought workers should be and above all for how the party leadership thought they should work. This was most evident in the constant series of activist campaigns, socialist competitions and brigade campaigns, beginning with the so-called 'Hennecke Movement' in 1948, whose purpose was to raise work discipline and productivity out of its postwar doldrums.

The genesis of the 'Hennecke Movement' was symptomatic of all these representative campaigns. What was supposed to be a 'spontaneous' decision of a 'progressive' miner was actually a carefully planned and closely directed stage presentation. This is obvious in the report of Otto Buchwitz, SED chief in Saxony and initiator of the movement, to the SED party executive:

> One should not imagine for a moment that this was a chance accomplishment; rather, we consciously developed the case. I would like to say a few words about this: our goal was to find a way that we would develop an activist movement. We said that for this we needed a central figure, a personality ... We looked for a man, and the district leadership helped us ... Director Wellershaus looked for a long time, and then found the coal miner Hennecke, whose production already always surpassed that of his colleagues. In the course of the following weeks, he was brought along by Wellershaus. Therefore, the record was prepared in advance and, to be sure, the goal was set before comrade Hennecke: see that you fulfil your norm by 250 per cent! ... We developed the man in such a way that we sent him first to the district party school [in August 1947] [and we] had him take part in political life until he declared that he was ready to take on [the achievement] despite all the resistance he believes it will encounter.[18]

And encounter resistance it did. But this was not part of the script. Instead, Buchwitz claimed that Hennecke's achievements were greeted by 'a storm of enthusiasm among the workers'. Workers in other industries supposedly emulated him, and telegrams poured in announcing amazing new production records all across the Soviet Occupation Zone. Party and union propagandists launched a massive and well-coordinated effort to popularize

Hennecke and his 'heroic deeds'. Newspapers were filled with impressive statistics and reports of local activists' feats. Activist posters were pasted everywhere, billboards were covered with Hennecke's face, pins and medals were produced, even schools and streets were named after Hennecke. There was also a spate of embarrassingly puerile poems and songs about Hennecke, which one can only imagine hindered the movement more than helped it. One example suffices to offer a taste of their iconographic flavour:

> Hennecke! Du bist der Mann, der uns begeistert!
> Hennecke! Mit Dir wird unsere Not gemeistert!
> Hennecke! Wir schwören Dir, wir wollen uns bemühen!
> Hennecke! Durch Dich wird unsere Wirtschaft wieder blühen!
> Hennecke! Du bist ein Held von unserer Klasse!
> Hennecke! Du bist mit uns die starke Masse!
> Hennecke! Wir wollen stets von Dir als Vorbild sprechen!
> Hennecke! Du wirst der Brüder Knechtung auch im Westen brechen![19]

By mining 387 per cent of his normal coal quota in one shift, Hennecke and the movement named after him were supposed to inspire other workers to fulfil their potential by demonstrating how easy it was to overfulfil one's quota. But reports from the factories offer little evidence that it worked, as few workers were willing to become 'norm-breakers'. Most workers were sceptical of production increases so long as problems of supply continued, and moreover had little desire to work harder 'for the Russians'. Furthermore, the majority correctly doubted the verity of Hennecke's heroic performance and knew good and well that a normal work day simply did not allow for such production increases. Simply put, most were well aware that it was stage production. As one retired worker put it:

> I've worked in factories and know what one can manage to do. But the idea that a worker nowadays triples his performance or even increases it sixfold seems impossible to me as long as everything happens in a normal way. In my opinion the Henneckes prepare everything hours in advance, pick out the best tools for themselves and get provided with the necessary materials. In short, it's actually just a big song and dance [*ein Theater*] that is being performed.[20]

Despite occasional successes, the Henneckists gained little influence over their fellow workers. In fact, their efforts won them more anger and hostility than admiration, as Hennecke himself had feared and quickly found out:

> When I came to the shaft the next day the lads [*Kumpel*] did not look at me anymore. That's anything but a nice feeling when you look them in the eyes and say '*Glückauf*' and they nod, yes, but you don't hear anything anymore. I used to be simply Adolf, a miner like any other. But now there was a wall between us.[21]

Although much of the resentment stemmed from the understandable aversion to the idea of working harder and being a 'norm-breaker', part of it stemmed from the 'Sovietness' of the movement. Most of the denunciatory letters sent to Hennecke not only denigrated him as a 'traitor to workers' and 'worker-murderer', but also also clearly associated him with what was widely viewed as the Soviet exploitation of Germany: 'For a whole year now you've sold the sweat of your comrades to the Russians and taken your blood money [*Judaslohn*]. You won't live another year, you scoundrel!'[22]

In its attempts to mobilize East German workers, the SED had slightly more success with more familiar ploys from the German, instead of Soviet, past. Concepts such as 'professional honour' (*Berufsehre*) and titles such as 'Heroes of Work' – which distinguished itself from the Hennecke Movement in taking the overall behaviour of workers into account, not just their measureable output – were consciously introduced by the party and union leadership as a means of stimulating performance by latching on to the symbols, traditions and values of the pre-war German workers' movement. This practice was especially visible in the propagation of a curiously nationalistic notion of 'German quality', which had also been used as an integrating factor for workers during both world wars.[23]

Yet most workers remained sceptical towards the party's mobilization attempts regardless of the particular symbols used. The 1958–60 campaign to found 'brigades of socialist work' offers another example of this. Although it encountered less shopfloor opposition than the Hennecke Movement, it too largely failed as a means of mobilizing the broad masses of workers by means of creating idealized representatives of the 'working class'.

Production brigades, modelled on Soviet 'shock brigades' of the 1920s and 1930s, were first introduced in the GDR in 1950. Their aim was not merely to increase productivity, but also to serve as an instrument for the control and 'education' of workers – in the words of the Free German Trade Union (FDGB) deputy chairman Rudi Kirchner, to 'shatter the individualist and rogue tendencies through collective work in the brigades and the closely related education towards collective responsibility, and to turn the brigade into the basic cell for the full unfolding of the creative energies of the workers'.[24] By the second half of the 1950s, production brigades had become an integral part of the world of work in the GDR. But as their numbers expanded over the years,[25] their value as models for workers' organization was diluted. The introduction of the 'brigades of socialist work' in 1959 was an attempt by the SED to revitalize the brigade movement and reassert control over it. As a 'higher form' of collective organization, these were supposed to offer a more suitable framework for the development of the 'new man'. The 'brigades of socialist work' were even more clearly intended as instruments for control and enhancing work-discipline than the previous brigades, as was particularly visible in their system of mutual control and prescribed practice of 'self-education'. But what distinguished them most clearly from their forerunners was their 'educational' and social functions outside the realm of work – not just 'sozialistisch zu arbeiten', but also 'sozialistisch zu leben und zu lernen'. Even the families of members were to be involved in the life of the brigade, which might include weekend trips, recreational activities, sporting events, and the like.

After a youth brigade at the Elektrochemisches Kombinat Bitterfeld supposedly initiated the 'movement' on 3 January 1959 (after careful planning by the FDGB executive), party and FDGB propagandists launched a huge campaign across the GDR heralding the founding of 'brigades of socialist work'. Yet despite the massive publicity efforts and thousands of factory assemblies, it proved difficult at first to find willing participants. The main problem was the new emphasis on one's behaviour and activities away from the factory. It was one thing to declare oneself willing to be more efficient or diligent at work, but it was quite another to play the role of upstanding 'socialist worker' at home as well. Even among groups of workers well-disposed to the idea of founding or joining a 'brigade of socialist work', few could picture to themselves what 'socialist living' would entail. As one report put it: 'It appears that the call "sozialistisch lernen und leben" (especially live) presents greater problems compared to the call "sozialistisch arbeiten."'[26] Among younger workers in particular, union functionaries again and again heard the question: 'Do we have to become a socialist brigade? We can fulfil our economic tasks like that as well, and can arrange our private lives however we like!' Women workers in Berlin often asked about shopping in the West: 'They say that if one forbids them to do this, they could not work in a socialist brigade.'[27] Some workers refused to join because they feared that their religious activities would be curtailed, above all that their children would have to undergo the secular *Jugendweihe*. Some Christian workers even went so far as to declare that 'joining a brigade of socialist work is a profession of atheism'. Even SED members by and large refused to join socialist brigades because 'there would be too many stipulations for one's personal life and they therefore feel hindered in their personal matters'.[28]

According to official statistics, it did not take long to overcome these problems and find enough workers willing to join. By the end of 1959 there were officially 59,324 'brigades of socialist work' with 706,657 members; by the end of 1960 the number had risen to 130,024 brigades with 1,669,208 members. But as the FDGB leadership itself was well aware, these statistics were themselves part of yet another stage production over which they themselves had little control: namely that of the lower levels of the party and union apparatus for the benefit of their superiors at the top of the hierarchy. Warnke himself complained as early as March 1959 that many lower-level functionaries were not taking the movement seriously, but merely indulging in 'Zahlenhascherei' ('throwing numbers around'). Otto Lehmann complained in July 1959 of 'many empty promises and much empty participation in this movement', estimating that around one-half of the brigades existed merely on paper.[29] Much worse than the self-serving reports of lower-level functionaries was the fact that even most of the 'brigades of socialist work' that did exist were hardly functioning as the models of socialist behaviour they were intended to be. For one thing, there was a tendency to use the brigade structure as a means of improving one's wages and maintaining the social and economic distinctions within the factories – forming brigades only out of the best workers, youth brigades refusing older workers because they were not as fit, all-male brigades excluding women, and so forth.[30] Moreover, social events such as the 'brigade evenings' were in practice little more than traditional *Stammtische*, and attempts to instrumentalize such social gatherings were utterly futile. As one brigadier in Brandenburg complained: 'If there is going to be a political talk and I have to pay for my own beer, I'm not coming!'[31]

Throughout the course of 1959 and 1960, the campaign for 'brigades of socialist work' ran well out of the SED's control. Not only did it fail as a means of mobilization, it in some ways made the task more difficult than before. By offering a 'higher form' of collective organization, the 'brigades of socialist work' also (completely contrary to the intentions behind them) offered workers a more effective framework for the articulation of interests *independent* of the SED and FDGB – interests which, as we have seen, were central to the regime's self-legitimatory claims. During 1959 and 1960 the brigadiers and in particular the new, relatively independent brigade-councils played a key role in the formulation and expression of wide-ranging demands concerning the interrelated questions of wages, norms and working conditions. The 'special rights' that some of the brigades demanded were unnerving to the party leadership. These included, for instance, the right to work out their own plan figures, to determine their own norms, to establish their own vacation schemes as well as to calculate and administer the payment of bonuses. Furthermore, the regulatory demands of brigades eventually extended well beyond purely material matters to include a certain measure of self-administration and insulation from factory managers, including the rights of punishment for poor work discipline. In some factories these competences were indeed temporarily transferred from the factory management to the brigades. As a result, attendence lists replaced old punch cards (which workers argued was an affront to the honour of a worker and member of a socialist brigade), tardy workers thereafter had to check in with the *Meister* or brigadier instead of the head office, and some brigades even began to make their own decisions regarding vacation, hiring, firing and transferring workers.[32]

The SED and FDGB leadership could not help but view this as a hollowing-out of their monopoly of power, and responded with an aggressive campaign in 1960 against 'syndicalism', as the tendency towards self-regulation was incriminatingly called.[33] This was tantamount to an admission that one of the SED's major stage productions of the 'working class' had gone badly awry. Yet maintaining appearances was of the utmost importance even in the manner of the crackdown. The fact that both Ulbricht and Warnke blamed functionaries and 'failures of leadership' more than the brigades themselves points back to a more fundamental problem of staging the 'workers' state'. The party and FDGB could under no circumstances be seen as failing to represent workers' interests. In this line of thought, the derailing of the socialist brigades campaign was not viewed as a structural problem, but rather one of not having done it quite right.[34]

Although the socialist brigades hardly constituted an internal threat to the regime, it is worth noting that the SED did not try this particular kind of stage production of the 'working class' again. Instead, the inability to increase productivity meaningfully via either the brigades or occasional administrative wage-reforms made older methods of mobilization, in particular the activists' movement and related 'socialist competitions', more attractive. After the initially disappointing results of the activists' movement, the numbers of workers participating in it constantly rose throughout the following decades (though it was clear that the monetary rewards and bonuses were the primary motivation, not the ideology behind them). Workers were literally playing the roles assigned to them and taking whatever advantages they could from the competitions. It was clear to party officials early on, especially those at the local level responsible for organizing them, that the competitions were of very limited economic use. Yet for a number of reasons these mobilization efforts never died out. On the contrary, over the years the activists' movement and socialist competitions became central features of the GDR economy – not for economic reasons, but rather because they were an indispensable political ritual of public affirmation of the regime, a necessary staging of the ideologically sound relationship between the working class and 'their' state. In the competitions, workers 'obligated' themselves to work more, to achieve something new, not for themselves, but for the party and its productivity goals. By agreeing, even if only symbolically, to do something 'extra', workers were in effect publicly displaying their support for the party. Like the socialist 'elections', which had little to do with deciding who ran the country, the socialist competitions were a ritual of working-class affirmation of the party and its industrial policies. What made them so indispensable and popular among the party hierarchy was not their effectiveness as a means of raising productivity, but rather the fact that at the local level they allowed party secretaries in the factories to demonstrate their authority, and at the central level, they nourished the double illusion of widespread worker support for the regime as well as the idea that productivity gains could be made by tapping into these reserves of 'working-class' loyalty to the SED's cause – an illusion that rapidly broke down during the summer and autumn of 1989.

The socialist competitions and activists' movement thus served more as a public ritual of outward support in exchange for material gifts than as a stimulus for increasing productivity. In fact, during the 1970s and 1980s this political theatre was the essence of SED social policy more generally. Under the slogan of the 'Unity of Social and Economic Policy', the party leadership under Honecker tried for almost two decades to secure the '*mißmutige Loyalität*'[35] of East German workers – by now officially presented as around three-fourths of the population – via a range of social concessions, an improved material living standard and better social services. The problem was that the GDR could barely afford such an expensive policy at the best of times, and piled up insurmountable debts in the 1980s under the effects of rising international oil prices, increasing trade competition and the high investment requirements of the electronics boom. Despite rising wages, which increased by 162 per cent between 1971 and 1988, labour productivity stagnated.[36] Whereas East German GDP per person stood at 67 per cent of the West German level in 1967, by the time the GDR collapsed this had declined to merely 40 per cent. East German workers may not have felt it at the time, but during the 1970s and 1980s they were becoming increasingly overpaid, and the GDR as a whole was living beyond its means. Yet for political reasons it was impossible to couple social policy and expenditure *vis-à-vis* the East German working masses with actual economic growth based on their productivity. The show of prioritized social expenditure for the 'working class' went on for as long as possible, but it could not last forever.

Conclusions

Ironically, then, the representation of the 'working class' as the majority ruling class in the GDR and the prioritization of social expenditure on 'workers' not only failed as a means of mobilizing them to overcome the problems in the economy, it became one of the main problems itself. Yet it would be wrong to conclude that the constant staging of the East German 'working class' was an unmitigated failure from the party's point of view. While it is clear that the SED leadership did not succeed in generating widespread positive support for the regime among the majority of 'workers', there seems little doubt that the social concessions did contribute to the regime's political stability during its latter decades, however immeasurable this contribution was. And while workers were clearly nothing like the models the SED presented to them and hardly responded to the various overtures of the regime as it would have wished, the vast majority still more or less willingly participated in the staging of the 'workers' state' – marching in the parades, signing the declarations of solidarity with striking workers in the West, paying dues to the SED-controlled union, signing up for the latest 'socialist competition' – however half-heartedly and however guided by their own interests.

Even though the SED could derive little long-term political or economic use out of this stage production, it was not without its effects. Whatever the regime's failures in creating a working class that conformed to Marxist-Leninist theory, it largely succeeded in constructing and maintaining a 'proletarian norm' in the GDR very different from the icon of the young classless

consumer in the West. Put another way, it managed to sustain and propagate a broad 'working-class' identity in the GDR, just not the particular one
it wanted. Whatever the popular resonance of the SED's constant class-
struggle rhetoric, belonging to the 'working class' remained a source of pride
and identity for many East Germans in a way and to an extent that it did
not in the West – hardly surprising, since the vast majority of East Germans
were constantly being told they were 'workers'.

This is not to say that the post-1989 East–West cleft in class identities is
just an innocuous cultural 'hangover' of forty years of East German socialism easily transformed by a new hegemony of western cultural symbols.
Indeed, its echoes have been clearly heard in the far more tangible realm of
social and political debates, for the cleft between East and West in unified
Germany has, after all, also been a very concrete social and economic one.
East German dislike of 'Wessis' and West German ways has not seldomly
been overladen with class terminology and connotations: for instance in the
resentment about former 'People's Own' factories being bought up by West
German businesses – particularly among the thousands who were thrown
out of work as a result – or about 'bourgeois' western landlords buying up
(or laying proprietary claim to) residential properties in the former GDR,
especially if rents were increased as the result of speculative renovations.
Although post-*Wende* feelings of relative deprivation in the new *Bundesländer* do not by themselves offer a satisfactory explanation for the fact that so
many former East Germans consider themselves 'lower and working class',
they should not be underestimated.

Of course the remarkable cleft in self-understanding and cultural values
between eastern and western Germany, still clearly visible a decade after
unification, has to do with more than just notions of vertical social status
and feelings of being the 'underdog'. Indeed, questions of class, material
wealth and the wider issue of 'national identity' in the new *Bundesländer*
cannot be neatly separated. Whatever the SED's success in building and sustaining a broad and diffuse 'working-class' identity in the GDR, it is clear
that one of main reasons for the collapse of communism and rapid unification with the West was the failure of the SED to construct a new, appealing,
socialist *East German* identity. There are numerous reasons for this, an
important one being the GDR's perennially disappointing economic performance compared with that of West Germany, which both officially and unof-
ficially served as the standard of comparison. In terms of material living
standards, many East Germans felt like second-class citizens in a capitalist
world, and what drove along the process of dissolution in the GDR and unification with the West with such breathtaking speed in 1989–90 was not
just an abstract sense of national oneness, but also the desire for immediate
economic improvement and the belief in economic prosperity, an East German variant of the oft-cited *Wirtschaftspatriotismus* of the Federal Republic.
Since then, however, many East Germans have been profoundly disap-

pointed with the results – little surprise, given CDU promises in 1990 that no one would be materially hurt and that the East could be brought up to the level of the West in only five years.

It is here that issues of class identity, feelings of relative deprivation and 'national' identity in the new *Bundesländer* intersect. If the post-*Wende* project of creating new identities in eastern and western Germany has anything to learn from the history of representations of the 'working class' in the GDR, and in particular the notion of a specifically *East German* working class, it is that identities are constructed and sustained largely independent of 'official' representations. While these can help give shape to patterns and frameworks of self-understanding, far more important are one's everyday social experiences. As long as Germans in the new *Bundesländer* are given concrete reasons to feel like members of the 'lower and working class' in their everyday lives (and there are still numerous reasons for this, even if the socio-economic differences between East and West are continually shrinking), official representations of a unified nation and German 'togetherness' are not likely to be very effective.

Notes

1 Statistisches Bundesamt, *Datenreport 1992. Zahlen und Fakten über die Bundesrepublik Deutschland*: Bundeszentrale für politische Bildung, (Bonn, 1992), p. 539.
2 Ibid.
3 For the East German case after 1989, see Michael Hofmann/Dieter Rink, 'Die Auflösung der ostdeutschen Arbeitermilieus. Bewältigungsmuster und Handlungsspielräume ostdeutscher Industriearbeiter im Transformationsprozeß', in *Aus Politik und Zeitgeschichle*, B 26–27/93 (25 June 1993), pp. 29–36. For the case of West Germany, see Josef Mooser, 'Auflösung der proletarischen Milieus: Klassenbildung und Individualisierung in der Arbeiterschaft vom Kaiserreich bis in die Bundesrepublik Deutschland', *Soziale Welt*, vol. 34, no. 3 (1983), pp. 270–306.
4 *Datenreport 1992*, p. 58.
5 Dietrich Storbeck, *Soziale Strukturen in Mitteldeutschland. Eine sozialstatistische Bevölkerungsanalyse im gesamtdeutschen Vergleich* (Berlin: Duncker & Humblot, 1964), pp. 152–3.
6 Ibid., pp. 283–4.
7 In 1961, the percentage of former refugees in the FRG possessing a higher degree was 7.2 per cent for men and 2.1 per cent for women, compared to 3.4 per cent and 1.0 per cent possessing higher degrees in West German populace as a whole. Students in higher education also comprised 0.7 per cent of all refugees from 1952 to 1961 but only 0.34 per cent of the entire GDR population over the same period. See Helge Heidemeyer, *Flucht und Zuwanderung aus der SBZ/DDR 1945/9–1961: Die Flüchtlingspolitik der Bundesrepublik Deutschland bis zum Bau der Berliner Mauer* (Düsseldorf: Droste Verlag, 1994), p. 50.
8 Gunnar Winkler, *Sozialreport '90: Zahlen und Fakten zur sozialen Lage in der DDR* (Berlin: Verlag Die Wirtschaft, 1990), p. 71; Rainer Geißler, *Die Sozialstruktur*

Deutschlands, (Opladen: Westdeutscher Verlag, 1992), p. 109.

9 Bertolt Brecht, *Gesammelte Werke*, vol. 10, (Frankfurt am Main: Suhrkamp, 1967), p. 1009.

10 For an overview of the uses of the anti-fascist founding myth, see Mary Fulbrook, *German National Identity after the Holocaust* (Cambridge: Polity Press, 1999).

11 Stiftung Archiv der Parteien und Massenorganisationen der ehemaligen DDR in Bundesarchiv (hereafter SAPMO-BA) FDGB-BV 20772, report of 5 May 1955.

12 SAPMO-BA DY30/IV2/5/983, 'Zusammenfassender Bericht über den Verlauf des 10. Jahrestages der DDR in Berlin', 8 October 1959.

13 *Statistisches Jahrbuch* (hereafter *StJB*) 1955 (Berlin, 1956), p. 33; *StJB* 1966 (Berlin, 1967), p. 72; *StJB* 1989 (Berlin, 1990), p. 111.

14 Winkler, *Sozialreport*, p. 73.

15 *Protokoll des V. Parteitages der SED*, vol. 1 (Berlin, 1959), p. 204. Party membership statistics are taken from *DDR-Handbuch*, 3rd edn, (Cologne, 1985), p. 1186.

16 *Protokoll des X. Parteitages der SED*, vol. 1 (Berlin, 1981), p. 133; *Protokoll des XI. Parteitages der SED*, vol. 1 (Berlin, 1986), p. 94.

17 *StJB* 1959, p. 14; *StJB* 1967, p. 479.

18 SAPMO-BA DY30/IV2/1/28, bl. 49–51, quoted from Norman Naimark, *The Russians in Germany: A History of the Soviet Zone of Occupation, 1945–1949* (Cambridge, Mass.: Belknap, 1995), pp. 198–9.

19 SAPMO-BA NY 4177/3, bl. 43. The literal translation of the poem is: 'Hennecke, you are the man who inspires us! Hennecke, with you we will overcome our distress! Hennecke, we swear to you that we will work hard! Hennecke, through you our economy will blossom again! Hennecke, you are a hero of our class! Hennecke, with us you are the powerful masses! Hennecke, we want to hold you up as a model! Hennecke, you will also destroy the enslavement of the brothers in the West!'

20 Brandenburgisches Landeshauptarchiv (hereafter BLHA) Ld. Br. Rep. 202G, Nr. 48, 'Stimmen zur Hennicke [*sic*!] -Bewegung aus Potsdam', 10 December 1948, bl. 42.

21 A. Hennecke, 'Der Durchbruch aus dem Teufelskreis', in Erwin Lehmann *et al.* (eds), *Aufbruch in unsere Zeit: Erinnerungen an die Tätigkeit der Gewerkschaften von 1945 bis zur Gründung der Deutschen Demokratischen Republik*, 2nd edn, (Berlin: Verlag Tribüne, 1975), p. 197.

22 SAPMO-BA NY 4177/3, bl. 66.

23 See Alf Lüdtke, '"Helden der Arbeit" – Mühen beim Arbeiten. Zur mißmutigen Loyalität von Industriearbeiter in der DDR', in H. Kaelble, J. Kocka and H. Zwahr (eds), *Sozialgeschichte der DDR* (Stuttgart: Klett-Cotta, 1994), pp. 188–213.

24 From a speech at the Third Congress of the FDGB in 1950, quoted from Peter Hübner, *Konsens, Konflikt und Kompromiß. Soziale Arbeiterinteressen und Sozialpolitik in der SBZ/DDR 1945 bis um 1970* (Berlin: Akademie Verlag, 1995), p. 215.

25 By 1957 there were 179,000 brigades with 1.9 million members. Jörg Roesler, 'Die Produktionsbrigaden in der Industrie der DDR. Zentrum der Arbeitswelt?', in Kaelble, Kocka and Zwahr (eds), *Sozialgeschichte*, pp. 144–170.

26 SAPMO-BA DY30/IV2/5/422, report of 8 July 1959, bl. 54.

27 SAPMO-BA DY30/IV2/5/422, 'Informationsbericht über den Stand des Wettbewerbes um den Titel "Brigade der soz. Arbeit" in Berlin', 19 August 1959, bl. 82.

28 SAPMO-BA DY30/IV2/5/422, bl. 47, 54, 60, 84.

29 Hübner, *Konsens, Konflict und Kompromiß*, pp. 223–4.

30 SAPMO-BA DY30/IV2/5/422, bl. 71.

31 BLHA Bez. Pdm. Rep. 530, Nr. 1218, 'Betr.: Argumentation im BTW', 28 October 1961.

32 SAPMO-BA DY30/IV2/6.11/52, 'Zu einigen Fragen der sozialistischen Gemeinschaftsarbeit', 18 May 1960, report from SED-ZK Abt. Gewerkschaften und Sozialpolitik to Alfred Neumann, bl. 223–8.

33 See, for example, Ulbricht's criticism in *Neues Deutschland*, 10 June 1960, p. 4.

34 See the discussion between Ulbricht and the Sekretariat of the FDGB-BV: SAPMO-BA DY30/IV2/6.11/12, 'Information an den Genossen Neumann', 25 May 1960, bl. 25–7.

35 See Lüdtke, '"Helden der Arbeit"'.

36 Günther Kusch *et al.*, *Schlußbilanz – DDR: Fazit einer verfehlten Wirtschafts- und Sozialpolitik* (Berlin: Duncker & Humblot, 1991), p. 108.

9

Re-presenting the nation: history and identity in East and West Germany

Mary Fulbrook

What do interpretations of the past (in the broad sense of historical consciousness) have to do with identity in the present? A great deal. At an individual level, a sense of where one has come from, the struggles and successes of one's past, strongly influences a sense of what one is doing and where one is going: it can summarize a view of abilities, skills and shortcomings, values, aspirations and strivings, defeats and determination, attributes and relationships, definitions of good and bad, self and other. But before one simply transposes these insights onto collective identities, and anthropomorphizes whole societies or nations, it should be remembered that the constitution of individuals has a basic difference from collective entities: the 'boundaries' of human beings as biological, if not social and cultural, identities are firmly defined, their lives circumscribed by the biological events of beginning and end, birth and death. This is not the case with collective entities such as the nation. The articulate, collective representation of a common past thus in some respects becomes all the more important in the attempt at construction of a broadly acceptable collective identity: for if a story of a common past with an apparently unified, persisting set of actors cannot be written, then the notion of a community persisting through time cannot be sustained.

The Federal Republic of Germany and the German Democratic Republic had, on the face of it, the 'same' pre-1945 past to represent. But professional historians in the two opposing states – mutually hostile creations of the Cold War – represented their common past very differently. Representations of the past were intimately bound up with the construction of new forms of identity in the present; and on both sides of the Wall accusations and counter-accusations were hurled about concerning ideology and political bias. The selection of topics from the past, the character of the stories told about these topics, and the wider 'historical pictures' (*Geschichtsbilder*) into which they were inserted differed across the two states and over time. So too did the styles in which the stories were told, the theoretical terminology or concepts with which they were narrated, the empathic and emotive force with which they were presented, and the broader socio-political context in which they were received and interpreted.

This set of assertions should, on the face of it, give some instant succour to a postmodernist view of history, as outlined in the Introduction to this volume. In principle, one might begin to think the tales told by those authors we shall consider in this chapter are little different – or at least not more 'true', more 'objective' – from the tales told by other authors, in other media, analysed in other chapters of this book. I shall argue that this is not, however, the case: history is not literature. But nor is the situation simply (as frequently depicted in Cold War versions) one of 'objective truth' versus 'wilful political distortion'.

If we examine a select range of examples of East and West German historical writing on aspects of the Third Reich, we can see more clearly the spectrum of degrees of political colouring and constraint, and the degrees to which different accounts are or are not *'realitätsnahe'* – or at least susceptible to critique and revision on the basis of some conception of 'empirical adequacy'.[1] Professional history is *not* simply mimetic representation of the past 'as it actually was'; and it *is* relevant to the representation and indeed construction of present identities; but it is nevertheless of a distinct order, different from some of the other modes of representation we consider in this book (which may, in fact, play a greater role in the construction of identities than do the writings of professional historians).[2] A comparative analysis of professional attempts to re-present the past in the two Germanies allows us some interesting insights into debates on representation, objectivity and fictivity in history. This chapter argues for a course between views stressing the priority of 'facts' and 'objectivity' on the one hand, and the implicit or explicit relativism of postmodernist approaches on the other.

Politics and historians

Let us first look briefly at the character of those doing the interpreting: at the professional historians in East and West; and at their respective views of the endeavours of their colleagues on the other side of the Iron Curtain.

It has to be emphasized at the outset that historians in the GDR were specifically charged with the creation of a new form of historical consciousness: their task was precisely to alter popular conceptions of history and identity inherited from the discredited past. The historical profession in the GDR was thus a crucial element in the Marxist-Leninist political scheme, driven as much by a desire to transform consciousness in the present and future as to understand, reconstruct and represent the past. As such, its representations ran very much in line with other state-controlled representations of the past, such as exhibitions in museums and at memorial sites (of which the most notable example was perhaps the 'shrine' of GDR identity, Buchenwald), or the messages put across in propaganda, parades, commemorations and the press. Discussions in creative literature (as in Christa Wolf's *Kindheitsmuster*) could, given the vicissitudes of censorship and self-censorship (what was known as the 'scissors-in-the-head' syndrome), only at certain times become more exploratory; what is remarkable, in retrospect, is the extraordinary strength of an almost subterranean tradition of historical consciousness passed down through private conversations in the circles of family and friends. Even here, however, the impact of the official message – while not reproduced in substantive detail – was evident in the general moral drawn from upbeat official tales about 'overcoming the past'.

This was quite different from the situation in the West, where there was a clear formal separation between the academies of research and learning on the one hand, and the political arena on the other, accompanied by a widespread commitment to the notion that 'politics' and 'historical knowledge' were to be held somewhat apart. There were thus multiple strands to the development of patterns of historical consciousness in the Federal Republic, where, very often, political speeches and commemorations (Adenauer's speech on 'restitution' in 1951, Reagan and Kohl's ill-judged meeting at Bitburg in 1985, Jenninger's address on the anniversary of Kristallnacht in 1988), or events in film and television (the 'Hitler-wave' in films of the 1970s, the showing of the American mini-series *Holocaust* in 1979), or discussions in the highbrow and popular press (from *Die Zeit* and *Der Spiegel* to *Bild*) were of far greater significance in shaping popular historical consciousness than were the abstruse writings of academic historians. This is not to deny the political relevance of academic historical intepretations – a relevance which was, as we shall see, inescapable throughout the history of divided Germany – but rather to highlight a crucial difference in the prevailing framing assumptions and conditions of reception of academic historical inquiry and representation on each side of the Wall.

Who then were the historians in each state? In the West, the ostensible situation was one of pluralism, diversity, 'objectivity'. This was however far from the case in practice. Few historians who had emigrated from Germany during the Third Reich because of persecution on 'racial' or political grounds chose to return.[3] The prevailing climate among historians in the 1950s was one of muted, generally nationalist conservatism, to some extent chiming in well with the more general political climate of Adenauer's Germany, with – as we shall see in a moment – the demonization and effective exclusion of Hitler as an aberration in the long sweep of an acceptable cultural/national past. The majority of historians showed, if anything, far greater restraint in even touching, let alone pronouncing on, matters of political relevance than did their contemporaries in the media and politics.[4] This picture changed dramatically in the course of the 1960s, with the explosion of new approaches following the 'Fischer controversy' and in the context of the general radicalization associated with the '1968' phenomenon. In the 1970s and 1980s, a diversity and range of historical voices could be heard in West Germany, although it has to be said that practitioners of 'the history of everyday life', feminists, socialists, and adherents of the history workshop movement, for example, tended to remain professionally marginalized. The variants of neo-Marxism current in Britain, France, Italy and the USA in the 1970s barely found a foothold in West German academia, where Marxism was unduly tainted by association with political terrorism (a fall-out on the far left of the 1968 phenomenon) on the one hand and orthodox GDR communism on the other. Even what was sometimes termed the 'new orthodoxy' of the Bielefeld style of societal history, deriving its primary inspiration from Weber rather than Marx, remained numerically a minority – if a securely established one – in a still predominantly conservative profession. Nevertheless, in the explosive *Historikerstreit* (historians' dispute) of 1986–87, it was the left-liberal camp who appeared at the time to gain the upper hand in what effectively became a war of attrition which fizzled out and was then overtaken by the more dramatic events of 1989.[5]

In any event, political diversity and the possibility of no-holds-barred debate in the public sphere were key characteristics of the conditions for the practice of history in the Federal Republic. Far from being some 'value-free, objective' scientific inquiry carried out in ivory towers, history in West Germany became a highly politicized affair, directly and centrally relevant to the key issues of the day. Given the widely held if not universal commitment among western historians to a conception of history as objective recovery of the past, what is slightly odd about the development of West German historical approaches, when one pauses to reflect on it, is the way in which different methodological and substantive concerns appeared to reflect, rather than inform, wider political commitments. Although there are some idiosyncratic exceptions, one can relatively easily map certain types of historical inquiry onto political sympathies – conservative, left-liberal, radical left-wing. And many approaches seemed to be assessed on their political implications rather than their 'empirical adequacy' (or other notion of historical 'truth').[6]

Being less internally diverse, and explicitly state-driven, the political relevance of history in the GDR was of course even more readily apparent. The self-avowed, explicit goal of historical writing in the GDR was precisely to have an impact on political consciousness in the present: to transform people's consciousness and to assist in the bringing about of socialism. As Heinz Heitzer, an official spokesperson for GDR history, put it, the purpose of history is for people 'to gain insights from the battles of the past and to draw inspiration from them to meet today's and tomorrow's challenges'.[7] In the late 1940s and 1950s, those historians who refused to go along with the increasing communist control of historical writing were subjected to Stasi surveillance and political pressure; many of those who were not willing or able to bow to the pressure to conform chose to emigrate to the West while the border was still open before 1961. Thereafter, the historical profession in the GDR was increasingly streamlined within institutional constraints which permitted a limited degree of professional autonomy under the over-all control of the ruling communist SED.[8] By the late 1980s, the historical profession had become a secure part of the GDR establishment, its practi-tioners to a large degree themselves socialized within and constituted by the already internalized goals of the state, although there were a few corners (ancient history, medieval history) of little direct relevance to con-temporary politics where less committed (although still conformist) spirits could escape.

What did East and West German historical colleagues think of each other? Did they indeed share any notion of participating in a common endeavour, a common profession committed to uncovering ever greater parts of a com-mon past – or did they rather see each other as hostile protagonists in Cold War ideological sniping, one side 'telling the truth' while the other was the chief manufacturer and purveyor of politically ordained lies?

During the period of division, the majority of western historians (insofar as they had any interest in the matter at all) tended to denounce GDR his-torical writing as politically biased to the point of outright distortion. Some western scholars, such as Hermann Weber, took a delight in the game of identifying 'blank spots' (*weisse Flecken*), or absences and omissions, as well as positive distortions in East German historical accounts; most, however, simply ignored the best part of GDR historical production as scarcely wor-thy of their attention, a political activity which did not constitute part of the same serious and 'objective' enterprise of historical investigation.[9] It was only a minority, relatively late in the GDR's existence, who sought to take East German historical writing more seriously. Western scholars such as Jür-gen Kocka, Georg Iggers and Konrad Jarausch, who made an honest effort to distinguish between the more and the less interesting historical scholar-ship of the GDR, were in a tiny minority.[10]

For their part, GDR historians took a great interest in western historical writing, but in a spirit of political competition, and with an equal measure of denunciation. From the official GDR point of view, western historical scholarship was 'bourgeois ideology' masquerading as truth; lavishly illus-trated textbooks and biographies of great men were produced simply to rein-force the 'capitalist-imperialist, militarist, revanchist' (and so on) world-view among the duped populace of the West. In symmetrical contrast to the west-ern interpretation, the official GDR view held that it was Marxism-Leninism that was 'non-ideological', in that it was based on a 'scientific' world-view which aimed to elucidate the 'laws of social progress'. Yet at the same time (and echoing a contradiction present also in Marx's original opus) these allegedly scientific 'laws' needed a little helping hand from the vanguard of the working class, the Party. Hence history was at the same time one of the tools in the arsenal of the ruling communist party, the SED, in seeking to raise the appropriate socialist class-consciousness among a population which had been subjected to twelve years of Nazi indoctrination prior to its 'liberation' by the communist Red Army. So history in the GDR was not only 'true', but also partisan: it was specifically designed to affect and alter people's political consciousness.

Westerners would have accepted the latter part of this GDR self-designation, but not the linked notions that Marxist-Leninist history was 'scientific' while western would-be objective history was merely 'bourgeois ideology'. Yet, after the *Wende*, there was a marked explicit re-politicization of history in the west. Analyses of the GDR which had not sufficiently castigated the dictatorship for its repressive character were indicted as, at best, the products of woolly-headed liberals who had been duped by the regime, or, more seriously, the malign outpourings of those who had colluded in upholding an illegitimate regime.[11]

These, then, were the authors: the professional creators of 'truthful' historical re-presentations of the past, and also – depending on which side of the Wall they found themselves – to some extent charged with, or relevant to, the construction of new political and national identities in the present. What pictures did they paint, and what devices did they use to construct new and differing views of a common past?

The cast: heroes, villains, bystanders and victims

The 'elements' out of which the past is to be reconstructed and from which the 'true story' is to be written, or at the very least the real historical individuals who played crucial roles in the events which 'actually happened', should, according to a traditional view of history, be 'the same' whoever tells the story. This should also to some extent be the case for those postmodernists who focus less on the traces of the past than on the writing of the historical text in the present, emphasizing the different ways in which the 'same' elements might be creatively woven into a variety of interpretive tales. But not even the historical cast, the set of actors whose story was to be written, was an area of common ground for historians on the oppposite sides of the Wall. And this is because the choice of cast in accounts of the past was in no way neutral with respect to the present.

A sense of acceptable national identity is usually constructed, in part, by singing tales of heroes and martyrs; to do this in Germany after Hitler was an extraordinarily complex matter, beset with potential pitfalls and sensitivities. Dissent and opposition to Nazism were crucial ingredients, in both German states, in the attempts at self-legitimization and representation of an acceptable version of German national identity after the Holocaust. In short, 'good' traditions in the past had to be found and celebrated as forebears of the present, while those responsible for the evils of Nazism had to be both identified and dealt with, both in reality (denazification, restructuring) and in interpretation (the tales told about the nation's history).

The developments on this front in the GDR are by far the simplest to recount concisely. The Communist Party (KPD) and its Soviet allies were of course designated as the primary heroes throughout the history of GDR historiography. Through their leadership and organization, communists had been able to spearhead active resistance to the Nazi terror. Often, too, they were able to gather together under their wing those of other political persuasions in the common fight against Hitler's tyranny, as in the Nationalkomitee Freies Deutschland.[12] More broadly, and with different emphases at different times, other traditions and individuals could be given what one might wish to term an 'honourable mention': other left-wingers, including members of the SPD, and a few Christians might deserve mention on occasion; and, in the apparently more 'pluralistic' historiographical climate of the 1980s, even the July Plotters and other members of the conservative resistance finally gained a modest place in the East German historical record.[13] Nevertheless, organized resistance under the auspices of the Communist Party retained its central role as the leading light in the fight against the forces of darkness.

The cast of heroes was significantly different in the Federal Republic. In the 1950s, it was primarily the July Plot which enjoyed primary pride of place as the 'other Germany', the legitimate forefathers of Federal Democracy (although, it should be noted, this was still a rather sensitive and by no means uncontested pride of place).[14] A few other groups and individuals received a lesser place in the ideological sun: the Catholic students of the Weiße Rose (White Rose) group in Munich, and some prominent churchmen, such as Martin Niemöller and Dietrich Bonhoeffer of the Bekennende Kirche (Confessing Church) were explicit also-rans at this time. The real explosion in the scope of what counted as legitimate resistance came with the diversification of historical approaches following the changed climate of the late 1960s. In the 1970s and 1980s, research carried out by, for example, those associated with Martin Broszat at the Munich Institut für Zeitgeschichte (Institute of Contemporary History) and others, expanded both the conceptual distinctions and the substantive focus of analyses of 'resistance'. With the new interest in the 'history of everyday life', shadings of grey were introduced into a previously black-and-white framework, to encompass varieties of dissent, non-conformity, *Resistenz*, and so on, in addition to active, organized opposition to the Nazi regime.[15] At the same time, scholars such as Hans Mommsen revealed the feet of clay of former heroes, laying bare the essentially autocratic, anti-democratic views of members of the conservative resistance who were now represented as harking back to Imperial Germany rather than prefiguring the democracy of the Federal Republic.[16]

Which individuals and groups were cast in the role of villains? In both Germanies, of course, Hitler had to play a central role. But – and this is crucial – even the character of Hitler's undoubtedly central role could be conceived in extraordinarily different ways. In the East, Hitler was cast as but an unwitting puppet of the manipulative forces of monopoly capitalism; it was collective class interests – anthropomorphized as key actors in the grand historical narrative – which played the vital moving role. In the West, particularly in the early decades, a 'Great Man' theory of history predominated, with a focus on individuals as major historical actors – those with sufficient charisma being deemed capable of overwhelming other traditions, other forces, even those which had prevailed over centuries. The self-same Hitler who in the GDR was a mere puppet of class interests was in the West cast more or less as a magician leaping into German history from somewhere completely different, dazzling and blinding the innocent masses and leading them off their allotted historical course. There was however a broader political lesson even behind this 'Great Man' view of Hitler – but a lesson which came to quite opposite conclusions to those of the GDR. In Gerhard Ritter's version, the 'modern' masses could be so easily led astray only because of their release from the binding structures of authority in pre-democratic regimes; some form of more authoritarian order than that provided in the Weimar Republic was clearly necessary to prevent the successes of such evil Pied Pipers in modern 'totalitarian' regimes. In Friedrich Meinecke's version, the solution was to return to the German cultural classics, particularly Goethe.[17]

Curiously, alongside more sophisticated versions of historical analysis in the 1970s and 1980s, in many quarters the fascination with Hitler continued – as almost an exonerating psychological explanation of mass indoctrination, the collective duping of a whole populace. Nevertheless, there were also more differentiated attempts to insert Hitler's role into a wider picture of structures of power which allowed and even exacerbated the radicalization of Nazi policies. Although in some versions of what came to be called functionalist approaches, the 'structures' of an increasingly chaotic, 'polycratic' regime linguistically almost took on the role of actor in place of real human beings, the role of Hitler remained crucial to otherwise quite different interpretations of the genesis of genocide (on which more in a moment).

Beyond Hitler, there were key differences in the casting of the other villains who were to play major roles in the stories told. In the GDR, the villains were again collective class actors: the Junkers and monopoly capitalists were the agents of the devil, while the workers and peasants were the innocent victims of fascist oppression.[18] Even when, in the 1970s and 1980s, it was officially conceded that certain workers and peasants had worn the uniforms of the SA and SS, and had collaborated in the Nazi system of terror and racial oppression, this was 'explained away' through the notion of 'false consciousness'. Under capitalism, as in previous systems, the labouring classes had been easily duped by those in power, and misled such that they were unaware of the real implications of their actions, or the real interests of those whose orders they were obeying. They were thus unwitting participants in their own oppression, and, again, irrespective of their actions, were exonerated.[19] Not real actions, but assumed underlying class interests (or the presumed class functions of actions, rather than the conscious motives for those actions) remained both the determining criterion for casting in the role of villain, and the focus of explanation for actions, even in the apparently less dogmatic East German historiography of the 1980s.

In West Germany in the 1950s, the villains remained a relatively tightly drawn and delimited circle of specific individuals. Not only in West German historical writing, which emphasized what has often been called the *Betriebsunfall* or 'spanner in the works' version of German history, but also in Adenauer's political speeches, and in the belated and unbelievably lenient war crimes trials in the period up to the mid-1960s, there was a demonization of Hitler, the SS, and a few 'criminals' who had helped to run the system of terror.[20] Beyond that the vast mass of the German people were pronounced (as in the GDR, but for quite different reasons) effectively innocent; while they had to play a role in the current story of collective shame for acts which had been committed 'on German soil', 'in the name of the German people', they need not have any real sense of guilt.

From the later 1960s onwards, however, in West Germany the circle of 'villains' was drawn more widely. By the 1980s, a variety of groups were being put in the frame by different historians: in the works of western scholars (including Anglo-American and Israeli, as well as West German, historians) the roles of bureaucrats, scientific and economic experts, members of the previously supposedly honourable Wehrmacht, and ordinary citizens who were only too willing to denounce their neighbours to a relatively understaffed Gestapo, all now came under much closer scrutiny. All in all, a much more complex, and in part less simplistically judgemental, picture of the Third Reich began to emerge: no longer could it, at least among a majority of academic historians, be recounted as purely a moralizing (and often self-exonerating) tale of heroes and villains. In some respects, one might say that the increasingly diverse set of castings was also increasingly 'empirically adequate', in the sense that this more complex picture corresponded better with the complexity of traces left by the real historical past.

But this did not necessarily mean it was deemed to be universally acceptable, politically irrelevant (as, according to the 'traditional' view of history, it perhaps should have been: a cumulatively 'better', 'fuller' picture of the past should have been acceptable across political and moral boundaries). There remained highly controversial and heated debates over the issue of whether the history of the Third Reich could be 'normalized' in Martin Broszat's sense.[21] And attempts to 'normalize' in a dramatically different sense, such as Hillgruber's plea for 'empathy' with the soldiers and civilians battling to sustain western civilization against the Bolshevik hordes on the eastern front (an extraordinary throwback to the Nazi version of heroes and villains), even at the expense of further murders in the concentration camps, were even more highly controversial.[22] Moreover, popular coffee table and even highbrow accounts for consumption by the educated public still retained the curious combination of denunciatory tone but at the same time broadly exculpatory message prevalent in the 1950s.[23]

Hence, not even the castings – the identification of actors in the story – were the same across the two sides of the Wall. Even before there was any attempt at broader historical explanation, implicit presuppositions and prior assumptions had – in different ways – influenced the identification and labelling of the historical parts out of which the contemporary narratives were to be constructed.

The plot: historical pictures (*Geschichtsbilder*)

These specific castings of heroes and villains were in turn located within wider 'historical pictures' or *Geschichtsbilder*. These historical pictures are difficult to categorise in terms of postmodernist debates: they correspond perhaps best to what Ankersmit calls 'narrative substances', or Hayden White's (rather idiosyncratic) distinction between 'events' and 'facts' rather than being ostensible 'narratives' proper.

In a curious way, the concept of 'totalitarianism' which was prevalent in West Germany in the 1950s fulfilled much the same exonerative functions as did the concept of 'fascism' favoured in the GDR. Both tended to pronounce the majority of ordinary Germans as effectively innocent, although through different interpretive frameworks. And these frameworks had crucial implications for the representation (or, rather, the hoped-for construction) of new identities in the present, by showing the ways in which each new German state could claim it had 'overcome the past' more completely than its Cold War opponent. For the GDR, the class interpretation of Nazism as 'fascism' set the Third Reich in the same historical frame as Italian fascism, as a product of a capitalist system. It meant that the socio-economic and political revolution undertaken under communist auspices had rooted out the historical bases of Nazism in the GDR, while, in this view, the continuities in socio-economic structure and personnel in the West meant that West German democracy represented a continuity with Nazi fascism, although disguised under a new political superstructure. For the Federal Republic, the 'totalitarianism' theory of Nazism meant that precisely the converse was true: it set the Third Reich in the context of 'modern mass society', on a par with Soviet Russia and other communist states. Thus there were, in the West German view, marked continuities between the repressive dictatorship of the Third Reich and that of the GDR, while the juridical proceedings against the key war criminals, along with the adoption of a new democratic political system in the West, meant that the Nazi past had been more effectively 'mastered' in the Federal Republic.

From the 1960s, the pictures in West German historical writing began to diversify in a variety of ways. For one thing, one spin-off from the renewed wave of war crimes trials in the 1960s (particularly the Auschwitz trial) was a more energetic engagement with the Holocaust on the part of professional historians.[25] For another, the rise of both neo-Marxism among the New Left, and the renewed interested in sociological approaches to history, such as that of Max Weber among left-liberal academics associated with the Bielefeld School, put a range of alternative 'historical pictures' on the table. The 'spanner in the works' view was challenged by alternative frameworks: that of 'fascism' again placed the emphasis on modern capitalism; while the hugely provocative and for a long time quite influential notion of the German *Sonderweg* (special path to modernity) laid the emphasis rather on the alleged long-term peculiarities of German history which set it on a path towards dictatorship rather than democracy.[26] Yet, it should be noted, the more traditional view of Nazism as totalitarianism, as a repressive dictatorship in part rooted in the general conditions of modernity interpreted as mass society, was never entirely quiescent. This resurfaced with a vengeance in the revisionist views of Andreas Hillgruber, Ernst Nolte and others in the *Historikerstreit* of the mid-1980s.

The general point to be underlined here is that, in the main, the developments just outlined were rooted less in the 'sudden discovery of new facts' than in shifts in the interpretive frameworks imposed on generally recognized sets of 'facts'. The Escher-like quality of alternative paradigms for perceiving 'reality' (as in the extraordinary prints of Escher, where one can either see, for example, the white angels or the black devils, the young woman or the old crone, the stairs going up or the stairs going down, but never all perspectives simultaneously) is very clear in the so-called 'functionalist-intentionalist' controversy over the origins of genocide.[27] One set of interpreters, the 'intentionalists', can see primarily, and centrally, the role of Hitler's intentions, which were carried out as soon as circumstances would allow. The other group, the so-called 'functionalists', see rather a 'twisted road to Auschwitz', in which mad intention only became ghastly reality through the chaotic pattern of functioning of a regime which, far from being a streamlined totalitarian dictatorship, was in fact 'polycratic', with much autonomy for regional leaders to seek to solve practical problems on the ground or compete for Hitler's favour by 'working towards the Führer'. This controversy has in fact been to some degree empirically fruitful, in that it stimulated increasingly detailed work on patterns of decision-making in the summer and autumn of 1941. In principle, then, and contra the postmodernist view of an almost arbitrary imposition of this sort of *Geschichtsbild*, there does appear in this case to be at least some possibility of 'appealing to theoretically neutral evidence' to seek to adjudicate between the two frameworks and produce views which attempt, in a more sophisticated way, to combine analysis of Hitler's central role with an awareness of the power of structures.[28]

Less fruitful, empirically, were the clashes of competing paradigmatic interpretations of the uniqueness or comparability of the Holocaust unleashed in the *Historikerstreit*. Here, competing interpretive frameworks were not so readily susceptible to empirical testing and revision in the light of evidence. Nevertheless, this illustrated perhaps more clearly the direct political relevance, and implications for constructions of national identity, of competing historical representations. Indeed, one might suggest that in this case, a historical consciousness derived in part perhaps from family experience, but certainly from personal political sympathies, more directly influenced the interpretive frames of the key historians (such as Hillgruber) than vice versa.

Thus, again, one finds – to different degrees – a considerable element of prior assumption (or metatheoretical presupposition) informing the way in which overall pictures are framed, the broader conceptual settings for specific historical accounts within which particular narratives may be told, or explanations developed. When these are deeply held for political reasons – particularly denunciation, whether of modern mass society as 'totalitarian' or of modern capitalism as 'fascist' – they are considerably harder to dislodge in the light of new empirical evidence than when less hinges on them. But when historians are prepared to step back for a moment with genuinely open minds, some at least of these overall interpretive frameworks (such as the antinomy between structure and intentions) may be open to improvement and change.

Style and presentation

In what sorts of style, what kinds of presentation, were such interpretations put across? Clearly matters of style and presentation are affected by intended impact and intended audience.

While the East German historians strove very explicitly to achieve a significant impact on historical consciousness, the presentation of their results left a lot to be desired. On the one hand were the clearly propagandistic documents, such as the glossy brochures produced on key historical anniversaries, such as 8 May 1985, commemorating 'liberation' in 1945.[29] On the other were the immensely weighty, densely written, largely tedious accounts in unappealing books with many pages of small print.[30] No part of this spectrum was necessarily instantly accessible to or credible for the East German public. Yet the message was unremittingly, insistently consistent – and consistent with far more instantly accessible and ubiquitous images, such as the numerous statues, commemorations and use of names of resistance heroes (notably the cult of Ernst Thälmann), and the compulsory trips with the Free German Youth or other organizations to the sacred sites of resistance such as Buchenwald or Sachsenhausen. By the 1980s, young East Germans had a distinctly one-sided view of their past, in which there was virtually no element of a guilt complex of the dimensions prevalent in the West.[31]

West German historians benefited from the better conditions of capitalist production, where print runs were determined more by marketing and audience demand than by politically determined allotments of paper, and from the possibility of public debate and a diversity of perspective. These conditions did not, however, necessarily guarantee much about the kinds of historical consciousness that were transmitted by the work of professional historians. The abstruse prose of academics, and the tendency to write in the driest possible manner (often in the passive tense) even – or perhaps especially – when writing about as emotive a topic as the Holocaust, inevitably limited the appeal of some of the cutting edge academic works.[32] It is also notable that the most popularly accessible texts, of the lavishly illustrated coffee-table variety, tended not to engage in the finer nuances of academic interpretation, but rather simply to reproduce the 'sob story' version of Nazism: collective shame and the pieties of public penance took the place of sober historical explanation.[33] Exculpation was achieved simultaneously with condemnation. At the same time – and for very understandable reasons – most of the educational presentation of the past was consciously trying hard to arouse anti-Nazi sentiments, often to the detriment of differentiated understanding.

Re-mapping the past, or creating the truth effect?

What of such mundane tools of the historian's craft as the use of empirical evidence and the role of the falsifiability of competing historical accounts? This is, I would contend, where the real differences between historiography in the GDR and the Federal Republic are to be found.

It has to be conceded that what counts as 'fact' or 'empirical evidence' varies with theoretical framework and associated metatheoretical assumptions. From the point of view of the variety of Marxism officially upheld in the GDR, no amount of empirical evidence on the actual attitudes and actions of ordinary working people in the Third Reich would serve to falsify the interpretation that pronounced them innocent – suffering, as they were, from 'false consciousness'. And from this perspective, of course, any alternative view would be merely a case of 'bourgeois subjectivism'. Moreover, if the task is not only to understand the world, but also to change it, then the way in which the past is represented is itself a political act.

Even from a non-Marxist, neo-Kantian position, 'facts' (or the empirical world out there) can only be 'known' through theoretical spectacles. But what is found 'out there' can at least have a limiting form of veto power, even if we concede, with Hayden White, that the whole picture, the framing narrative, is not given in the surviving traces of the past. Moreover, it is possible to pursue hypotheses which lead to the uncovering of more pieces of the puzzle, and give us more to play with when (creatively) seeking to paint the broader picture.

'Remapping' the past is in fact a useful analogy. Maps can be designed on different scales, with different landmarks, for different purposes. We all know they are drawn according to certain conventions, and do not claim to be realistic, accurate, totally mimetic representations of reality. But we certainly also know when maps are wrong, misleading, do not take us where we want to go, or fail to tell us about key reference points or features of the landscape. Of course there are stylistic, aesthetic criteria which form part of the evaluation of a map; but probably most important is its faithfulness to the 'reality out there' – and hence its usefulness to users in finding their way in unknown territory.

The record of developments within even the highly politicized world of West German historiography suggests that there is the possibility of developing views which are increasingly empirically adequate, and producing more sophisticated, more complex, and more balanced ways of recounting and reinterpreting the records of the past. This is not just the wilful construction of a 'truth effect': this is, rather, the drawing of ever more detailed maps, with better means of representing contours, key landmarks, paths through the wilderness.

Historical consciousness, national identity and collective memory

The sense of a common past can only be fractured, partial; and it is formed through many and diverse influences. Let me briefly conclude by placing the works of professional historians in a broader context of patterns of historical consciousness.

Historians delude themselves if they think they are the key to shaping popular historical consciousness. Of arguably far greater impact are the – emotionally more easily accessible, if sometimes intellectually less rigorous – media of novels and dramas (as discussed in other chapters of this book), films, television documentaries, museum exhibits, commemorations and reconstructions in the 'authentic locations' of the past, the 'sacred sites of collective memory'. Quite apart from factual content, or imparting of real 'knowledge', a major role is played by the tone or moral message conveyed by political commemorations and gestures: contrast the vague penumbra of collective shame which characterized western public political culture with the official façade of innocence and victory in the GDR. Of importance too are the collective memories passed down through family stories, through oral recollections, through the informal landscapes of memory which are given different significations by those who pass through them.

These different facets of collective memory provide frameworks of interpretation into which the 'facts' are inserted. They provide penumbra of meanings and indications of 'appropriate' emotional responses, which are very often deeply contentious.

An analysis of public, often official West German representations of the Holocaust over the years shows a continuing streak of emotional distancing: the reprehensibility of the absolute evil of the Nazi genocide is emphasized, while at the same time suggesting that this was carried out by only a small number of individuals (Hitler, Himmler, and their henchmen) who have, in one way or another, been adequately punished. But because these crimes 'were committed' (politicians' speeches from Adenauer onwards prefer the passive tense) 'on German soil', 'in the name of the German people', the latter have a peculiar burden of responsibility, without admission of guilt, which lays on them the duty to be peculiarly moral, peculiarly vigilant, to make retribution for evermore. The sins of the fathers are indeed visited upon succeeding generations. Political education in West German schools and youth groups, in television and public debate, relentlessly repeated the message that one could only be ashamed to be German. And the 'educational' impact of the mass media was primarily to endorse the emotive impact of the message, to arouse the tears without furthering sober causal understanding of the true extent of real responsibility and guilt. As a result, by the 1980s, the West Germans were the least 'proud' of their national belonging of any citizenry in Europe.

Quite the opposite was the case in the GDR. From the very beginning, East Germans were led to believe that, if they had not actually been actively involved in the heroic (and mainly communist) anti-fascist resistance to Hitler, they had at least been the innocent victims of fascist oppression, liberated by the Red Army of the Soviet Union. The 'racial' aspects of Nazism were downplayed, highlighting instead an interpretation of Nazism as rooted in class struggle. These official pictures were everywhere: in street names, memorials, statues, exhibitions in former concentration camps, as well as in history textbooks. They were perhaps never transmitted with quite the emotional impact of the western media, but nevertheless prevailed in excluding alternative possible images from the public sphere.

Of at least equal – at some times possibly even greater – importance are the tales told in families, in workplaces and pubs, the presentations of the past articulated and conveyed through family folklore, through self-representations in professional and private life. 'Memory', in popular parlance, should in some senses be more 'authentic' than 'history'. It is, allegedly, what is actually known by those who lived through it. But, as most individuals also know all too well, 'memory' can be misleading, patchy, reinterpreted and re-remembered. This is all the more the case when we are dealing with the phenomenon of 'collective memories'. These provide a framework of meaning for salient events in a common past, selected, reinterpreted and re-presented for new purposes in the new contexts of the present. What we find in the case of the two Germanies after 1945 is a series of dissonances, of fractures in historical consciousness. On neither side of the Iron Curtain was there any generally accepted, common tale of a common past. Within each state, there were crucial fractures between the 'official versions' and different patterns of popular consciousness. In the West, public penance and philo-Semitic pieties jarred with unresolved yearnings and private grief, as a combination of collective shame and restricted attribution of real guilt came to stamp its mark on public political culture. In the East, the official version of collective heroism and innocence allowed a quiescence about the past such that for younger generations of East Germans it was no longer a major issue; but the disjunctures between public heroism and socialist propaganda on the one hand, and private patterns of political culture on the other, were too great to allow the development of a securely anchored official version of GDR identity.

At the same time, there were other currents at work with respect to the definition of the nation. During the period of division, the Federal Republic officially retained an essentially ethnic-cultural definition of citizenship entitlement, which was combined with the commitment – constitutionally enshrined in the Basic Law – to the reunification of all 'Germans'. East Germans (and others who were 'German' under the terms of citizenship entitlement) had a constitutional right to settle as citizens in the territory of the Federal Republic. But this official commitment to an ethnic-cultural notion of 'German' was decreasingly shared by younger West Germans. Whatever their views (if any) on the debates over 'constitutional patriotism' among left-liberal intellectuals, younger generations of West Germans increasingly identified with region, with Europe, with 'the West', or even (though with some sensitivity about the taboo notion of patriotism) with the Federal Republic as a democratic state with a high standard of living. What happened on the other side of the Iron Curtain was of ever less relevance and interest for them; East Germans were not, for the most part, present in their active mental universe.

Almost exactly the opposite was the case in the GDR. Here, in 1974, the notion of 'nation' was officially redefined: no longer did it apply to the ethnic-cultural community, but now, rather, to the 'socialist state of workers and peasants'. Class and social structure became the key defining characteristics of 'nation', in contrast to the retention of a sense of a community of descent, with common language and customs, as 'nationality'. But this theoretical sleight of hand, enshrined both in the new constitution of 1974 and in SED theoretical literature, did not catch on among the East German populace. West Germany always remained a salient reference point (in a way that the East never was among West Germans); a sense of common 'German' identity remained very much alive and well in the 'socialist state of workers and peasants'. At the same time, given the very different pattern of historical consciousness and mode of 'overcoming the past' in the East, there were not the same sensitivities and taboos about what it meant to be

German; there was no public culture of shame. Then, when the Wall fell – for quite other reasons – it was quite possible for East Germans to mobilize the sense of the ethnic-cultural nation and to claim, without embarassment, *Wir sind ein Volk*, in a way that arguably could never have been done without accusations of right-wing extremism in the West.

Yet, when the Wall fell and 'Germans' were reunited, it became manifest that very different behaviour patterns, ways of looking and of seeing the world, had developed in the two states which had been founded on the soil of the defeated Third Reich. The notions of 'Ossis' and 'Wessis' soon characterized in popular parlance the dramatic socio-psychological differences which had arisen through forty years of political separation. 'National identities' are as much rooted in everyday experiences, and related conceptions of self and other, as in any intellectual constructions of collective community.

Conclusion: history, identity and representation

If these other influences played such a major role in the shaping of historical consciousness, and if the discipline of history is itself so shaped by and imbued with political relevance, what then of the status of historical inquiry as the 'pursuit of truth'? What light does the case of history as a professional discipline in the GDR and the Federal Republic shed on more general debates on the nature of history as a creative mode of re-presentation of the past from particular perspectives in the present?

For all the areas of overlap and the mutual, not always symmetrical, patterns of influence, clear distinctions need to be made between cultural, political and everyday understandings of past and present identities, and the work of professional historians. The creative works of film, drama, narrative prose, explored in previous chapters, can set up imaginative strategies of inquiry, creatively shaping their chosen casts and plots, and exploring different possible answers, often within a deliberately ambiguous, unresolved field of tensions and contradictions. Political representations are concerned not only with exploration (and not always with truth), but primarily with effective change in the light of certain judgements of goals, values, strategies and tactics: utterances about the past may be wilful and conscious interventions in the present, precisely in order to shape what is perceived to be a 'better' future. And the understandings of identity in lived experience – ranging from popular perceptions rooted in family anecdotes, or seeping in through daily exposure to newspaper reports and cartoons, or the impact of architecture and travel guides, or the development of active strategies and responses to living in certain socio-economic and political circumstances – may well be at odds with the kinds of collective conversation about identity engaged in through the creative or political media of the public arena.

Historical representations share many features with these other media and modes of reconstructing and representing the past. Even the knowledge of the 'real' elements out of which the stories have to be constructed is itself in large measure a product of present concerns, as we have seen in the discussion of different casting, characterization and emplotment of a common past in the two Germanies, above. This is even more the case with the insertion of specific stories into wider pictures of the broader sweep of history. But note the use of the qualifying phrase, 'in large measure': such representations are never entirely products of the present; nor are they arbitrary representations, without anchorage in and reference to an assumed – if never perfectly known – past. They can be rationally discussed, debated, and amended or rejected, not because of personal preferences or political inclinations, but rather because alternatives may be seen to account better for new or different evidence.

I am not arguing here for a return to an (allegedly) a-theoretical empiricism; but I am pointing to the possibility of rational debates both within and across different theoretical perspectives in history, premised on a widely shared set of general rules about honesty in debate and a willingness to contemplate revision. (Consider for a moment the very word 'revision': re-vision, see differently, 'in a new light'.) Such open debate and amenability to revision require a degree of intellectual security (consider the notion of 'academic freedom', important also under democratic conditions) where political or personal implications are not a relevant yardstick for the adjudication of historical interpretations. In different ways in both postwar German states, history has been of such political resonance and sensitivity that this distance has been extraordinarily hard to achieve – even in the democratic West. But difficulty in practice does not necessarily entail impossibility in principle.

Nevertheless, disciplined historical inquiry is not the only route for imaginative engagement with and interpretation of past and present identities; it is but one among many, interrelated ways in which human beings participate in collective conversations – to which there are never definitive conclusions – about who they are and where they have come from. It has both its limits (not least the loss of the kind of emotional immediacy possible in the creative arts) and its strengths (not least a belief in at least some version of veracity or falsifiability). We hope in this book at least to have illustrated the variety of, and interrelationships among, different modes of construction of German identity in the twentieth century, and to have clarified some of the points at issue in current debates about literary and historical routes to the representation of 'reality'.

Notes

1 Admittedly, adjudication of the latter presupposes some metatheoretical standard (or supra-paradigmatic possibility) of 'evaluation in the light of empirical evidence'. There is not space here to explore this crucial theoretical issue further; I

shall simply attempt here to make the case in respect of the particular example. I discuss the broader issues more generally in *Historical Theory* (Routledge, forthcoming).

2 See the wider arguments made in my book, *German National Identity after the Holocaust* (Cambridge: Polity Press, 1999).

3 Cf. particularly Winfried Schulze, 'Der Neubeginn der deutschen Geschichtswissenschaft nach 1945: Einsichten und Absichtserklärungen der Historiker nach der Katastrophe' in Ernst Schulin and Elisabeth Müller-Luckner (eds.) *Deutsche Geschichtswissenschaft nach dem zweiten Weltkrieg (1945-1965)* (Munich: Oldenbourg, 1989); see also Winfried Schulze, *Deutsche Geschichtswissenschaft nach 1945* (Munich: Oldenbourg, 1989).

4 There were of course highly important exceptions; but such developments as, for example, the opening of the Munich Institute for Contemporary History were accompanied by much controversy.

5 On the *Historikerstreit*, see the key texts reprinted in Piper Verlag, *Historikerstreit* (Munich: Piper, 1987). See also: Hans-Ulrich Wehler, *Entsorgung der deutschen Vergangenheit?* (Munich: C. H. Beck, 1988); C. Maier, *The Unmasterable Past* (Cambridge, Mass.: Harvard University Press, 1988); Richard J. Evans, *In Hitler's Shadow* (London: I. B. Taurus, 1989).

6 This carries over even into a very detailed survey of the development of German historical writing: see Stefan Berger, *The Search for Normality* (Oxford: Berg, 1997).

7 Heinz Heitzer, *GDR: An Historical Outline* (Dresden: Verlag Zeit im Bild, 1981; German orig. 1989), p. 7.

8 On East German historiography, see for example A. Fischer and G. Heydemann (eds), *Geschichtswissenschaft der DDR*, vol. 1 (Berlin: Duncker & Humblot, 1988); A. Dorpalen, *German History in Marxist Perspective* (London: Tauris, 1985); Jan Herman Brinks, *Die DDR-Geschichtswissenschaft auf dem Weg zur deutschen Einheit* (Frankfurt: Campus Verlag, 1992); and further references in Fulbrook, *National Identity*.

9 Hermann Weber, 'Die "weissen Flecken" in der Geschichte', in *Aufbau und Fall einer Diktatur* (Cologne: Bund-Verlag, 1991).

10 Cf., for example, Georg Iggers (ed.), *Marxist Historiography in Transformation* (Oxford: Berg, 1991); Konrad Jarausch (ed.), *Zwischen Parteilichkeit und Professionalität. Bilanz der Geschichtswissenschaft in der DDR* (Berlin: Akademie Verlag, 1991); and the attacks by Armin Mitter and Stefan Wolle on Kocka and the 'Bielefelder Weg'. It is notable that both Iggers and Jarausch had their primary professional bases not in Germany, but in north America.

11 Cf., for example, Jens Hacker, *Deutsche Irrtümer* (Berlin: Ullstein, 1992); Klaus Schroeder (ed.), *Geschichte und Transformation des SED-Staates* (Berlin: Akademie Verlag, 1994); see also M. Fulbrook, *Interpretations of the Two Germanies, 1945–1990* (Basingstoke: Macmillan, 2000).

12 See for example Zentralinstitut für Geschichte der Arbeiterbewegung, *Grundriß der deutschen Geschichte* (Berlin: VEB Deutscher Verlag der Wissenschaften, 1979), pp. 474–81.

13 See for example Ines Reich, 'Das Bild vom deutschen Widerstand in der Öffentlichkeit und Wissenschaft der DDR', in Peter Steinbach and Johannes Tuchel (eds), *Widerstand gegen den Nationalsozialismus* (Berlin: Akademie Verlag, 1994).

14 See for example C. Toyka-Seid, 'Der Widerstand gegen Hitler und die westdeutsche Gesellschaft: Anmerkungen zur Rezeption des "anderen Deutschland" in den frühen Nackkriegsjahren', in Steinbach and Tuchel (eds), *Widerstand*.

15 The best guide in English to the relevant literature is Ian Kershaw, *The Nazi Dictatorship*, 3rd edn (London: Longman, 1993).

16 See for example H. Mommsen, 'Social Views and Constitutional Plans of the Resistance', in H. Graml *et al.*, *The German Resistance to Hitler* (London: Batsford, 1970).

17 See for example Gerhard Ritter, *Europa und die deutsche Frage* (Munich: Münchner Verlag, 1948), pp. 193–4; see also Friedrich Meinecke, *Die deutsche Katastrophe* (Wiesbaden: Eberhard Brockhaus Verlag, 1946).

18 See for example Jürgen Kuczynski, *Die Geschichte unseres Vaterlandes von 1900 bis zur Gegenwart* (Berlin: Dietz Verlag, 1953), pp. 7–8.

19 See for example the tendentious introduction to the otherwise useful collection of documents edited by Kurt Pätzold, *Verfolgung, Vertreibung, Vernichtung* (Frankfurt am Main: Röderberg Verlag, 1984; orig. Leipzig, 1983), particularly p. 19.

20 Cf the echoes of this view in Hochhuth's *Der Stellvertreter*, analysed by Judith Beniston in Chapter 6, above. On the trials, see for example H. G. van Dam and Ralph Giordano (eds), *KZ-Verbrechen vor deutschen Gerichten* (Frankfurt am Main: Europäische Verlagsanstalt, vol. I 1962; vol. II 1966); Hermann Langbein, *Im Namen des deutschen Volkes. Zwischenbilanz der Prozesse wegen nationalsozialistischer Verbrechen* (Vienna: Europa Verlag, 1963); Hermann Langbein, *Der Auschwitz-Prozeß. Eine Dokumentation* (Vienna: Europa Verlag, 1965); Jürgen Weber and Peter Steinbach (eds), *Vergangenheitsbewältigung durch Strafverfahren? NS-Prozesse in der Bundesrepublik Deutschland* (Munich: Olzog, 1984); Adalbert Rückerl (ed.), *NS-Vernichtungslager im Spiegel deutscher Strafprozesse. Belzec, Sobibor, Treblinka, Chelmno* (Munich: Deutscher Taschenbuch Verlag, 1977). For a selection of the rather large literature on the politics of 'overcoming the past' in Adenauer's Germany more generally, see for example Ulrich Brochhagen, *Nach Nürnberg. Vergangenheitsbewältigung und Westintegration in der Ära Adenauer* (Hamburg: Junius Verlag, 1994); Norbert Frei, *Vergangenheitspolitik* (Munich: C. H. Beck, 1994); Jörg Friedrich, *Die kalte Amnestie. NS-Täter in der Bundesrepublik* (Frankfurt: Fischer, 1985).

21 See the exchange between Martin Broszat and Saul Friedländer, reprinted in Peter Baldwin (ed.), *Reworking the Past. Hitler, the Holocaust and the Historians' Dispute* (Boston: Beacon Press, 1990), part 2.

22 The work by Hillgruber, *Zweierlei Bewältigung. Die Zerschlagung des deutschen Reiches und der Untergang des europäischen Judentums* (Stuttgart: Siedler, 1986), was of course one of the key texts unleashing the *Historikerstreit*.

23 See for example Helmut Diwald, *Geschichte der Deutschen* (Frankfurt am Main and Berlin: Ulstein, 1978); Gerhard Schulz, *Deutschland seit dem ersten Weltkrieg*, *Deutsche Geschichte* vol. 3 (Göttingen: Vandenhoeck and Ruprecht, 1985).

24 Cf F. R. Ankersmit, 'Reply to Professor Zagorin', *History and Theory*, vol. 29, no. 3 (1990), pp. 275–96; Hayden White, 'Response to Arthur Marwick', *Journal of Contemporary History*, vol. 30, no. 2 (1995), pp. 233–46.

25 See particularly the *Gutachten* developed specifically for these trials by historians at the Munich Institute of Contemporary History: Hans Buchheim, 'Die SS – das Herrschaftsinstrument. Befehl und Gehorsam', *Anatomie des SS-Staates*, vol. 1;

Martin Broszat, 'Konzentrationslager', Hans-Adolf Jacobsen, 'Komissarbefehl', and Helmut Krausnick, 'Judenverfolgung', *Anatomie des SS-Staates*, vol. 2 (Munich: Deutscher Taschenbuch Verlag, 1967). On the unwillingness on the part of West German historians even to deal with what was essentially ghettoized as 'Jewish history', see for example Konrad Kwiet, 'Die NS-Zeit in der westdeutschen Forschung 1945–1961', in Schulin and Müller-Luckner (eds), *Deutsche Geschichtswissenschaft*.

26 The work of Hans-Ulrich Wehler on Imperial Germany was of course particularly stimulating in this connection.

27 Key intentionalists include Lucy Dawidowicz and Gerald Fleming; key 'functionalists' include Hans Mommsen and Martin Broszat. Moderating views include works by Christopher Browning and Philippe Burrin. See Kershaw, *Nazi Dictatorship*, and Nicholas Stargardt, 'The Holocaust', in M. Fulbrook (ed.), *German History since 1800* (London: Arnold, 1997), for overviews of the debate.

28 See particularly Ian Kershaw's biography of *Hitler* (London: Penguin, 1998), vol.1, for an approach of this sort. For more detailed discussion of the theoretical issue, see Fulbrook, *Historical Theory*.

29 See for example *Upholding the Antifascist Legacy* (Dresden: Verlag Zeit im Bild, 1985).

30 For example Autorenkollektiv, on behalf of the Zentralinstitut für Geschichte der Akademie der Wissenschaften der DDR, *Grundriß der deutschen Geschichte* (Berlin: VEB Deutscher Verlag der Wissenschaften, 1979).

31 For further details, see Fulbrook, *German National Identity*.

32 This seems to have played something of a role in Hans Mommsen's difficulties in conveying his (far more differentiated) view of Nazism against the simplistic but highly emotive presentation in Daniel Goldhagen's book, *Hitler's Willing Executioners. Ordinary Germans and the Holocaust* (New York: Knopf, 1996).

33 See for example Diwald, *Geschichte der Deutschen*, pp. 163–5.

Index